D1112367

Climate Change

Recent Title in Contemporary Debates

The Affordable Care Act: Examining the Facts
Purva H. Rawal

CLIMATE CHANGE

Examining the Facts

Daniel Bedford and John Cook

Contemporary Debates

ABC-CLIO™

An Imprint of ABC-CLIO, LLC
Santa Barbara, California • Denver, Colorado

Library of Congress Cataloging-in-Publication Data

Names: Bedford, Daniel. | Cook, John (Climatologist)
Title: Climate change : examining the facts / Daniel Bedford and John Cook.
Description: Santa Barbara, California : ABC-CLIO, [2016] | Series:
    Contemporary debates | Includes bibliographical references and index.
Identifiers: LCCN 2016011069 | ISBN 9781440835681 (alk. paper) |
    ISBN 9781440835698 (ebook)
Subjects: LCSH: Climatic changes. | Global warming. | Climate change
    mitigation.
Classification: LCC QC903 .B43 2016 | DDC 551.6—dc23
LC record available at http://lccn.loc.gov/2016011069

ISBN: 978-1-4408-3568-1
EISBN: 978-1-4408-3569-8

20 19 18 17 16   1 2 3 4 5

This book is also available as an eBook.

ABC-CLIO
An Imprint of ABC-CLIO, LLC

ABC-CLIO, LLC
130 Cremona Drive, P.O. Box 1911
Santa Barbara, California 93116-1911
www.abc-clio.com

This book is printed on acid-free paper ∞

Manufactured in the United States of America

Contents

Acknowledgments

Several people provided invaluable assistance in bringing this book to completion. Mark Biddle did magnificent work on many of the graphics. Several scientists contributed data, background information, quotations, and/or permissions to use them as examples of some of the issues discussed in the book. Richard Alley, Barry Bickmore, Kerry Emanuel, Andrew Dessler, Mauro Rubino and Pieter Tans all contributed in one or other of these ways. The generous assistance of all of these individuals is gratefully acknowledged.

Introduction

Climate Change: Myths and Realities

Each winter, the oceans around the poles get so cold that they can freeze over, forming sea ice several feet thick. Each summer, it melts again, but not completely—even in the summer, the Arctic is still chilly. How much ice is left at the end of the summer is a good indicator of how warm the previous year was. In September 2012, satellite measurements showed that Arctic sea ice reached a record for its lowest extent, at 3.41 million square kilometers. The previous record low was in September 2007. The record before that was 2005. Then 2002. Then 1995. Every few years, a new record low has been set for Arctic sea ice extent. Experts at the National Snow and Ice Data Center in Boulder, Colorado, have extended the measurements of Arctic sea ice as far back as 1953, combining information from satellites with reports from ships. As time goes on, they have found less and less of the Arctic Ocean has been staying frozen by the end of the summer.

Other bodies of ice have fared no better in recent years. Measurements of the gravitational field exerted by the Greenland ice sheet, using the twin satellites of National Aeronautics and Space Administration (NASA)'s Gravity Recovery and Climate Experiment (GRACE) have found a similar steady decline in the mass of this huge body of land ice. GRACE finds the same trend occurring with smaller glaciers in the world's mountainous regions. Measurements from the satellites match observations on the ground: a large fraction of the world's ice is melting.

The obvious conclusion to draw when ice melts in large quantities is that the planet is getting warmer, and other measurements confirm that this is indeed the case. The multiple independent assessments of thermometer measurements worldwide show that 2015 was the globe's warmest year ever recorded by a wide margin, with 2014 the second warmest. U.S. government scientists at the National Oceanic and Atmospheric Administration (NOAA) agree with independent assessments from NASA and the Berkeley Earth project, a nongovernmental effort to track global temperatures. In Britain, the Met Office finds the same thing. The World Meteorological Organization has recently reported that 15 of the world's 16 warmest years on record took place in the 21st century. The evidence, from many different places and from many different scientists and scientific organizations, is pointing in one direction: Earth's climate is changing. Global warming is real.

In May 2013, instruments at NOAA's Mauna Loa Observatory, which is located on top of a 13,000-foot mountain in the middle of the Pacific Ocean, measured levels of carbon dioxide (CO_2) in the air at their highest since measurements began in 1958. This in itself is not particularly unusual—CO_2 in May of every year has been higher than in May of the previous year, as CO_2 levels keep going up—but May 2013 was striking because CO_2 concentrations exceeded 400 parts per million (ppm) for the first time in that 55-year record. In keeping with the pattern of progressively higher CO_2 levels each year, May 2014 broke the record again, exceeding 400 ppm by slightly more than the previous year. According to measurements of CO_2 retrieved from bubbles of air trapped in ancient ice deep in Antarctica, today's levels are higher than at any time in the last 800,000 years.

A warming globe, ever-higher levels of CO_2 in the atmosphere. What's the connection? CO_2 is a heat-trapping gas, one of several known as greenhouse gases because, like the glass of a greenhouse, they let sunlight pass through them but don't let heat escape back out again. The heat-trapping properties of greenhouse gases were first measured in 1859 by an Irish physicist named John Tyndall, and they are now very well established aspects of basic physics. Scientists have improved on Tyndall's measurements, to be sure—the U.S. Air Force studied greenhouse gases in detail in the 1970s to make sure their heat-seeking missiles would work properly—but no scientist seriously challenges the fact that CO_2 and its relatives trap heat. Over the last few decades, increasingly sophisticated computer simulations of Earth's climate have shown with greater and greater confidence that more greenhouse gases in the atmosphere should produce a warmer climate. The details in the simulations provide a more complicated picture, but at a basic level, you don't need a computer to tell you the obvious: the more of a heat-trapping gas there is in the atmosphere, the more heat is going to be trapped.

Where is the CO_2 coming from? In the late 1800s and early 1900s, Swedish scientist Svante Arrhenius suggested that the prodigious amounts of coal being burned to fuel the Industrial Revolution could put enough carbon into the atmosphere to change Earth's climate. Throughout the 20th century, as technology, measurements, and analytical techniques improved—in short, as science progressed—scientists studying the climate became more and more convinced that Arrhenius's basic idea was correct. Today, measurements of the different isotopes of carbon found in the CO_2 in the atmosphere can tell scientists where that carbon came from—and it's coming overwhelmingly from coal, oil, and natural gas, the fossil fuels we rely on to power our modern industrial civilization.

The basic science, then, is clear: global warming is real, and it's happening because when we burn fossil fuels we put carbon into the atmosphere that reacts with oxygen to form carbon dioxide, which is a heat-trapping gas. These basic facts have been reaffirmed with ever-increasing confidence by the United Nations Intergovernmental Panel on Climate Change (IPCC), a large body of scientists and government officials from around the world that produces a comprehensive review of the science of climate change every five or six years (IPCC members include representatives from major oil exporters such as Kuwait and Saudi Arabia). Several other studies of the scientific literature, using different methods, have concluded that roughly 97% of the relevant peer-reviewed scientific papers agree that global warming is happening and is caused by the buildup of greenhouse gases from burning fossil fuels. This level of agreement constitutes an overwhelming scientific consensus.

Why, then, is there any controversy or confusion surrounding this issue? For controversy there certainly is—not among climate scientists, but among politicians, some media outlets, and the general public. For many Americans, according to opinion polls, this issue is met with misunderstanding, apathy, or outright rejection of the reality, seriousness, and human origins of climate change. What accounts for this?

There are several explanations. First, climate change is a complicated field, cutting across multiple scientific disciplines, including atmospheric physics, chemistry, geology, glaciology, biology, oceanography, economics, and political science, and it sometimes must rely on advanced statistical analysis techniques. This makes the phenomenon difficult to understand for the average person, and scientists have often not been effective communicators of their research. Some of the complexities of climate change also show up in counterintuitive aspects of global warming, such as melting Arctic sea ice possibly causing colder, snowier winters in parts of Europe. Not every place is warming at the same rate, or even at all, leading to arguments about what to even call the phenomenon: global warming or climate change? Even the terms "global weirding" or "climate chaos" have been suggested, to convey the idea that the world is not warming uniformly, and more extreme and unusual weather events may be on the way. A scientific issue of this breadth and technical complexity is ripe for misunderstanding, even by those who accept that climate is changing: one recent study found that the important misconception of confusing global warming with the Antarctic ozone hole was most widely held among those who were most concerned about climate change.

Second, climate itself is somewhat intangible, lending itself more readily to being understood in the dry language of statistics and trends. Climate is the sensible older sibling to weather, which is more unpredictable and chaotic than climate, but gets all the attention. Climate is often described as the long-term average weather, giving a picture of "typical" monthly temperatures and precipitation, but it can also be described as setting the boundary conditions in which weather occurs. If weather bounces around erratically like a pinball, climate is the pinball machine within which the ball bounces. We directly experience weather but cannot directly experience climate—and there's no substitute for direct experience in shaping peoples' opinions. Peoples' recent experience with weather has been shown to affect their views on the reality of climate change, even though weather and climate are different things: on a brutally, unseasonably cold or snowy day, it can be hard to remember that you're experiencing weather, not climate, and that it's the climate that's changing.

Similarly, it's hard to pin any given extreme weather event, such as a hurricane or a heat wave, definitively on climate change. Each new weather extreme adds a new data point to the emerging pattern, and it's the pattern, more than the individual event, that tells the story of a changing climate. Climate scientists use the pattern of data to identify the probability that global warming was a contributing factor. But even if the odds are strong that global warming played a role, there's still a chance, however small, that an extreme weather event would have occurred naturally. This gives people predisposed toward skepticism about climate change an escape clause, a way to persuade themselves that extreme weather events have nothing to do with global warming.

Third, climate change is not only a scientifically huge issue—it's a huge issue for human society as a whole. Climate change has the potential to literally transform our lives, one way or another—either through how we choose to tackle it, or through the impacts from a changed climate if we don't (or more likely, a combination of both). Cutting our emissions of carbon means reducing and eventually ending our reliance on fossil fuels, which have powered the extraordinary advances in human material well-being enabled by the Industrial Revolution, and which have subsequently acquired a central role in our civilization. This means the findings of climate science have significant implications for energy policy—which in turn means climate science has political implications, and science and politics are often awkward roommates. The political and financial implications of moving away from fossil fuels as our primary energy source have led to public relations (PR) efforts intended to sway public opinion in one direction or another, much as the tobacco industry spent years, and millions of dollars, manufacturing uncertainty about the connection between smoking and lung cancer. These PR campaigns often employ the language of science—indeed, they sometimes employ scientists themselves, in the role of professional skeptics—and exploit the caveats inherent in science to amplify small areas of uncertainty to the point where they appear to be overwhelming, when in reality they are minor issues.

Because some of this PR is dressed up to look like science, it can be hard for ordinary people, the stereotypical intelligent layperson, to know what to think. If you don't have specialized knowledge helping you to discern spin from science, most people tend to listen to the message they like the most—the message that resonates best with their core beliefs, or one delivered by a trusted messenger, such as a talk radio host, movie star, or Internet blogger. Opposing messages are greeted with distrust, so the result is that people tend to accept or reject the reality, seriousness, and human origins of climate change based a lot more on their gut than on their knowledge of climate science. Research in psychology has shown that this is an innate human tendency and has nothing to do with how intelligent or well-educated people are (if anything, more intelligent and well-educated people are more prone to this effect)—and the PR campaigns have exploited this innate human tendency in order to manufacture doubt about the science of climate change.

The convergence of these factors—the complexity of climate science, the intangibility of climate and climate change, the policy implications of addressing the problem, and the emergence of political "spin" around the issue—has produced a fertile environment for the planting and growing of misconceptions or myths about climate change. And that brings us to the purpose of this book. In the pages that follow, we present 35 of the most common questions about our understanding of climate change. Many of these questions directly address pervasive or misleading myths surrounding the issue. Some myths are innocent mistakes, simple misunderstandings, or conflations of terms, such as the ozone hole and global warming mentioned earlier, or mistaking weather for climate. Others have distinctive origins in PR efforts and have been repeated widely by sympathetic news outlets. While some are simply flat-out wrong, many of the most enduring and misleading myths have a grain of truth, but gloss over important details, context, or key interpretations.

The questions are organized into five chapters. Chapter 1 examines the evidence that the climate is changing; chapter 2 delves into the science demonstrating that human activities are the cause of the recently observed changes in climate; chapter 3 focuses on the impacts of climate change, both currently experienced and projected for the future; chapter 4 discusses the robust scientific consensus supporting fundamental aspects of the science on climate change; and chapter 5 considers the prospects for addressing the challenges posed by climate change, both now and in the future.

Each chapter presents a fact-based response to the question posed, in many cases explaining how myths and misunderstandings have distorted or obscured those facts. By examining these myths and misunderstandings, it is our hope that readers will build a clearer, more robust understanding of climate change science—but also that critical thinking skills will be sharpened by exploring the techniques of misinformation used to distort the science. Ideally, we hope, readers will be able to dismantle new myths when they encounter them 'out in the field'—in social media, in conversations with friends and family, and in news reports. We hope that this book can become a starting point for respectful conversations about climate change, which might then shift beyond the basic questions that have been settled for some years: global warming is happening, and it's caused by greenhouse gases released when humans burn fossil fuels. It's time to start talking about solutions, and we hope this book will help move the conversations toward that point.

1

The Evidence Regarding
Climate Change

Q1. WHAT IS HAPPENING TO SEA ICE
IN THE ARCTIC?

Answer: Arctic sea ice has undergone a rapid and dramatic decline in extent, area, and thickness in recent decades, and is showing no sign of recovery.

The Facts: There are few clearer or more compelling indicators of a warming world than melting ice, and the sea ice cover of the Arctic Ocean is melting at an astonishing rate. Since 1979, satellites have measured how much of the Arctic Ocean is frozen at any given time. Scientists at the U.S. National Snow and Ice Data Center (NSIDC), among others, analyze these measurements and compile them into an index of sea ice extent and area. Sea ice extent is always greater than total sea ice area because there are gaps of open water between the chunks of ice. Regardless of whether sea ice extent or area is analyzed, the complete satellite record from 1979 to the present shows that Arctic sea ice is in dramatic decline. NSIDC scientists calculate that winter sea ice extent has declined by around 3–4% per decade since 1979. Sea ice extent in September—the end of the summer melt season and therefore the minimum amount of sea ice for the year—has declined by an astonishing 11.5% per decade between 1979 and 2012 (Figure 1.1).

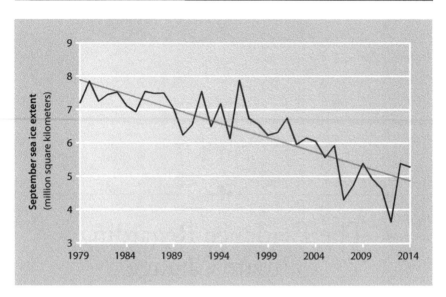

Figure 1.1 Arctic sea ice extent in September, 1979–2014.
Source: NSIDC.

However, even the full length of the satellite record is relatively short by climate standards—less than 40 years. Therefore, the satellite measurements are sometimes criticized for being too short in length to say anything truly meaningful about Arctic sea ice. Maybe natural variations in the past, before satellite measurements began, produced declines just as remarkable as those of the present day. To learn more about the long-term behavior of Arctic sea ice, scientists have worked to reconstruct ice extent using a wide range of historical records, including reports from ships, and charts maintained by government agencies with an interest in monitoring sea ice, such as the U.S. Naval Oceanographic Office, the Danish Meteorological Institute, and the Icelandic Glaciological Society. Using many independent sources allows scientists to cross-check sources against each other and improve the accuracy of the historical reconstructions. Furthermore, where historical data overlap with satellite measurements—as in the case of some of the shipping reports—the accuracy of the historical data can be verified by comparing with the satellite data.

Using these techniques, scientists have extended our estimates of Arctic sea ice extent into the pre-satellite era. One reconstruction used these historical sources to reconstruct sea ice extent as far back as 1870 (Walsh and Chapman, 2001). Yet another study took a different approach to go even further back in time, by using 69 proxy measures of sea ice extent—indirect estimates of sea ice derived from other environmental indicators, such as ice core data or tree rings (Kinnard et al., 2011). This reconstruction pushed back estimates of Arctic sea ice extent to 1,450 years ago.

The historical data show the larger context of Arctic sea ice decline than that measured by the satellites. In this context, it's clear that the recent melting of Arctic sea ice is not simply part of a long-term cycle. Sea ice extent was relatively stable until about 1960 and then began its dramatic decline. The current melting of Arctic sea ice is unprecedented in nearly 150 years, using historical sources. The scientists using the proxy measurement approach suggested that the magnitude, rate, and duration of the current melting of Arctic sea ice seem to be unprecedented in the past 1,450 years (Figure 1.2). Melting on this scale does not seem to have happened as part of a recurring natural climate cycle. It is an extraordinary, and clear, signal of a warming world.

If the evidence is so clear, why do some media outlets and think-tank reports sometimes claim that Arctic sea ice has recovered or that its

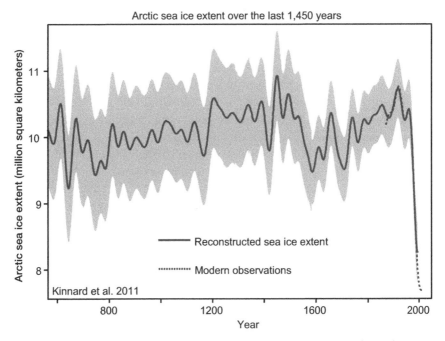

Figure 1.2 Late summer Arctic sea ice extent reconstructed for the past 1,450 years.

Source: Kinnard et al. (2011).

decline has been exaggerated? Articles in Britain's *Daily Mail,* opinion columns in the *Wall Street Journal,* comments by conservative media figures like Rush Limbaugh, reports from the Heartland Institute and other conservative think-tanks, and at least one nationally syndicated cartoon strip (Mallard Fillmore) all attempt to make this argument in some form. They generally do so using statistical sleight of hand, typically relying on confusion between short-term variation and long-term trends.

This confusion is central to many myths about climate change and will be explained in more detail elsewhere in this book. However, the basic idea is straightforward, especially as it applies to sea ice: some winters are colder than others, and some summers are warmer or stormier than others. Colder winters mean more freezing, and more ice to be melted the following summer; warmer summers melt more ice, more quickly, than cooler summers; and more storms can break up the ice, making it easier to melt. The result is that Arctic sea ice extent and area show lots of variability from one year to the next.

Concerns about climate change, however, are not about year-to-year variations but about the long-term pattern of those variations. The key question is whether the "downs" outweigh the "ups" over many years (the more years the better). For Arctic sea ice, since 1960, they clearly do. Over many years, the trend in Arctic sea ice extent and area is down, even as short-term variability superimposes fluctuations on top of that trend.

This is where the myth comes in. Whenever some aspect of Arctic sea ice—often extent, but sometimes area or thickness—breaks a new record, those natural variations mean that the following year is unlikely to be yet another new record. It would be surprising, given the natural pattern of ups and downs, if sea ice extent did not increase, at least slightly, after a new record low. However, this natural variability can be manipulated to calculate some misleading statistics. For example, the NSIDC sea ice index reports Arctic sea ice area for September 2012 as 2.15 million square kilometers, the lowest on record. For the following year, September 2013, sea ice extent increased slightly, as natural variability would lead one to expect, to 3.54 million square kilometers. This was an increase of 1.39 million square kilometers over the 2012 sea ice extent. When reported as a value relative to the 2012 record low, any increase can look quite large. That 1.39 million square kilometers of growth in the Arctic sea ice area from 2012 to 2013 represents an increase of almost 65%—and suddenly, news articles, op-eds, blogs, think-tank reports and cartoons are claiming that Arctic sea ice has grown dramatically from 2012 to 2013, suggesting that fears of global warming are overblown. In reality, however, 2013's 3.54 million square kilometers of Arctic sea ice area was the eighth lowest on record. In addition, a focus only on the 2013 total requires ignoring that new records for lowest sea ice area were set four times between 2002 and 2014.

This approach for distorting the scientific evidence for climate change is known as cherry-picking, and it involves selecting a few data points that show the desired result, while ignoring the inconvenient bigger picture. It can be applied to places as well as times. For example, the Heartland Institute's 2009 report, *Climate Change Reconsidered*, as well as a follow-up report in 2013, discusses several studies of small individual locations within the Arctic Ocean where sea ice patterns are reported to show small increases, often over quite short time periods. By focusing on a few small trees and ignoring the very large forest, reports such as these can foster the impression that Arctic sea ice is not receding and may even be growing. This may be true for a handful of places within the Arctic, but it is categorically untrue for the Arctic Ocean as a whole.

Other variations on the myth of Arctic sea ice recovery misdirect attention away from the obvious melting of Arctic sea ice toward the role of storms in recent record low sea ice extent events. According to this line of argument, storm events broke up the sea ice in those years. While this is true, it glosses over the fact that sea ice has become much thinner in recent decades due to melting, making it more vulnerable to those storm events. Suggesting that Arctic sea ice decline is simply an accident of a few freak storms ignores the longer-term decline and glosses over the main causes of melting sea ice: warmer air temperatures and warmer water temperatures. These climate changes are the likely drivers of Arctic sea ice decline, and while global temperatures continue to warm, that decline shows no sign of stopping any time soon. Arctic sea ice has not recovered.

FURTHER READING

The Cryosphere Today, website based at the University of Illinois, maintained by John Walsh. Available at http://arctic.atmos.uiuc.edu/cryosphere/. Accessed January 30, 2015.

Idso, C. D., Carter, R. M., and Singer, S. F. (2013). *Climate Change Reconsidered II*: 2013 Report of the Nongovernmental International Panel on Climate Change (NIPCC). Nongovernmental International Panel on Climate Change.

Idso, C. D., and Singer, S. F. (2009). *Climate Change Reconsidered*: 2009 Report of the Nongovernmental International Panel on Climate Change (NIPCC). Nongovernmental International Panel on Climate Change.

Kinnard, C., Zdanowicz, C. M., Fisher, D. A., Isaksson, E., de Vernal, A., and Thompson, L. G. (2011). Reconstructed changes in Arctic sea ice over the past 1,450 years. *Nature, 479*(7374), 509–512.

National Snow and Ice Data Center. (2015). Sea Ice Index. Available at http://nsidc.org/data/seaice_index/; data on Arctic sea ice extent and area; available at ftp://sidads.colorado.edu/DATASETS/NOAA/ G02135/Sep/N_09_area.txt. Accessed January 29, 2015.

National Snow and Ice Data Center. (2015). State of the Cryosphere: Sea Ice. Available at https://nsidc.org/cryosphere/sotc/sea_ice.html. Accessed January 29, 2015.

Walsh, J. E., and Chapman, W. L. (2001). 20th-century sea-ice variations from observational data. *Annals of Glaciology, 33*(1), 444–448.

Q2. WHAT IS HAPPENING TO SEA ICE IN THE ANTARCTIC?

Answer: The Southern Ocean surrounding Antarctica has warmed up since the 1960s. Despite this warming, Antarctic sea ice has expanded slightly in recent years, but the growth is small and probably attributable to stronger winds in the region.

The Facts: Climate change has many aspects that appear counterintuitive with a superficial understanding of the climate system, but actually make sense with a deeper understanding. Many of the myths propagated by climate change denialists exploit this situation, relying on the fact that most people are not climate scientists and therefore lack a deep understanding of climate change. A prime example is the apparently contradictory behavior of sea ice in the Southern Hemisphere. Here, despite warming temperatures, sea ice extent and area have grown slightly since satellites began their measurements in 1979.

The most important point to make about the situation in Antarctica is that temperatures have been going up. Several different independent studies of the available data conclude that the Southern Ocean, the body of water surrounding the Antarctic continent, has been warming since the 1960s (Zhang, 2007). This is evident in both sea surface temperatures and surface air temperatures. The evidence from the continent of Antarctica is somewhat less clear, with some places possibly cooling, but overall, the continent as a whole also appears to have warmed since the 1960s, especially in the Antarctic Peninsula, which has warmed more than any other place in the Southern Hemisphere. As a whole, the picture from Antarctica is clear: it is getting warmer.

At the same time, however, sea ice around Antarctica is increasing, setting new record highs for both sea ice extent and area several times in the past few years, including the greatest sea ice extent on record in September 2014. How can this be happening? Surely more ice must mean that the region around Antarctica is getting colder. This is the superficial understanding promoted by several different sources, including opinion columns at *Forbes Online*, websites such as Climate Depot and CO_2 Science, and Steve Goreham's 2013 book *The Mad, Mad, Mad World of Climatism*, which was distributed free and unsolicited, courtesy of the Heartland Institute think-tank, to thousands of colleges across the United States.

These documents emphasize the growth in Antarctic sea ice and imply that it must mean cooling in the region. As James Taylor, writing for *Forbes Online*, put it in May 2014, "Antarctic polar ice extent has set another new record, defying alarmist global warming claims." This myth works, in part, by misdirection: persuading people to focus on one piece of the story rather than the complete picture. The emphasis in these misleading sources is on the expanding Antarctic sea ice, not on the overall warming of temperatures in the region.

Reconciling these two seemingly contradictory patterns—warming temperatures and growing sea ice—requires digging a little deeper into two areas of climate science: the mechanics of sea ice formation and changes in the upper atmosphere of Antarctica. First, sea ice forms during the southern winter of June, July and August, the opposite of the Arctic, because seasons are reversed between the Northern and Southern Hemispheres. During these months, in the high latitudes close to the South Pole, the sun never rises and temperatures plummet, getting cold enough that even salty seawater can freeze into ice several feet thick.

Cooling the sea surface to temperatures where freezing can happen requires that the ocean lose heat to the extremely cold air above it, which happens through the processes of evaporation, conduction, and radiation. The transfer of heat from the oceans to the atmosphere is much more effective where the sea surface is directly exposed to the atmosphere—so as ice starts to form, it effectively inhibits its own growth, as the skin of ice over the water starts to block the transfer of heat. Consequently, sea ice grows progressively more slowly as it gets thicker. This means that rapid sea ice growth can occur only if something moves the ice away from where it originally formed, exposing the open water underneath in a sort of sea ice conveyor belt.

One of the most powerful forces for moving sea ice around in this way is the wind. Strong winds circulating around Antarctica turn the Southern Ocean into an efficient sea ice production line every winter. Ice forms at the colder, higher latitudes close to the Antarctic continent; then winds push the ice away northward, toward lower latitudes, exposing the open water again and allowing new ice to grow. This production line is so efficient that the sea ice pack melts back almost completely to the coast of Antarctica each summer, and then grows again almost from scratch each winter, adding over two million square miles of ice extent in six months.

This understanding of the importance of wind in forming sea ice helps explain why recent growth in Antarctic sea ice can occur even while the temperatures are rising, but it requires examining the full range of other changes taking place in the region's climate. First, in addition to the surface warming, the winds around Antarctica have become stronger. Several measures of wind strength indicate this, and the expected result would be a faster-moving sea ice production line leading to more ice formation, assuming that the winter is still cold enough to form ice at all—which, of course, it is. Although the Southern Ocean has warmed overall since the 1950s, this is still Antarctica and *warmer* does not mean *warm*. Stronger winds in these warmer—but still frigid—temperatures would be expected to produce more sea ice.

Why have the winds become stronger? This is where the second part of digging into climate science comes in: examining the complete set of changes in Antarctica's climate. While the surface air around the South Pole has, for the most part, warmed since the 1960s, a layer of the upper atmosphere called the stratosphere has become colder. This is likely to have been caused by two separate, but related human impacts on the atmosphere.

One is increasing levels of carbon dioxide in the atmosphere, due to burning fossil fuels. While this is the main cause of global warming and the warming of the lower atmosphere, it also makes the stratosphere colder. This is expected by theoretical considerations of how the greenhouse effect works and has been confirmed by observations.

At the same time, a second impact is the breaking down of ozone in the stratosphere by industrial chemicals called chlorofluorocarbons, producing the infamous ozone hole over Antarctica. Because stratospheric ozone absorbs ultraviolet light from the sun, less ozone makes for less absorption and a cooler stratosphere. Global warming is not caused by the ozone hole, but these two separate problems produce one common outcome: a colder stratosphere over Antarctica. Because the winds around Antarctica are a result of the temperature difference between the pole and lower latitudes, a colder Antarctic stratosphere should theoretically produce stronger winds—and this is exactly what has been observed (Thompson et al., 2011).

Antarctic sea ice, then, is growing despite warmer surface water and air temperatures, and seems to be doing so because of human-induced cooling of the Antarctic stratosphere, driving stronger winds that promote more growth of sea ice in the winter. The superficial implication that more ice must mean colder temperatures, present in some reports on Antarctic sea ice growth, is not supported by the facts.

There are several variants of this myth, all quite straightforward to deal with. One variant simply suggests that if sea ice is growing, then ice all across the Antarctic continent must also be growing, implying that all Antarctic ice is the same. Land ice and sea ice are very different, and measurements from satellites find that, overall, the huge ice sheets of Antarctica—land ice—have been losing hundreds of billions of tons of ice since roughly 2005.

The other common variant is that the observed small growth in Antarctic sea ice somehow cancels out the catastrophic decline of sea ice in the Arctic, leaving little or no change in the total amount of sea ice for the world as a whole. The Heartland Institute's 2013 report *Climate Change Reconsidered II* states this, for example, as does the website CO_2 Science. This is perhaps the easiest myth to address. The NOAA State of the Climate Report for 2014 states that global sea ice extent is decreasing at an average rate of 123,000 square miles per decade. The Arctic is losing an average of 200,000 square miles per decade, while the Antarctic is gaining an average of 77,000 square miles per decade.

Clearly, loss of ice in the Arctic is not being balanced by ice growth in the Antarctic. But even if the areas of gain and loss were roughly in balance, sea ice at the two poles plays very different roles in the Earth's climate system. In the Arctic, sea ice persisting through the summer serves to reflect sunlight back out to space, helping to keep the Earth cool. This effect happens only during the summer, because in the Arctic winter the sun never rises. The reduced area of summer sea ice is important because it exposes the dark, absorbent ocean beneath the ice, triggering a kind of reverse snowball effect where, once the ice starts to melt, the process builds on itself and ice area gets smaller and smaller as the oceans are exposed to warm sunlight, melting ever more ice.

In Antarctica, remember that the sea ice melts almost all the way back to the coast, so this reflection effect is minimal in the Southern Hemisphere. Large growth in winter sea ice is irrelevant here, because the sun does not shine near the South Pole in winter. Growth in winter sea ice in Antarctica cannot balance loss of summer sea ice in the Arctic, even if the numbers were similar.

FURTHER READING

co2science.org. (2003). Trends in Arctic and Antarctic Sea Ice Extent. Available at http://www.co2science.org//articles/V6/N44/C1.php. Accessed January 31, 2015.

Gillis, J. (2012). Running the numbers on Antarctic sea ice. Posted to the *New York Times*'s Green blog, October 3, 2012, available at http://green.blogs.nytimes.com/2012/10/03/running-the-numbers-on-antarctic-sea-ice/?_r=0. Accessed January 30, 2015.

Goreham, S. (2013). *The Mad, Mad, Mad World of Climatism: Mankind and Climate Change Mania*. New Lenox Books.

National Snow and Ice Data Center. (2014). State of the Cryosphere: Ice Sheets. Available at https://nsidc.org/cryosphere/sotc/ice_sheets.html. Accessed February 1, 2015.

NOAA National Climatic Data Center. (2014). State of the Climate: Global Snow and Ice for Annual 2014. Available at http://www.ncdc .noaa.gov/sotc/global-snow/. Accessed January 31, 2015.

Steig, E. (2014). Clarity on Antarctic sea ice. Posted to RealClimate. org, December 19, 2014, available at http://www.realclimate.org/ index.php/archives/2014/12/clarity-on-antarctic-sea-ice/. Accessed January 30, 2015.

Taylor, J. (2014). Record Antarctic Ice Extent Throws Cold Water on Global Warming Scare. Published online at Forbes.com, May 16, 2014. Available at http://www.forbes.com/sites/jamestaylor/2014/05/16/record-polar-ice-extent-debunks-antarctic-global-warming-scare/. Accessed February 1, 2015.

Thompson, D.W., Solomon, S., Kushner, P.J., England, M.H., Grise, K.M., and Karoly, D.J. (2011). Signatures of the Antarctic ozone hole in Southern Hemisphere surface climate change. *Nature Geoscience*, 4(11), 741–749.

Zhang, J. (2007). Increasing Antarctic sea ice under warming atmospheric and oceanic conditions. *Journal of Climate*, 20(11), 2515–2529.

Q3. WHAT IS HAPPENING TO GLACIERS AND ICE SHEETS?

Answer: Ice sheets on Greenland and Antarctica, as well as most mountain glaciers worldwide, have been rapidly losing mass in recent decades.

The Facts: As with the rapid decline of Arctic sea ice (see question 1), melting glaciers and ice sheets are a powerful image of a warming planet.

The Extreme Ice Survey, led by photographer James Balog, has captured the disintegration of 23 glaciers around the world, including Alaska, Greenland, Iceland, and Antarctica, using time-lapse video sequences, viewable at various locations online and in the documentary film *Chasing Ice* (2012). Repeat photography—replicating an old photograph to see how conditions have changed in the intervening years—provides a less detailed but longer-term view of the pattern of melting glaciers.

Careful measurements of the mass of glaciers and ice sheets over time, both on the ground and from satellites, support the anecdotal, but visually powerful, photographic evidence. The conclusion is clear: glaciers and ice sheets around the world are rapidly losing mass. In fact, the evidence for melting glaciers and ice sheets is so clear and strong that it is difficult to see just how a myth to the contrary could gain any traction. To understand the myth, it is necessary first to understand more about the details of glaciers and how they are measured.

Glacier ice forms as snow accumulates year after year, so that the weight of the snow on top gradually compresses the snow at the bottom. This squeezes out the air, making it denser over time, so that the snow is eventually transformed into ice. Consequently, glaciers will only form where more snow falls during the winter than melts away in the summer, because only then will there be a surplus of snow to build up year after year. This situation, where more snow falls than melts, is known as a *positive net mass balance*—the net result of adding mass by snowfall and subtracting mass by snowmelt is positive—and this allows a glacier to grow. Positive net mass balances are found where snowfall is heavy, or the snowmelt is small, that is, places that are generally cold, by virtue of either high altitude or high latitude or both. This explains why glaciers are found in high mountains or near the poles.

Conversely, if more snow and ice melt in summer than snowfall adds in winter, a glacier will have a negative net mass balance. If this persists for long enough, the glacier will shrink. Net mass balance, and its translation into visible changes in the size of a glacier, means that glaciers can act as indicators of climate change. A prolonged cold or snowy spell should see glaciers advancing, while a warm or dry spell should see the opposite. The available evidence tells us that most of the world's glaciers and ice sheets are shrinking, or losing mass.

How is this known? After all, there are an estimated 160,000 glaciers in the world, not counting those on the edges of the big ice sheets of Greenland and Antarctica. Only a handful of these have been surveyed. Climate scientists, however, have devised several ways to address this challenge. First, the World Glacier Monitoring Service (WGMS) coordinates an international program to monitor 37 "reference" glaciers located in 10 different mountain ranges around the world. These reference glaciers have continuous on-the-ground measurements of mass balance stretching back to 1980 or earlier.

Many other glaciers have been monitored for much shorter periods of time, but because there are so many more of them, they cover a larger area than just the reference glaciers, though the total number of measured glaciers is still small compared with the estimated total number of glaciers in the world. WGMS regularly compares the mass balance for the reference glaciers with the mass balance for all glaciers in the archive. The two sets of mass balance data agree closely. For surveyed glaciers, there has been a striking loss of ice since 1980, with an overwhelming majority of monitored glaciers retreating since that time. Given that almost all the glaciers surveyed around the world are losing mass, this suggests that, even though there are large gaps between glaciers, they are in fact capturing an accurate picture of global glacier behavior.

Credence is added to these on-the-ground measurements by recent satellite observations. Measurements of the Earth's gravitational field have been made since 2003, using NASA's twin satellites called GRACE. Since gravity is a function of mass, changes in the gravitational field can indicate changes in mass.

Recent measurements of the mass of mountain ranges in Alaska and South America show striking mass losses, indicating melting glaciers. GRACE provides similarly clear evidence of accelerating mass loss for the great ice sheets of Greenland and Antarctica.

Measuring the changing gravitational field of the Earth from space is a serious technical challenge, and the difficulties of accurately measuring changes in glacier and ice sheet mass with GRACE should not be underestimated. However, other satellite measurements provide a cross-check for the GRACE data. Instruments measuring the extent of the summer melt area on the Greenland ice sheet since 1979 show a progressive increase in melt area over time. Although the natural variability of Earth's climate means some summers are colder and others warmer, the long-term trend is evident: more and more of Greenland's surface is melting in summer.

For Antarctica and Greenland, satellite-mounted laser altimeters have measured the height of the ice sheets and recorded changes over time. These measurements also largely agree with the GRACE data: Greenland and Antarctica are losing mass. Currently, Greenland alone is losing more than 300 billion tons of ice every year. That's more than the entire weight of Mount Everest.

Finally, a long-running scientific project to monitor changes in mountain glaciers using satellites is now coming to fruition. The GLIMS project (Global Land Ice Measurements from Space) is using space-based visual observations—essentially, pictures of glaciers—to map modern-day glacier locations, lengths, and shapes, and compare them to historical records. In one application of these techniques, to the Cordillera Blanca mountain range in Peru, scientists found the glacier-covered area shrank from 665.1 km^2 in 1970 to 516.1 km^2 in 2003, a reduction of 23% (Racoviteanu et al., 2008). In another recent study, of the eastern Himalayas, every single one of over 500 glaciers in the study was found to have retreated since the 1960s, giving a total reduction in the area covered by glaciers of around 12%—and the rate of retreat is accelerating (Racoviteanu et al., 2014). GLIMS is significantly increasing the number of glaciers being monitored, and finding results consistent with the surface observations: glaciers are melting.

Given the overwhelming evidence to the contrary, how can anyone say that glaciers and ice sheets are not melting? One way is simply to make inaccurate statements. The Heartland Institute's 2013 report *Climate Change Reconsidered II* and Steve Goreham's 2013 book *The Mad, Mad, Mad World of Climatism* state that the Greenland ice sheet's mass balance is stable, in flat contradiction of the available data.

Another approach is to focus on a small number of glaciers around the world that are not shrinking and ignore the rest. A third approach is to emphasize how small the number of measured glaciers is compared with the estimated total number of glaciers worldwide. This approach is evident in the *Climate Change Reconsidered II* report, as well as in the work of the late science fiction writer Michael Crichton, who presented this myth (along with many others related to global warming) in his 2004 novel *State of Fear*.

It is true that the number of directly measured glaciers is very small compared with the global total—at most a few hundred ever surveyed, out of 160,000, with long-term detailed measurements for only 37, the WGMS reference glaciers. However, to emphasize the uncertainty is misleading, because so many of the glaciers that have been surveyed, which are widely separated in space and scattered all across the globe, show similar patterns of mass loss. The GRACE and GLIMS measurements also confirm this view. Multiple lines of evidence all point to the same conclusion: glaciers and ice sheets worldwide are losing mass, in some cases rapidly.

A final variant on this myth comes in the form of *exaggerations* of the rate of glacier melt. In an unfortunate case of bad proofreading and editing, the Intergovernmental Panel on Climate Change (IPCC)'s 2007 report included a statement that the Himalayas would lose 80% of its glacier area by 2035. The original source for this claim appears to be a 2005 World Wildlife Fund report, which cited an interview in *New Scientist* with Indian scientist Syed Hasnain. In this interview, Hasnain speculated that the glaciers might disappear by 2035, although this speculation was not supported by peer-reviewed research. Unfortunately, the rigorous IPCC processes were not followed in this case, which underscores the importance of adhering to their stringent standards and reliance on peer-reviewed scientific research (see Cook, 2010, for a complete account). The IPCC is the world's most authoritative source on climate change and has an exhaustive process of peer review, so letting such a mistake slip into its final report was a serious error. However, the IPCC eventually recognized the mistake and issued a correction. The facts about the melting of glaciers and ice sheets worldwide are serious enough in their own right. They do not need to be exaggerated.

FURTHER READING

Barry, R., and Gan, T. Y. (2011). *The Global Cryosphere: Past, Present and Future.* Cambridge University Press.

Chasing Ice. (2012). Documentary film. Available at http://www.chasingice .com/.

Cook, J. (2010). Himalayan Glaciers: How the IPCC Erred and What the Science Says. Available at https://www.skepticalscience.com/IPCC-Himalayan-glacier-2035-prediction-intermediate.htm. Accessed April 17, 2016.

Crichton, M. (2004). *State of Fear.* HarperCollins, New York, New York.

Extreme Ice Survey. Extreme Ice Survey—A Program of Earth Vision Institute. http://extremeicesurvey.org/. Accessed February 7, 2015.

Goreham, S. (2013). *The Mad, Mad, Mad World of Climatism: Mankind and Climate Change Mania.* New Lenox Books.

Idso, C. D., Carter, R. M., and Singer, S. F. (2013). *Climate Change Reconsidered II:* 2013 Report of the Nongovernmental International Panel on Climate Change (NIPCC). Nongovernmental International Panel on Climate Change.

Kargel, J. S., Leonard, G. J., Bishop, M. P., Kaab, A., and Raup, B. (Eds.). (2014). *Global Land Ice Measurements from Space.* Springer-Praxis. 33 chapters, 876 pages. ISBN: 978-3-540-79817-0.

Parry, M. L. (Ed.). (2007). *Climate Change 2007: Impacts, Adaptation and Vulnerability: Contribution of Working Group II to the Fourth Assessment Report of the Intergovernmental Panel on Climate Change* (Vol. 4). Cambridge

University Press. Available at http://www.ipcc.ch/publications_and_data/ar4/wg2/en/contents.html. Accessed February 7, 2015.

Racoviteanu, A., Arnaud, Y., Williams, M., and Manley, W. F. (2014). Spatial patterns in glacier area and elevation changes from 1962 to 2006 in the monsoon-influenced eastern Himalaya. *The Cryosphere Discussions*, 8(4), 3949–3998.

Racoviteanu, A. E., Arnaud, Y., Williams, M. W., and Ordonez, J. (2008). Decadal changes in glacier parameters in the Cordillera Blanca, Peru, derived from remote sensing. *Journal of Glaciology*, 54(186), 499–510.

World Glacier Monitoring Service. (2008). Global Glacier Changes: Facts and Figures. UNEP/WGMS. Available at http://www.wgms.ch/downloads/wgms_2008_ggc.pdf. Accessed February 1, 2015.

Q4. DO GLOBAL AVERAGE SURFACE AIR TEMPERATURES SHOW WARMING?

Answer: Yes. When averaged together and analyzed by multiple independent teams of scientists using different methods, surface air temperature measurements from thermometers at weather stations around the world indicate a general warming trend for the Earth.

The Facts: In the summer of 2012, the Berkeley Earth project, a team of scientists studying annual changes in the Earth's average temperature, released its results. The team had spent more than two years painstakingly collecting measurements of air temperature near the Earth's surface, taken by thermometers in weather stations all over the world. They then compiled the readings into a single value representing the average temperature for the Earth as a whole, one global average temperature value per year stretching all the way back from the present to 1750. To publicize their findings, one of the project's founders, Richard Muller, a physicist at the University of California-Berkeley, did the rounds of the television news media and wrote opinion columns for the *New York Times* (e.g., Muller, 2012). By the standards of climate science, it was a media blitz.

Many climate scientists, however, greeted the Berkeley Earth results with interest, but not much excitement. This was because several teams of scientists at leading research universities and government agencies around the world, such as NASA and NOAA in the United States, and the Climatic Research Unit (CRU) at Britain's University of East Anglia, had been doing the same thing for years or, in some cases, decades.

Berkeley Earth was simply the latest addition to an already-crowded field. And although Berkeley Earth used its own, independently developed methods, its results were practically identical to those of the other teams. To nobody's surprise, Berkeley Earth had found that the world had warmed up by about 0.8°C over the 20th century, that most of the warming had occurred since 1970, and that the rate of warming was accelerating—exactly what all the other teams had found years ago (Figure 1.3). Berkeley Earth's results were a welcome addition but hardly a game changer.

To understand why a team of accomplished scientists would spend years replicating results that had already been verified several times, it helps to understand what goes into calculating global average temperature. Ultimately, this is a challenge of isolating a signal from some quite noisy data. Imagine a radio operator listening for a distress message coming in through a sea of static. The message is there, but the static makes it hard to hear. The radio operator might use different techniques to enhance the distress signal digitally, making it stand out more clearly. Data scientists working on global average temperature are a little like the radio operator straining to hear the emergency signal, and there are several sources of static that they must contend with.

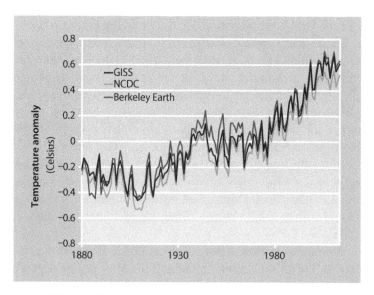

Figure 1.3 Three different, independent reconstructions of global average surface temperature from weather station thermometers.
Source: GISS/NCDC/Berkeley Earth.

First, crunching the numbers from hundreds, sometimes thousands, of thermometers around the world into a single value requires allowing for the fact that the thermometers are not equally spaced around the world—so not every place on Earth is equally represented. Weather stations tend to be set up where people are, so Europe and the eastern United States have a lot of measurements, while the Amazon Rainforest and the Sahara Desert have very few. Notable gaps also exist for the oceans, where measurements are made of air temperature and sea surface temperature by ships, and for the polar regions.

Adjusting for this uneven coverage is a technical challenge that many scientists relish, and there is more than one reasonable way to do it—and there are plenty of arguments about the best way to do it. Rather like knowing the quickest way across town, or the smartest way to load the dishwasher, everyone seems to have his or her own method of accounting for the gaps in weather station coverage. Britain's CRU, for example, more or less ignores the Arctic because there are so few readings from there, while NASA's Goddard Institute for Space Studies (GISS) uses statistics to fill in the gaps between stations. Because the Arctic is warming a lot faster than the rest of the planet, CRU's global average temperature for any given year tends to be a bit cooler than GISS's in recent years. Other teams use slightly different approaches as well, yielding slightly different global average temperatures. Even though the data have been analyzed many times, in many different ways, the idea of coming up with a new approach just that little bit better than everyone else's can be irresistible to many scientists, and that was one of the motivations for the Berkeley Earth project. Ultimately, however, the differences in the final results have turned out to be very small, and the trend of warming over time is fundamentally the same, no matter how the numbers are crunched—as Figure 1.3 shows. This is a strong indicator that the warming trend is a real one that is actually in the data, and is not a consequence of how the average is calculated.

But uneven distribution of weather stations is just one of the challenges in figuring the Earth's average temperature. Many weather stations have gone out of service over time, for example due to war, or economic or political collapse. Even those weather stations that have continuous records for long periods of time have almost certainly upgraded their instruments as newer, more accurate thermometers became available, or undergone other changes in observation methods, such as a shift in the time of day when the temperature was recorded. For example, the U.S. weather observation network underwent just such a shift between the 1940s and the 1990s, from recording temperatures at sunset to recording them at sunrise.

Temperatures are colder at sunrise, so this shift in observation time has made the temperatures for the United States over this period appear to be colder than they really are. Scientists have adjusted for this change by estimating the temperatures for each station in the network based on the time of sunrise and height of the Sun in the sky, and verifying the estimate against the times of the day when measurements are available (see Karl et al., 1986, and Vose et al., 2003, for technical details). The corrections are different for each station, but combined, they add about 0.2°C to U.S. temperatures as a whole from the 1940s to the 1990s, filtering out some of the static from the data.

Other ways that the temperature readings can be influenced include changes in the landscape around the thermometer, either because the thermometer has been moved or because the land has changed—over time, trees get cut down, or fields get paved over and turned into parking lots and shopping malls. Different land surfaces respond to the Sun's energy differently, giving different heating and cooling patterns. One especially important example of this is known as the urban heat island effect: cities are warmer than the surrounding countryside, partly because dark parking lots and roads absorb sunlight more easily and partly because fields and plants contain lots of water, which helps keep them cool through evaporation. Suddenly relocating a weather station from a rooftop to a nearby field would introduce an artificial cooling, just as moving it to an airport containing large expanses of paved surfaces would make the temperatures suddenly jump upward.

Cleaning out influences in the temperature data from these kinds of changes in the surrounding landscape is another of the challenges facing data scientists working on global average temperature, and once again there are several different possible ways to do it. Some teams, like Berkeley Earth, try to use only weather stations that can accurately be described as rural, eliminating any chance of contamination from the urban heat island effect. Other teams compare the trend over time for rural stations compared with urban stations, and adjust for any differences that might appear in the urban stations' trend. However, once again, it does not really seem to matter all that much which of the various cleaning-up techniques is used. Figure 1.3 shows that several different teams, all using their own methods, all ultimately arrive at very similar results. The thermometer data show that the world is warming, with most of the recent warming having taken place since 1970, and the warming is accelerating.

Furthermore, the warming trend in the thermometer data matches other, more indirect observations of Earth's temperature, such as melting glaciers or measurements of air temperature taken from satellites.

Just about every indicator we have points to a warming planet, with the possible exception of Antarctic sea ice (as discussed in question 2)—and even there, the growth of Antarctic sea ice is happening against a backdrop of warming temperatures. The record of surface air temperature from thermometers is simply one more piece of the puzzle. As climate scientist Richard Alley has put it, the scientific case for climate change hangs not from a single thread, but from a strong cable of many threads woven together. Multiple different analyses of the surface air temperature record all point toward warming—and so do multiple other indicators of temperature. This strongly suggests that the surface air temperature record is in fact a reliable indicator of a warming world.

Myths about the surface temperature record tend to focus on the technical challenges associated with cleaning out the static and strengthening the signal. Specifically, the existence of those challenges is used to suggest that the surface temperature record is inherently unreliable. This is a central argument of the late Michael Crichton's 2004 novel *State of Fear*, which draws particular attention to the uneven distribution of weather stations, the challenges of maintaining accurate records over a long period of time, and the contamination of temperature records from the growth of cities. As urban areas have sprawled out into what used to be green fields, any weather stations that were once located in the countryside might now find themselves in a suburban landscape of roads and buildings. The urban heat island effect would have reached out to affect their thermometers, so any warming over time could be an artifact of the changing landscape.

Influence on temperature data by factors other than the climate, such as the growth of cities, is a real issue. In an impressive work of citizen science, a group of over 650 volunteers was recruited by the SurfaceStations.org project to survey the location of as many U.S. weather stations as possible, ultimately checking over 860. The SurfaceStations team took photographs using infrared cameras to show the contaminating effect of nearby warm buildings and parking lots, and many of their images are visually very impressive. Ultimately, however, all the project really did was to draw attention to a problem that scientists were already well aware of. Filtering out the static from non-climatic effects such as urban heat islands is a core part of the challenge of constructing global average temperatures, and, as noted earlier, many different teams, trying many different filtering techniques—including using only rural stations—ultimately arrive at the same conclusion: that the world really is getting warmer. This conclusion is supported not only by all the independent reconstructions of global average temperature but by the overall behavior of the rest of the climate system, such as melting glaciers and Arctic sea ice. These various different lines of evidence all suggest that, despite the difficulties, the surface temperature record is showing a warming trend that is real, not artificially introduced by contaminating effects.

While the focus on urban heat islands suggests, incorrectly, that scientists have failed to remove an artificial warming trend, another version of the myth focuses on scientists filtering out artificial cooling. Without knowing, for example, that the U.S. weather observers gradually shifted their observing times from warmer sunset to cooler sunrise, it could easily look as though the adjustment necessary to correct for the artificial cooling is actually inflating the thermometer readings and introducing an artificial warming. Several concerned voices have pointed to adjustments of this nature. For example, Steve Goreham, in *The Mad, Mad, Mad World of Climatism*, writes, "The U.S. government makes 'adjustments' to the raw temperature data. . . . *So NOAA is adding a half-degree* [Fahrenheit] upward temperature bias to the raw thermometer data! This gives a whole new meaning to the phrase 'man-made global warming'" (pp. 150–151, emphasis in original). Similarly, Britain's *Daily Telegraph* has featured columns by Christopher Booker, accusing scientists of adjusting temperature readings upward to support a narrative of warming—basically, manipulating the data so that they show what scientists already believe to be happening.

Typically, however, sources of this myth do not explain the background of why the adjustments were made. A little additional research shows that the adjustments are not cases of malpractice by scientists, but are entirely appropriate attempts to correct biases in the data from other sources, such as the change in observing time described earlier. Furthermore, most sea surface temperature measurements taken from ships have been adjusted to account for changes in measurement practices: prior to about 1945, it was common to fill a bucket with seawater, pull it on deck, and measure the temperature with a thermometer. Evaporation meant that temperatures measured using this bucket technique are cooler than those using a technique common after 1945, measuring the temperature of water drawn in to cool ships' engines. The artificially cooler temperatures earlier in the record exaggerate the warming trend, so scientists have adjusted the earlier temperatures upward, bringing them closer to more recent temperatures. Because the oceans cover more than 70% of Earth's surface, the overall effect of these adjustments is to bring the global warming trend *down* when land and ocean temperatures are combined. The raw data for the Earth as a whole show *more* warming than the adjusted data. Climate scientists are not making global warming out to be more dramatic than it really is. (For an especially clear and readable account of these issues, see the 2015 post on SkepticalScience.com by Zeke Hausfather, 2015, a Berkeley Earth project scientist.)

In fact, concerns about exactly these issues were among the motivations of Berkeley Earth's Richard Muller to set up his own, independent analysis of the surface temperature record. By finding virtually identical trends to all the other teams engaged in this research, Berkeley Earth demonstrated clearly that the surface temperature record is, in fact, reliable and that the filtering techniques are not being applied in a biased way. The scientific challenge of improving on the existing techniques is still there, however, and Berkeley Earth has not been the last word on the subject.

In 2014, scientists Kevin Cowtan and Robert Way introduced yet another new approach to reducing the static and clarifying the signal, and again found results that are ultimately very close to all the other teams. Along with the many other indicators of climate change, such as melting glaciers and Arctic sea ice, this independent replication, repeated many times over, confirms the view that the surface temperature record is a reliable measure of a warming world. Just as the surface temperature record is one strand in the cable of evidence showing global warming, so any single analysis of the surface temperature record is one of several—all showing the same results.

FURTHER READING

Berkeley Earth (2015). Summary of Findings. Available at http://berkeley earth.org/summary-of-findings. Accessed February 25, 2015.

Booker, C. (2015). The fiddling with temperature data is the biggest science scandal ever. *The Daily Telegraph*, February 7, 2015, available at http://www.telegraph.co.uk/news/earth/environment/globalwarming/11395516/The-fiddling-with-temperature-data-is-the-biggest-science-scandal-ever.html. Accessed February 25, 2015.

Cowtan, K., and Way, R.G. (2014). Coverage bias in the HadCRUT4 temperature series and its impact on recent temperature trends. *Quarterly Journal of the Royal Meteorological Society*, 140(683), 1935–1944. Project website http://www-users.york.ac.uk/~kdc3/papers/coverage2013/background.html. Accessed February 25, 2015.

Crichton, M. (2004). *State of Fear*. HarperCollins, New York, New York.

Goreham, S. (2013). *The Mad, Mad, Mad World of Climatism: Mankind and Climate Change Mania*. New Lenox Books.

Hausfather, Z. (2015). Understanding adjustments to temperature data. Posted to SkepticalScience.com, February 26, 2015, available at https://www.skepticalscience.com/understanding-adjustments-to-temp-data.html. Accessed March 11, 2015.

Karl, T.R., Williams Jr, C.N., Young, P.J., and Wendland, W.M. (1986). A model to estimate the time of observation bias associated with monthly mean maximum, minimum and mean temperatures for the

United States. *Journal of Climate and Applied Meteorology*, 25(2), 145–160.

Muller, R. A. (2012). The conversion of a climate change skeptic. *The New York Times*, July 28, 2012 (published in print July 30, page A19), available at http://www.nytimes.com/2012/07/30/opinion/the-conversion-of-a-climate-change-skeptic.html?_r=0. Accessed February 25, 2015.

NASA Goddard Institute for Space Studies. (2015). GISS Surface Temperature Analysis (GISTemp). Available at http://data.giss.nasa.gov/gistemp/. Accessed February 25, 2015.

NOAA National Climatic Data Center. (n.d.). Monitoring Global and U.S. Temperatures at NOAA's National Climatic Data Center. Available at http://www.ncdc.noaa.gov/monitoring-references/faq/temperature-monitoring.php. Accessed February 8, 2015.

NOAA National Climatic Data Center. (n.d.). Global Historical Climatology Network. Available at http://www.ncdc.noaa.gov/data-access/land-based-station-data/land-based-datasets/global-historical-climatology-network-ghcn. Accessed February 25, 2015.

Vose, R.S., Williams, C.N., Peterson, T.C., Karl, T.R., and Easterling, D.R. (2003). An evaluation of the time of observation bias adjustment in the US Historical Climatology Network. *Geophysical Research Letters*, 30(20): DOI: 10.1029/2003GL018111.

Watts, A. (2009). Is the US surface temperature record reliable. The Heartland Institute, Chicago, IL. Available at https://wattsupwiththat.files.wordpress.com/2009/05/surfacestationsreport_spring09.pdf. Accessed February 8, 2015.

Q5. DO SATELLITES USING "THERMOMETERS IN SPACE" SHOW A WARMING TREND IN EARTH'S LOWER ATMOSPHERE?

Answer: Satellite measurements of the Earth's lower atmosphere, known as the troposphere, show warming—after one team's mistake in interpreting the data was found and corrected.

The Facts: As discussed in question 4, building a coherent, accurate global average surface temperature record is painstaking work. The appeal of trying to measure air temperature using satellites, which are unaffected by urban heat islands or the sampling problems that come with uneven distribution of weather stations, is clear, and in recent years, climate scientists have turned their attention to archives of satellite measurements of air temperature. In the late 1970s, NASA began launching a series of weather satellites intended to measure air temperature at various different altitudes. Although the satellites were originally intended to study weather, not climate, the data have now been collected for long enough to provide an important line of evidence showing global warming. Two different teams have analyzed the satellite data, one at the University of Alabama-Huntsville (UAH) and one at the private corporation Remote Sensing Systems (RSS). Both show warming of the lowest roughly 8 km of the atmosphere, a layer called the lower troposphere, of around 0.14°C per decade (according to UAH), and 0.12°C per decade (according to RSS) for the period 1979–2014 (Figure 1.4). Furthermore, the data products from UAH and RSS have themselves been scrutinized by two other independent teams, all of

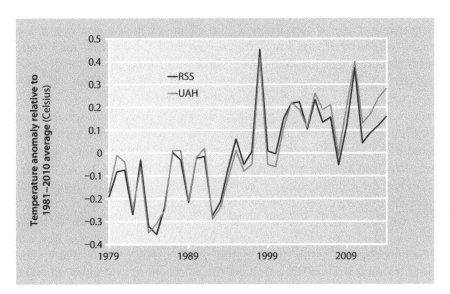

Figure 1.4 Two independent estimates of global average temperature changes of the lower troposphere 1979–2014, derived from satellite measurements of microwave radiation from oxygen molecules in the atmosphere at different heights. Temperatures are shown as differences from the 1981–2010 average, for the two most widely cited interpretations of the satellite data—Remote Sensing Systems (RSS) and the University of Alabama-Huntsville (UAH).

Source: Data archived by the National Climatic Data Center, available at http://www.ncdc.noaa.gov/temp-and-precip/msu/time-series/global/lt/jan/ann. Accessed March 11, 2015.

whom find warming of the lower troposphere to varying degrees—from around 0.11°C per decade for 1979–2001 (Fu et al., 2004) to around 0.18°C per decade for 1979–2006 (Zou and Wang, 2010).

If the instruments aboard the satellites are basically thermometers in space, why is there a need for multiple independent studies of the satellite data, and why are there slight differences between their findings? It turns out that measuring air temperature from space is a difficult thing to do. The satellites are not measuring temperature directly but are measuring microwave radiation from oxygen molecules at various levels in the atmosphere. The amount of microwave radiation is directly proportional to the air temperature, so in principle, converting the microwave measurements into a temperature reading should be fairly straightforward. In practice, though, just as with the surface temperature record from weather stations, there are numerous sources of static that need to be filtered out in order to get a clear reading of temperature.

For example, scientists trying to measure the temperature of the lower troposphere have to contend with the effects of the atmosphere above that layer, between the lower troposphere and the satellite taking the measurements. The air in between also contains oxygen molecules giving off microwaves. At a high-enough altitude, in the next layer up—the stratosphere—the atmosphere is actually cooling. In order to measure the temperature of the lower troposphere, the effects of the stratosphere must be filtered out. It's a bit like trying to read a road sign when your car's windshield is fogged up or iced over: you can make out roughly what the sign says, but the fog or ice on the windshield makes it harder to see. Clearing the windshield, or filtering out the effects of the atmosphere between the satellite and the lower troposphere, makes it easier to read.

Furthermore, the satellites' orbits shift very gradually over time. There are several reasons for this, but one of the more obvious is that there is slight frictional drag with the very thin upper atmosphere. This alters the orbit, causing the satellites to view the atmosphere in slightly different ways from one day to the next. Just as with the changes in the time of observation for the United States' surface temperature data examined in question 4, these orbital changes have to be taken into account in order to get a clear, accurate reading of temperatures for the various different levels of the atmosphere. And similar to the efforts to filter out static in the surface temperature record, different climate research teams have their own approaches.

What's striking about these different approaches is that they all yield essentially the same results: a warming troposphere (Figure 1.4) and a cooling stratosphere (Figure 1.5). This happens because the thickening

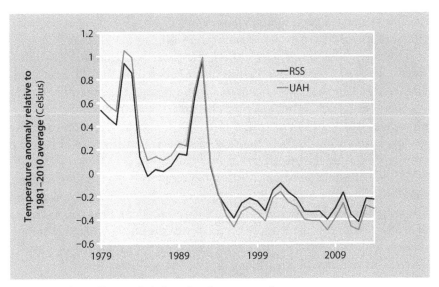

Figure 1.5 As Figure 1.4, but for the stratosphere.
Source: NCDC.

blanket of carbon dioxide and other greenhouse gases that trap heat in the troposphere prevents heat from escaping into the higher levels of the stratosphere. Consequently, tropospheric warming combined with stratospheric cooling is a key fingerprint of a human influence on global climate. There are differences between each team's estimates, to be sure, but these are small compared with the similarities. Having all of these different approaches converge on the same result is not, by itself, a guarantee that they're correct—but this convergence gives us a lot more confidence than if the results of different filtering methods were all radically different from each other.

In fact, for several years in the 1990s and early 2000s, the UAH team *did* have a radically different interpretation of the satellite data. They showed a lower troposphere that was warming very slowly, or even cooling slightly, compared with surface temperatures and climate model expectations (Christy et al., 1995). This finding was at odds with almost every other indicator of temperature change. The UAH studies provided a source for the myth that satellites do not show warming of the troposphere. As Michael Crichton wrote in *State of Fear* (2004): "Since 1979 we've had orbiting satellites that can continuously measure the atmosphere five miles up. They show that the upper atmosphere [meaning the troposphere] is warming much less than the ground is. . . . Trust me, the satellite data have been re-analyzed dozens of times. . . . They're probably the most intensely scrutinized data in the world" (pp. 99–100).

This last claim about how closely the data were examined is unfortunate, because this version of the myth is based on an old interpretation of the data that was later found to be wrong. Prompted by UAH's incongruous results, other scientists began to pore through the raw satellite data and UAH's processing methods. Eventually, a team from the private corporation Remote Sensing Systems found that UAH had not correctly adjusted for the orbital drift of the satellites (Mears and Wentz, 2005). When the adjustment was applied properly, UAH's measurements matched the other indications of warming in the lower atmosphere and at the surface, such as melting ice. This is an excellent example of science at work: results diverge from other evidence and from what theory predicts; scientists investigate the discrepancy; and the problem is eventually solved—in this case by identifying an error in one set of results.

Another version of the myth that satellites show no warming in the troposphere is more recent and emphasizes an absence of marked warming since 1998. While it's true that warming has slowed in recent years, this is for a relatively short period compared with the overall trend since 1979, shown in Figure 1.4. In other words, even though the entire record shows warming, the warming progresses in fits and starts, making it possible to isolate short segments that show no warming, or even cooling. We'll look at the claim of a global warming slowdown in more detail in question 7, but it's certainly applied to the satellite data by many blogs and websites, such as a 2015 article by David Rothbard at the website for the Committee for a Constructive Tomorrow (CFACT.org), and posts at Marc Morano's ClimateDepot.com. Focusing on short periods is a technique used to suggest that warming has stopped, or, as in question 1, that Arctic sea ice has recovered—but it's misleading, because it does not consider the full picture.

Claims that the satellites show no warming are often accompanied by claims that the satellite data are the most reliable indicator we have of global air temperatures. David Rothbard's (2015) CFACT.org article, for example, states that satellite temperature measurements are superior to those from the surface because "[t]heir coverage is more complete and the data they yield is much more difficult to manipulate." This glosses over the considerable challenges of taking measurements of microwave radiation from the lower troposphere, adjusting for the interference that the radiation encounters on its way through the atmosphere to reach an instrument on a satellite high up in space (which is itself subject to slight changes in its orbit), and finally converting it into a temperature reading.

As with selectively focusing on a segment of the record that happens to show cooling, these claims of superior reliability from the satellite measurements understate the difficulties with one measurement technique (the satellites) and overplay the difficulties with another (the surface temperature record).

FURTHER READING

Christy, J. R., Spencer, R. W., and McNider, R. T. (1995). Reducing noise in the MSU daily lower-tropospheric global temperature dataset. *Journal of Climate*, 8, 888–896.

Crichton, M. (2004). *State of Fear*. HarperCollins, New York, New York.

Fu, Q., Johanson, C. M., Warren, S. G., and Seidel, D. J. (2004). Contribution of stratospheric cooling to satellite-inferred tropospheric temperature trends. *Nature*, 429(6987), 55–58.

Mears, C. A., and Wentz, F. J. (2005). The effect of diurnal correction on satellite-derived lower tropospheric temperature. *Science*, 309(5740), 1548–1551.

Morano, M. (2015). Scientists balk at "hottest year" claims: ignores Satellites showing 18 Year "Pause"—"We are arguing over the significance of hundredths of a degree"—The "Pause" continues. Posted to ClimateDepot.com, January 16, 2015, available at http://www .climatedepot.com/2015/01/16/scientists-balk-at-hottest-year-claims-we-are-arguing-over-the-significance-of-hundredths-of-a-degree-the-pause-continues/. Accessed March 11, 2015.

Rothbard, D. (2015). Satellites: warming pause continues and 2014 not the hottest. Posted to CFACT.org, February 7, 2015, available at http://www.cfact.org/2015/02/07/satellites-warming-pause-continues-2014-not-the-hottest/. Accessed March 11, 2015.

Zou, C. Z., and Wang, W. (2010). Stability of the MSU-derived atmospheric temperature trend. *Journal of Atmospheric and Oceanic Technology*, 27(11), 1960–1971.

Q6. HOW MIGHT GLOBAL WARMING BE CAUSING RECORD COLD WINTERS IN SOME PLACES?

Answer: Global warming is a global-scale phenomenon, with different local consequences depending on a wide range of geographical factors.

Even as some places have recently experienced record winter snowfalls and cold winters, others have experienced record winter warmth.

The Facts: This chapter has already examined four clear indicators that the world is getting warmer: melting Arctic sea ice, melting land ice, warmer global temperatures in the lower atmosphere, and warmer global temperatures at the Earth's surface. Question 2, however, looked at a more complicated situation, where Antarctic sea ice is growing slightly even as the air and oceans in the region get warmer.

This phenomenon hints at a broader challenge with understanding climate change: the buildup of heat-trapping gases in the atmosphere may sometimes produce puzzling, counterintuitive results for the Earth's climate. While the big, global-scale picture is clear—the Earth is getting warmer over time—individual places or regions have recently experienced very cold, snowy winters. Focusing on these exceptions, however, is a little like focusing only on the lowest test scores in a student's record: it's not an accurate representation of the whole picture, because it ignores the high scores. However, understanding *why* some places are experiencing colder, snowier winters is an interesting question in climate science and is worth examining in some detail.

There is no doubt among scientists that burning fossil fuels has raised concentrations of CO_2 and other heat-trapping gases in the atmosphere to their highest levels in at least 800,000 years, and probably much longer. These gases are trapping ever-greater amounts of heat in Earth's atmosphere. The most obvious manifestation of this is the increase in air temperatures, discussed in questions 4 and 5.

However, this does not mean that the planet will experience a uniform, straight-line increase in temperature, with each day, month, or year progressively a little warmer than the last, nor should every place on Earth be expected to warm in the same way at the same rate. This is because the climate system consists of many interconnected parts besides just the atmosphere. Each of these parts influences and is influenced by the others, and some of those parts do not simply warm up when heat is added to the system. Water evaporates, for example, or ice melts. These are clear responses of the physical world to additional heat, but they don't result in a change in temperature (the change from solid to liquid or liquid to gas involves *latent*, or hidden, heat). Because the Earth has varied geography—ice and snow in some places, rainforests in others, oceans in others, mountains scattered unevenly across the globe—the exact ways that the additional trapped heat shows up vary from place to place. And the resulting changes can then go on to influence the weather, both locally and far away.

For example, question 1 documents that Arctic sea ice is in a state of dramatic collapse, especially in summer. As the shiny, reflective sea ice melts, it exposes the darker water underneath. The Arctic Ocean then absorbs more sunlight, getting warmer still and melting yet more sea ice. The whole process feeds on itself in what's known as a *positive feedback*, an amplifying mechanism that causes a small initial change to get bigger and bigger. Several positive feedbacks, collectively known as Arctic amplification, seem to be at work in this region, combining to warm the Arctic at more than twice the global average rate (Jeffries et al., 2013, has a useful summary). Other places, with other characteristics, are not warming as quickly.

Different places, then, respond differently to global warming because of the Earth's varied geography. But the consequences of a rapidly warming Arctic aren't confined just to that region. They may be spreading to the entire Northern Hemisphere by changing the speed of the jet stream. The jet stream—a belt of strong winds girdling the planet in the upper atmosphere—gets its power from the difference in temperature between the equator and the pole. Because the Arctic has warmed more than the equator, that temperature difference has gotten smaller, which should theoretically weaken the jet stream. When fluids slow down, they start to move in wavier patterns, and because fluids can be liquids or gases, this behavior can be seen in rivers of water or in rivers of air, like the jet stream. Just as a stream of water flowing out of the mountains starts to swing back and forth as it emerges onto the plains, so the jet stream might be expected to follow a more meandering path as it slows down because of the weaker temperature gradient between equator and pole. The bigger waves in the jet stream should produce sharp differences in temperature across large regions of the Northern Hemisphere, like the United States, as waves coming down from the North Pole bring very cold air toward the equator, and waves coming up from the equator bring much warmer air toward the pole. Recent heat waves in Russia might also fit this pattern. (See work by Jennifer Francis, the climate scientist most closely associated with this idea—e.g., Francis, 2015, or Francis and Vavrus, 2012.) The evidence for this particular phenomenon is growing, but is not yet conclusive, and the scientific community has not reached a consensus on the issue. But if the idea is correct, it would explain how long-term global warming can lead to short-term local cooling for regions stuck under a wave bringing very cold air southward from the Arctic.

Interconnections like the one between the warming Arctic and the jet stream not only explain counterintuitive local responses to global warming but also show how weather is inherently different from climate. The connections mean that small changes in one place can be amplified into much larger changes elsewhere. As meteorologist Ed Lorenz (1995) put it, a butterfly flapping its wings in Brazil could cause a tornado in Texas, giving the name to this area of atmospheric science: the butterfly effect. The climate system contains so many interconnected parts that a small disturbance in one place can have large consequences in another place and later in time. This makes the behavior of weather inherently variable over the short term, which is why it's hard to predict more than a few days in advance (see Gleick, 1987, for an accessible introduction to the butterfly effect and its older sibling, chaos theory). As question 7 will explain, the variability tends to decrease, and the predictability tends to increase, with progressively longer timescales and larger spatial scales.

This tendency is why it's very important to distinguish between weather and climate. Weather is short term and highly variable from day to day, week to week or month to month; climate is long term and much less variable. The long run of global warming can be punctuated by shorter-term events. Like going for a walk with a dog, or a small child, the overall direction of the walk might be interrupted by reversals, accelerations, small detours, or short pauses as new and interesting distractions appear, giving a pattern of short-term variability superimposed on top of the long-term overall direction (see University Corporation for Atmospheric Research Center for Science Education, 2015, for a helpful video showing this idea).

One such recent short-term detour has been record cold and snowy winters in the eastern United States and western Europe. While these record cold snaps have been a recurrent phenomenon in the past few years, and have brought significant difficulties to the people living in the affected areas, they have been counterbalanced by record warm winters elsewhere—exactly the pattern you'd expect if the jet stream was weakening, as described earlier. In the winter of 2014–2015, as cities across New York, Pennsylvania, Ohio, and Illinois set record low temperatures, Arizona, California, Nevada, Utah, and Washington had their warmest winter on record, and six more western states experienced a winter that was among their top 10 warmest, according to NOAA's State of the Climate Report for February 2015. Because most people in the United States live in the eastern states, more people have experienced colder winters recently, but this does not mean that the United States as a whole has experienced colder winters. In fact, data from NOAA's National Climatic Data Center show that, over time, the percentage of the U.S. land area experiencing very warm winters has increased relative to the percentage experiencing very cold winters (Figure 1.6).

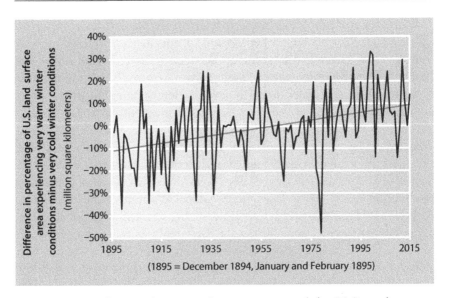

Figure 1.6 Difference between the percentage of the U.S. surface area experiencing very warm conditions and very cold conditions in winter, 1895–1896 to 2014–2015. Difference is calculated as very warm percentage minus very cold percentage. Winter is defined as December, January, and February.

Source: Data archived by the National Climatic Data Center, available at http://www.ncdc.noaa.gov/temp-and-precip/uspa/?area=warm-cold&year=2014&month=12. Accessed March 13, 2015.

Statistics like these show how misleading it is to focus on what's happening locally to claim the climate is not warming globally. It's understandable—when you're shoveling record amounts of snow out of the driveway, it's hard to remember that not everyone, everywhere is having the same experience—but it's still misleading. Unfortunately, there's no shortage of news reports and blog posts doing exactly this. Even elected representatives have made this mistake, as Sen. James Inhofe, R-Oklahoma, demonstrated in February 2015. According to *The Washington Post*, Senator Inhofe spoke out against "hysteria on global warming" by holding up a snowball on the Senate floor and saying, "I ask the chair, do you know what this is? It's a snowball, just from outside here. It's very, very cold out." He then reportedly tossed the snowball at the Senate's presiding officer. This assumption by Senator Inhofe, that what happens in Washington, D.C., must be happening everywhere in the country, or globally, has been evident in statements made by other members of the U.S. Congress as well (Friedman, 2010).

While Senator Inhofe's error was to focus on one *place* while ignoring the whole country (or planet), other versions of this myth get mixed up over issues of *time*, blurring the boundary between short-term and long-term change. Global warming will, in the long run, reduce the overall amount of winter snow, especially in the Northern Hemisphere; but in the short run, the fits and starts of the climate system's inherent variability—those distractions of the dog on its walk—mean that some places may, for a time, get colder and snowier. This is easy to make fun of—global warming explains both warmer conditions *and* colder conditions?—and Steve Goreham (2013) does exactly that in *The Mad, Mad, Mad World of Climatism*, in a section titled "Snow Is a Sign of Global Warming?" (pp. 120–124). Although it is counterintuitive to associate heavy snow with global warming, a moment's reflection shows that there really is no conflict between the two. The myth that more snow in the short run cannot coexist with global warming confuses the long-term trend with short-term variability, and ignores the variations from place to place.

The effects of global warming as we personally experience them will often be indirect results of changes in atmospheric circulation such as changes in the jet stream, and may not always be as intuitively obvious as hotter summers, warmer winters, more heat waves or more droughts. Strange weather of all stripes can be a reaction of the climate system to added energy, which is why the terms "climate change" or even "global weirding" have been used as alternative names for global warming (Friedman, 2010). It's also why a focus on short-term, local weather is misleading.

FURTHER READING

Francis, J. (2015). A melting Arctic and weird weather: the plot thickens. *The Conversation*, February 18, 2015, available at http://theconversation.com/a-melting-arctic-and-weird-weather-the-plot-thickens-37314. Accessed March 14, 2015.

Francis, J. A., and Vavrus, S. J. (2012). Evidence linking Arctic amplification to extreme weather in mid-latitudes. *Geophysical Research Letters*, 39(6), DOI: 10.1029/2012GL051000.

Friedman, T. L. (2010). Global weirding is here. *The New York Times*, A23, available at http://www.nytimes.com/2010/02/17/opinion/17friedman.html?_r=0. Accessed March 15, 2015.

Gleick, J. (1987). *Chaos: Making a New Science*. New York: Viking Penguin.

Goreham, S. (2013). *The Mad, Mad, Mad World of Climatism: Mankind and Climate Change Mania*. New Lenox Books.

Jeffries, M.O., Overland, J.E., and Perovich, D.K. (2013). The Arctic shifts to a new normal. *Physics Today*, 66(10), 35–40.

Lorenz, E.N. (1995). *The Essence of Chaos*. University of Washington Press.

NOAA National Climatic Data Center, State of the Climate: National Overview for February 2015, published online March 2015, available at http://www.ncdc.noaa.gov/sotc/national/. Accessed March 16, 2015.

University Corporation for Atmospheric Research Center for Science Education. (2015). From Dog Walking to Weather and Climate. Available at http://scied.ucar.edu/dog-walking-weather-and-climate. Accessed March 14, 2015.

The Washington Post Editorial Board. (2015). Sen. Jim Inhofe Embarrasses the GOP and the U.S. March 1, 2015. Available at http://www.washington post.com/opinions/a-snowballs-chance/2015/03/01/46e9e00e-bec8-11e4-bdfa-b8e8f594e6ee_story.html. Accessed March 13, 2015.

Q7. HOW AND WHY HAS THE PACE OF GLOBAL WARMING CHANGED OVER TIME?

Answer: Earth's climate system is gaining more energy than it loses every year; exactly how the extra energy is distributed across the climate system varies over time, resulting in periods of faster and slower warming.

The Facts: Climate scientists have documented striking changes in the Earth's climate, including melting Arctic sea ice, melting glaciers and ice sheets, and rising air temperatures. These changes are all symptoms of the same root cause: the Earth's energy budget is out of balance, causing the climate system to gain more energy than it loses, due to an ever-thickening blanket of greenhouse gases in the atmosphere. Current estimates are that the Earth is accumulating energy at a rate of 0.5 to 1.0 $W.m^{-2}$ (Hansen et al., 2013; Trenberth and Fasullo, 2013). This is the equivalent of four atomic bombs' worth of heat every second (Cook and Nuccitelli, 2013), and this accumulating energy is responsible for the melting ice and rising air temperatures. As dramatic as these effects are, however, they represent the work of less than 10% of the extra energy accumulating in the climate system. Over 90% of global warming is heating the oceans, according to measurements of temperature changes from the surface down to around 3,000 m, with only about 2% warming the atmosphere (Levitus et al., 2001). The remarkable fact is that, although the changes in our planet discussed so far in this book are significant from a human perspective, when considering the climate system as a whole, they're really no more than a sideshow to the oceans' main event.

These percentages do not stay constant over time, however. Although the oceans always receive the overwhelming majority of the energy, sometimes a little more goes into the atmosphere and a little less into the oceans; sometimes the opposite happens. These shifts alter the rate at which the oceans or the atmosphere warms up: more energy results in faster warming, less energy in slower warming. Periods of faster and slower warming of the atmosphere are evident in the surface temperature record, shown in Figure 1.7 (see also question 4). These periods indicate shifts in where the energy is being distributed.

A crucial point about these shifts in energy distribution is that they are cyclical. The climate system is full of cyclical patterns; in fact, one way to think about climate in general is that it's the net result of many

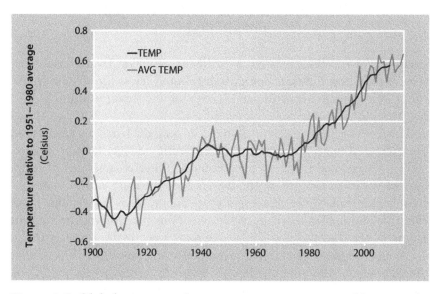

Figure 1.7 Global average surface temperature reconstructed from weather station thermometers by Berkeley Earth. Annual average temperature is shown in light gray, with an 11-year moving average, which filters out short-term variability, shown in black. Temperature is shown as difference relative to an estimated global average temperature for 1951–1980 of 14.771°C.

Source: Data from Berkeley Earth, available at http://berkeleyearth.lbl.gov/auto/Global/Land_and_Ocean_summary.txt. Accessed March 27, 2015.

cyclical patterns superimposed on each other, rather like a complex piece of music. Climate consists of many repeating patterns, all playing to their own rhythm, and scientists must tease apart the rhythms in order to better understand how climate works.

One of the best-known climate cycles occurs in the tropical Pacific Ocean, which alternates between two states known as El Niño and La Niña. Winds push the surface waters of the tropical Pacific westward, away from South America, allowing the ocean to accumulate energy from the intense sunshine of the tropics as it goes, building into a pool of warm water over a hundred meters deep by the time it reaches Australia. Much colder water from the deep ocean wells up to the surface off the coast of South America in the east Pacific, to replace the water moving west. This produces a distinctive pattern of sea surface temperatures across the tropical Pacific: very cold to the east, much warmer to the west.

In El Niño conditions, the winds weaken and the warm water slides back across the Pacific from Australia toward South America, covering the cold upwelling water and releasing heat to the atmosphere. In La Niña years, the opposite happens: the wind and ocean currents become exceptionally strong, building a large pool of cold water off South America that reaches into the central Pacific, cooling the atmosphere above it. El Niños therefore tend to produce noticeable upward spikes in global average temperatures, with sharp downturns during La Niñas. The record El Niño of 1998 shows up in Figure 1.7 as one such spike, followed by a sharp drop as the El Niño faded away. (See Herring, 1999, for a user-friendly account or Trenberth, 1997, for a more technical discussion of El Niños and La Niñas.)

In addition to affecting the global average temperature, El Niños and La Niñas affect the climate of many individual locations around the world, causing especially wet or dry seasons for the years when they occur. During an El Niño, for example, California experiences floods, and eastern Australia experiences droughts, with these conditions flipped for La Niña years. Scientists describe the El Niño/La Niña cycle as an example of *climate variability*, because it affects the day-to-day weather of these places for an extended period, up to a year in some cases. The average weather—that is, the climate—is especially wet or dry because of an El Niño or La Niña. However, because they are cyclical, they are different from climate *change*.

The difference between climate variability and climate change can be seen in Figure 1.7. Climate change is evident in the clear warming trend over the complete period of record. Climate variability is the up-and-down "wiggles" on top of the trend. Although there are other sources of climate variability, El Niños and La Niñas account for many of the wiggles. Climate change is a result of an overall buildup of heat in our planet's climate system. Climate variability is a result of the heat being moved across different parts of the climate system.

Another source of climate variability is the tendency of El Niños and La Niñas to cluster in groups where one or the other is dominant—strong El Niños paired with weak La Niñas or vice versa. These clusters of warm events (El Niños) and cold events (La Niñas) can last for several decades, so the climate variability they bring about lasts longer than the single-year effects of El Niños and La Niñas. This tendency to switch between clusters of warm and cold events is known as the Pacific Decadal Oscillation (PDO), and is shown in Figure 1.8. There is also a longer-lasting version, known as the Pacific Multidecadal Oscillation (PMO), and a cousin in

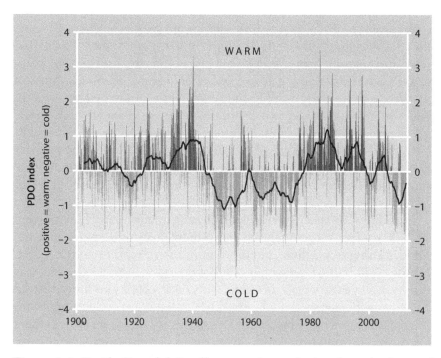

Figure 1.8 Pacific Decadal Oscillation index, calculated on the basis of sea surface temperatures in the North Pacific Ocean. Shown are monthly values (dark and light gray bars), and a roughly 5-year (61-month) running mean (black line), for the years 1900–2013.

Source: Data from the University of Washington's Joint Institute for the Study of the Atmosphere and Ocean, available at http://research.jisao.washington.edu/pdo/PDO.latest. Accessed March 27, 2015.

the Atlantic, the Atlantic Multidecadal Oscillation (AMO). Just as El Niños and La Niñas can affect the climate in the years when they occur, so these longer-lasting phases of warm versus cold water in the Pacific and Atlantic Oceans also seem to influence climate. However, these longer cycles are still manifestations of climate variability, not climate change.

A close examination of Figure 1.7 shows longer periods of more rapid warming separated by periods of stable or cooling temperatures, with the short-term "wiggles" of El Niño and La Niña superimposed on top. This gives the warming trend a stair-step pattern similar to an escalator (for an animated version, see Nuccitelli, 2011). A substantial body of research now shows that one of the flat steps in Figure 1.7, from around 1940 to the mid-1970s, was most likely caused mainly by air pollution, which reflects sunlight, offsetting the warming effects of carbon dioxide (see question 29 for more information on this phenomenon; see, e.g., Tett et al., 1999, Meehl et al., 2004, or Booth et al., 2012, for technical discussions). However, both the PMO and AMO were shifting into their cold phases around this time, so swings in sea surface temperatures may also have played a role.

Scientists are more confident that the swing to warm phases in the oceans in the mid- to late 1970s helped boost the warming from carbon dioxide. The swing back to cold phases after about 1998 helped slow the warming down again. As Figure 1.9 shows, global average air temperatures continued to increase after 1998—just not as quickly as they had in preceding decades when the ocean cycles were working with carbon dioxide's warming effects, instead of against them. Much as the 24-hour cycle of daytime warming and nighttime cooling occurs in the context of seasonal changes, warming as summer approaches and cooling as winter approaches, so El Niños and La Niñas are superimposed on the longer-term ocean cycles—and both are superimposed on the overall shift toward warming. Climate variability is superimposed on climate change.

Because of this, different features of the climate system come into sharp relief at different timescales. A focus on a period of a few decades will show climate variability clearly, but will probably hide the long-term trend, just as listening to only one or two seconds of music makes it almost impossible to hear the tune. It's there, but the short-term focus obscures it.

This is the root problem with one especially widespread myth about climate change, that global warming stopped in 1998 (or a similar recent year). The focus is on the short term, where the cyclical patterns of climate *variability* show up clearly, rather than on the long term, where the indications of climate change are apparent. The year 1998 may seem like a long time in the past, but in terms of patterns like the PDO, PMO, or AMO, it's still not even one typical complete cycle ago. From the

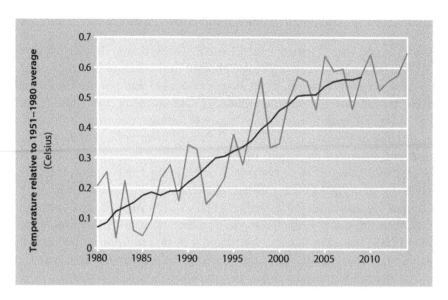

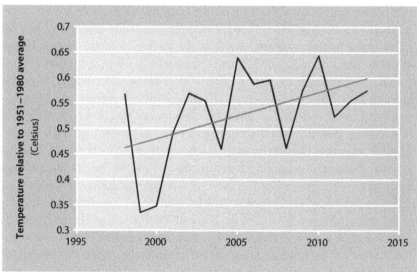

Figure 1.9 Global average temperature reconstructions from Berkeley Earth for 1980–2014 (top) and 1996–2014 (bottom). As with Figure 1.7, annual average temperature is shown in gray, as the difference relative to an estimated global average temperature for 1951–1980 of 14.771°C. For the top graph, an 11-year moving average, which filters out short-term variability, is shown in black, highlighting the slowdown in the rate of warming in recent years. For the bottom graph, the temperature trend is shown by the straight black line, calculated using linear regression of temperature against time.

Source: Data from Berkeley Earth, available at http://berkeleyearth.lbl.gov/auto/ Global/Land_and_Ocean_summary.txt. Accessed March 27, 2015.

perspective of the climate system, 1998 is very recent. This short-term focus makes it difficult to see the long-term trend.

The myth is expressed in several different ways. A 2013 report in *The Economist*, for example, stated, "Over the past 15 years air temperatures at the Earth's surface have been flat while greenhouse-gas emissions have continued to soar." Later reports in the same newspaper identified the period since 1998 as a "pause" in global warming (*The Economist*, 2013). It is true that the rate of warming since 1998 has been slower than in earlier decades, notably from around 1980 to 1998—but as Figure 1.9 shows, it has not been flat. Furthermore, periods of faster warming interspersed with periods of slower warming are to be expected, given climate variability superimposed on the warming trend. The warming slowdown coincides with the shift of the Pacific and Atlantic Oceans into cool phases, as noted earlier. To be fair, *The Economist* article took pains to point this out.

Some reports, however, erroneously assert that global warming did not just pause, but actually stopped in the late 1990s. The title of an article by Bob Carter (2006) in Britain's *Telegraph* states flatly that global warming stopped in 1998. Nigel Lawson (2009), of the climate-skeptic think-tank the Global Warming Policy Foundation, draws attention to "the absence of any recorded 21st century global warming" (p. 8), while Patrick Michaels (2011) asks, "Why hasn't the Earth warmed in nearly 15 years?" Christopher Monckton (2014), writing for the website ClimateDepot.com, claims that there has been no warming since 1996.

How can these claims be made, in light of surface temperature data graphed in Figure 1.9, showing warming since the late 1990s? Lord Monckton's claim is the easiest to illuminate, because it works by using only the data set which shows the smallest warming trend since 1996: the RSS satellite measurements of lower tropospheric temperature. Readers might recall from question 5 that there are challenges in interpreting the satellite data, and different teams get slightly different results. Over a short-enough time period, those slight differences are enough to give different trends, such that UAH shows a greater warming trend since 1996 than RSS. Figure 1.10 shows both the RSS and UAH temperatures since 1996, along with trend lines indicating the overall pattern of temperature change over that time period. Lord Monckton can say that there has been no warming since 1996 because he focuses on just one set of measurements while ignoring all the others. Interactive online graphing tools, such as Kevin Cowtan's, at the University of York in Britain, make it possible for readers to do their own comparisons of temperature trends from different data sets over different time frames

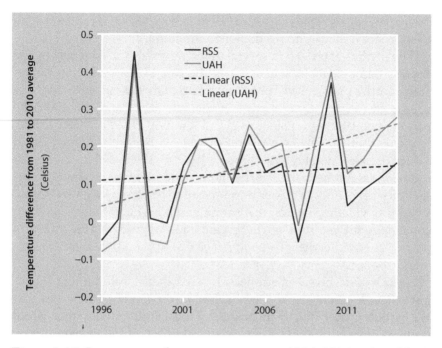

Figure 1.10 Lower tropospheric air temperature 1996–2014, inferred from satellite measurements of microwave radiation by two different teams (RSS and UAH). Trendlines are calculated using linear regression of temperature against time. The RSS trend since 1996 is essentially flat, while the UAH trend shows warming.

(see Further Reading), highlighting the fallacy of relying on just one set of measurements.

Other versions of the myth make the more sophisticated argument that no statistically significant warming has taken place since 1998 (or 1996). This claim may be true for some data sets but is misleading. As Figure 1.9 shows, there has been warming since that period. At such short timescales, however, the up-and-down wiggles of climate variability are large relative to the trend, making it impossible to say with confidence that the trend is anything different from the year-to-year variability. This claim is really only restating the obvious: as you zoom in to progressively shorter and shorter timescales, it becomes harder and harder to identify the trend amid the climate variability. Climate change is happening over longer periods than the past 20 years or so. While to most of us, 20 years seems like a long time, from the standpoint of climate, it's no more than a few notes out of a symphony.

FURTHER READING

Booth, B. B., Dunstone, N. J., Halloran, P. R., Andrews, T., and Bellouin, N. (2012). Aerosols implicated as a prime driver of twentieth-century North Atlantic climate variability. *Nature*, 484(7393), 228–232.

Carter, R. (2006). There IS a problem with global warming . . . it stopped in 1998. Posted to *The Telegraph*, April 9, 2006, available at http://www.telegraph.co.uk/comment/personal-view/3624242/There-IS-a-problem-with-global-warming . . . -it-stopped-in-1998.html. Accessed March 27, 2015.

Cook, J., and Nuccitelli, D. (2013). Four Hiroshima bombs worth of heat per second. Posted to SkepticalScience.com, July 1, 2013, available at http://www.skepticalscience.com/4-Hiroshima-bombs-worth-of-heat-per-second.html. Accessed March 27, 2015.

Cowtan, K. (n.d.). Temperature Trends. Interactive Plotting Tool. Available at http://www.ysbl.york.ac.uk/~cowtan/applets/trend/trend.html. Accessed March 28, 2015.

The Economist. (2013). A Sensitive Matter. March 30, 2013. Available at http://www.economist.com/news/science-and-technology/21574461-climate-may-be-heating-up-less-response-greenhouse-gas-emissions. Accessed March 29, 2015.

Hansen, J., Kharecha, P., Sato, M., Masson-Delmotte, V., Ackerman, F., Beerling, D. J., Hearty, P. J., Hoegh-Guldberg, O., Hsu, S.-L., Parmesan, C., Rockstrom, J., Rohling, E. J., Sachs, J., Smith, P., Steffen, K., Van Susteren, L., von Schuckmann, K., and Zachos, J. C. (2013). Assessing "dangerous climate change": required reduction of carbon emissions to protect young people, future generations and nature. *PloS One*, 8(12), e81648.

Herring, D. (1999). What Is El Niño? NASA Earth Observatory, April 27, 1999. Available at http://earthobservatory.nasa.gov/Features/ElNino/. Accessed March 23, 2015.

Lawson, N. (2009). *An Appeal to Reason: A Cool Look at Global Warming.* Duckworth Overlook, London and New York.

Levitus, S., Antonov, J. I., Wang, J., Delworth, T. L., Dixon, K. W., and Broccoli, A. J. (2001). Anthropogenic warming of Earth's climate system. *Science*, 292(5515), 267–270.

Meehl, G. A., Washington, W. M., Ammann, C. M., Arblaster, J. M., Wigley, T. M. L., and Tebaldi, C. (2004). Combinations of natural and anthropogenic forcings in twentieth-century climate. *Journal of Climate*, 17(19), 3721–3727.

Michaels, P. (2011). Why hasn't the Earth warmed in nearly 15 years? Posted to Forbes.com, July 15, 2011, available at http://www.forbes.com/

sites/patrickmichaels/2011/07/15/why-hasnt-the-earth-warmed-in-nearly-15-years/. Accessed March 22, 2015.

Monckton, C. (2014). Global warming "pause" extends to 17 years 11 months. Posted to ClimateDepot.com, September 7, 2014, available at http://www.climatedepot.com/2014/09/07/global-warming-pause-extends-to-17-years-11-months/. Accessed March 29, 2015.

Nuccitelli, D. (2011). Global surface temperature: going down the up escalator, part 1. Posted to SkepticalScience.com, November 5, 2011, available at http://www.skepticalscience.com/going-down-the-up-escalator-part-1.html. Accessed March 23, 2015.

Rahmstorf, S. (2014). Recent global warming trends: significant or paused or what? Posted to RealClimate.org, December 4, 2014, available at http://www.realclimate.org/index.php/archives/2014/12/recent-global-warming-trends-significant-or-paused-or-what/. Accessed March 22, 2015.

Tett, S. F., Stott, P. A., Allen, M. R., Ingram, W. J., and Mitchell, J. F. (1999). Causes of twentieth-century temperature change near the Earth's surface. *Nature*, 399(6736), 569–572.

Trenberth, K. E. (1997). The definition of El Niño. *Bulletin of the American Meteorological Society*, 78(12), 2771–2777.

Trenberth, K. E., and Fasullo, J. T. (2013). An apparent hiatus in global warming? *Earth's Future*, 1(1), 19–32.

Q8. WHAT DO THE "CLIMATEGATE" HACKED E-MAILS SHOW ABOUT CLIMATE SCIENCE?

Answer: In 2009, an anonymous hacker stole private e-mail correspondence between leading climate scientists and posted it on the web. A small number of these e-mails, taken out of context, show the scientists in a bad light, saying rude, even aggressive, things about their critics, and seeming to manipulate data. However, a more careful scrutiny shows that processes of science have confirmed again and again, using many independent methods, that the basic findings of climate scientists are accurate. The "climategate" e-mails show only that science is a rigorous, sometimes brutal, process.

The Facts: Science is a process through which we understand the world and the universe around us. Contrary to popular belief, there is no single "scientific method," but instead there are many related ways of doing science. Some involve constructing hypotheses and devising experiments to test them; others involve collecting data and identifying patterns within those data. What unites the many different approaches to science are, first, a reliance on data to support conclusions; and, second, the importance of peer review. A peer-reviewed journal is one that publishes work only after it has been approved by several independent, and usually anonymous, reviewers, other scientists—peers—who check the work for flaws, such as inappropriate methodology or inaccurate conclusions.

There are many, many peer-reviewed journals, some more general (e.g., *Nature* or *Science*), others more specialized (such as the *Journal of Climate*), and some have more rigorous standards than others. Peer review is not perfect, even at the higher-quality journals, and sometimes mistakes slip through. Consequently, an important aspect of peer review is that it does not stop when research is published. Instead, this is just a first step that leads to further review, this time by the broader community of scientists working on the particular subject of the publication. Interesting results will often prompt other scientists to try to replicate or improve upon the work, as scientists are professional skeptics and typically do not uncritically accept the word of other scientists. They want to check for themselves.

It's therefore not uncommon for different groups of scientists to find different results at first, and publications and counter-publications can go back and forth on an issue until finally reaching some form of resolution. This is the case, for example, with the idea that the rapidly warming Arctic might be causing a wavier jet stream, with important consequences for the weather in North America and Europe, as discussed in question 6. It's an interesting idea, with some strong evidence behind it, but not all the published research supports it and some climate scientists are still metaphorically kicking the tires, checking to see if the idea holds up under close inspection.

While the wavier jet stream idea is still being debated in the peer-reviewed literature, other issues have already been subjected to the scrutiny of other scientists and passed the tests. This is the case for reconstructions of the surface temperature record (question 4) and satellite measurements of air temperatures (question 5), where multiple independent analyses of the data all reach the same conclusion—that the world is getting warmer. This constitutes a *scientific consensus*, and while there is always the possibility that all those independent results are wrong, the chances are small—and get smaller with each new independent confirmation (we'll return to the idea of scientific consensus in question 26).

Another area of climate science where a scientific consensus has been reached is the effort to reconstruct global average temperature stretching back 1,000 years or more into the past. This is an area that has received special attention, not just from scientists but from interested members of the public, because such reconstructions help put the current observed warming in context: has the climate system periodically behaved in the same way over the past 1,000 years or so, or is the current warming unusual? Other instances of this kind of warming in the past might indicate a natural cause for the present warming.

Reconstructions of temperature this far back into the past can make only limited use of thermometer data, because accurate thermometers came into relatively widespread use only about 200 years ago. Instead, they rely on substitute measures of temperature known as *proxies*. There are many natural features that serve to "record" temperature, although they are usually influenced by other factors as well, and isolating the temperature signal can be technically challenging. For example, some species of trees grow better when it's warmer, producing wider growth rings. This allows scientists to estimate temperature in past years by measuring the width of the rings. However, wet and dry years can also affect tree ring width, so scientists try to use many different proxy measures to home in on the temperature signal.

A pioneering effort to combine many different proxy measures to produce an estimate of Northern Hemisphere average temperature 600 years into the past was published in the journal *Nature* in 1998 by Michael Mann, Raymond Bradley, and Malcolm Hughes. Their analysis showed global average temperature gradually cooling from the year 1400 onward, followed by a rapid warming in the 20th century—strong evidence that our current warming is unusual. As is the nature of science and scientists, other climatologists, after reading Mann, Bradley, and Hughes's paper, set out to see for themselves if the results were accurate. While a small number of papers highlighted flaws in the methods, some of those papers were themselves later shown to be flawed. Many subsequent analyses have found that the basic picture of gradual global cooling followed by rapid warming was fundamentally correct. This was the conclusion not only of multiple different studies but also of a review of those multiple different studies published by the U.S. National Research Council in 2006 (a useful short summary is provided by Chapman and Davis, 2010).

Science, however, is conducted by human beings with all our human failings: ego, pride, defensiveness, and so on. In these respects, scientists are basically like most other people, and some fairly ugly catfights litter the history of science. This is why the processes of science, such as peer review, are so important: over time, they help separate out the ideas that are supported by data from those that are simply being pushed aggressively by a few scientists convinced that they are right. While this sifting is going on, scientists in the thick of the process, being only human, can sometimes say rude things about each other, each other's work, and their own critics. Bill Streever's 2009 book *Cold: Adventures in the World's Frozen Places* includes discussion of several battles in climate science.

While such rudeness is a common feature of most, perhaps all, areas of science, this aspect of climate science was put on public display in 2009, when an anonymous hacker broke into a computer at the Climatic Research Unit (CRU) at Britain's University of East Anglia. The hacker stole private e-mails between several leading climate scientists and posted them online. Some of the stolen correspondence included some rude comments about critics and generally showed climate scientists to be every bit as human as scientists throughout history.

However, the contents of some of the e-mails were subsequently taken out of context or otherwise misconstrued to suggest a conspiracy among climate scientists to manipulate data and prevent contrary perspectives from being published in peer-reviewed journals. As a result, the episode became known as "climategate," a name coined by British newspaper columnist James Delingpole (2009), and quickly adopted worldwide.

Perhaps the most famous excerpt from one of these e-mails is a comment from CRU director Phil Jones, stating, "I've just completed Mike [Mann]'s *Nature* trick of adding in the real temps to each series for the last 20 years (ie from 1981 onwards) and from 1961 for Keith [Briffa]'s to hide the decline."

To fully understand Jones's comment, it is helpful to recall the earlier discussion of how tree ring width can be influenced not only by temperature but by other environmental variables as well. After 1961, those other environmental variables became more dominant in some high-latitude locations, and the relationship between tree ring width and temperature weakened, as documented in the peer-reviewed literature by, for example, Briffa et al. (1998). This feature of tree rings is known as the divergence problem, because tree rings no longer track temperatures but diverge from them. Quite why this happens remains unclear—some evidence indicates increasing levels of air pollution are a contributing factor—but what is clear is that after 1961, tree rings no longer serve as reliable indicators of temperature in some locations. Phil Jones's e-mail references his decision to stop using the tree ring data at 1961 and turn to thermometer data instead. Climate scientists assert that this was an appropriate step given the divergence problem, rather than an effort to mislead. Certainly, there are instances where climate scientists could and should have explained more clearly what was thermometer data and what was proxy data—but this is hardly a conspiracy to conceal global temperature trends.

However, Jones's choice of words left his private correspondence especially open to negative portrayals, and politicians and pundits jumped in to paint climate scientists as conspiring to hide a decline in the global average temperature itself. As previous questions (especially question 7) have explained, there has been no such decline, but numerous blog posts, books, and newspaper columns promoted the myth that climate scientists were manipulating data to further their own political agenda. For example, Sarah Palin, former governor of Alaska and one-time Republican candidate for vice president of the United States, wrote in a 2009 op-ed in *The Washington Post*: "The e-mails reveal that leading climate 'experts' deliberately destroyed records, manipulated data to 'hide the decline' in global temperatures, and tried to silence their critics by preventing them from publishing in peer-reviewed journals." Steve Goreham (2013) makes essentially the same accusation in *The Mad, Mad, Mad World of Climatism*. James Inhofe also draws attention to Jones's e-mail in his 2012 book *The Greatest Hoax*, although unlike Governor Palin he does at least mention the divergence problem.

As question 7 discussed, there has been no decline in global average temperatures. The decline to which Jones was referring was the decline in a selection of tree rings' ability after 1961 to serve as a stand-in for temperature. What about the claim that climate scientists were trying to silence their critics? This point mostly refers to e-mail exchanges addressing a 2003 paper in the journal *Climate Research* by Willie Soon and Sallie Baliunas, which was later demonstrated by several leading climate scientists to be riddled with basic errors (Mann et al., 2003a, 2003b; Soon and Baliunas, 2003; Soon et al., 2003). The concerns raised in the e-mails related to how such a flawed paper could have been published in the first place, and speculated about lapses in the peer review process at the journal. Subsequent events at *Climate Research* supported those worries: a new editor-in-chief was brought in, but remaining concerns about the quality of the peer review process at the journal led to his resignation, along with two other members of the editorial board (see Monastersky, 2003, and Kinne, 2003, for more detailed accounts). Discussions in the e-mails simply reflected concerns about the rigor of a journal that allowed substandard work to be published.

The aggressive and sometimes rude tone of the climategate e-mails prompted nine separate independent inquiries, four in the United Kingdom focusing on Phil Jones and CRU and five in the United States focusing on Michael Mann. Every one of them found that the claims made by Palin, Inhofe, and other climate change denialists were groundless, including Governor Palin's claim that scientists had deliberately destroyed data (details on the inquiries are provided at SkepticalScience.com by John

Cook [2014]). Although some scientists had discussed deleting e-mails, there is no evidence that they actually followed through, and there is every indication that discussions about doing so were simply scientists venting their frustrations at having to deal with quite aggressive people who were dismissive of the scientists' work.

There are also conspiratorial claims that the inquiries themselves were whitewashes, producing preordained results (see, e.g., Goreham, 2013, pp. 163–166). It seems unlikely that all nine inquiries, conducted in two countries by a range of different bodies, would fail to find evidence of wrongdoing if there was in fact any there to find. Nevertheless, a distinctive trait of conspiratorial thinking is that any evidence disproving the existence of a conspiracy (such as the exonerating investigations) is, in the eyes of conspiracy theorists, further proof that the conspiracy exists (the whitewashing hypothesis).

In many respects, however, the inquiries are irrelevant. Science has vindicated the work of Phil Jones, Michael Mann, and the others whose e-mails were stolen and made public. As mentioned earlier, multiple different studies, using different methods and sometimes different data, have found the same broad results: gradual global cooling over the past 1,000 years, followed by abrupt warming in the past few decades. Scientific perspective on any issue is typically a mountain made of many grains of evidence. Each peer-reviewed publication is one grain. It takes a lot to shift the overall balance of evidence, the shifting of many, many grains. The climategate e-mails do not alter the findings of many thousands of scientists that show glaciers and sea ice melting, with ocean heat content and surface air temperatures rising. As noted several times already in this book, almost every indicator we have shows that the world is getting warmer. Stolen e-mails, no matter how they're misrepresented, do not change this fact.

FURTHER READING

Briffa, K. R., Schweingruber, F. H., Jones, P. D., Osborn, T. J., Shiyatov, S. G., and Vaganov, E. A. (1998). Reduced sensitivity of recent tree-growth to temperature at high northern latitudes. *Nature*, 391(6668), 678–682.

Chapman, D. S., and Davis, M. G. (2010). Climate change: past, present, and future. *Eos, Transactions American Geophysical Union*, 91(37), 325–326.

Cook, J. (2014). What Do the "Climategate" Hacked CRU Emails Tell Us? Available at http://www.skepticalscience.com/Climategate-CRU-emails-hacked.htm. Accessed May 4, 2015.

Delingpole, J. (2009). Climategate: the final nail in the coffin of "Anthropogenic Global Warming"? Posted online at Telegraph.co.uk, November 20, 2009, available at http://blogs.telegraph.co.uk/news/jamesdelingpole/100017393/climategate-the-final-nail-in-the-coffin-of-anthropogenic-global-warming/. Accessed April 4, 2015.

Goreham, S. (2013). *The Mad, Mad, Mad World of Climatism: Mankind and Climate Change Mania*. New Lenox Books.

Inhofe, J. M. (2012). *The Greatest Hoax: How the Global Warming Conspiracy Threatens Your Future*. WND Books, Washington, DC.

Kinne, O. (2003). Climate Research: an article unleashed worldwide storms. *Climate Research, 24*(3), 197–198.

Mann, M., Ammann, C., Bradley, R., Briffa, K., Jones, P., Osborn, T., Crowley, T., Hughes, M., Oppenheimer, M., Overpeck, J., Rutherford, S., Trenberth, K., and Wigley, T. (2003a). On past temperatures and anomalous late-20th-century warmth. *Eos, Transactions American Geophysical Union, 84*(27), 256–258.

Mann, M., Ammann, C., Bradley, R., Briffa, K., Jones, P., Osborn, T., Crowley, T., Hughes, M., Oppenheimer, M., Overpeck, J., Rutherford, S., Trenberth, K., and Wigley, T. (2003b). Response "[to Comment on 'On past temperatures and anomalous late-20th-century warmth'"]. *Eos, Transactions American Geophysical Union, 84*(44), 473–474.

Mann, M. E., Bradley, R. S., and Hughes, M. K. (1998). Global-scale temperature patterns and climate forcing over the past six centuries. *Nature, 392*(6678), 779–787.

Monastersky, R. (2003). Storm brews over global warming. *The Chronicle of Higher Education, 50*(2), A16.

National Research Council. (2006). *Surface Temperature Reconstructions for the Last 2,000 Years*. National Academies Press, Washington, DC, available at http://www.nap.edu/download.php?record_id=11676#. Accessed April 9, 2015.

Palin, S. (2009). Sarah Palin on the politicization of the Copenhagen climate conference. *Washington Post*, December 9, 2009, available at http://www.washingtonpost.com/wp-dyn/content/article/2009/12/08/AR2009120803402.html. Accessed April 9, 2015.

Soon, W., and Baliunas, S. (2003). Proxy climatic and environmental changes of the past 1000 years. *Climate Research, 23*(2), 89–110.

Soon, W., Baliunas, S., and Legates, D. (2003). Comment on "On past temperatures and anomalous late-20th century warmth." *Eos, Transactions American Geophysical Union, 84*(44), 473–476.

Streever, B. (2009). *Cold: Adventures in the World's Frozen Places*. Little, Brown.

2

The Causes of Climate Change

Q9. IS HUMAN ACTIVITY THE MAIN DRIVER OF MODERN CLIMATE CHANGE?

Answer: Climate changes when it is forced to do so. While climate has changed in the past due to natural causes, currently human activity is the main driver of modern climate change.

The Facts: The year 1816 is sometimes referred to by historians and climate scientists as "the year without a summer." The early colonists on the east coast of North America who survived it gave the year a more dramatic name: "Eighteen Hundred and Froze to Death." Unusually cold weather across the Northern Hemisphere resulted in terrible harvests, prompting starvation and disease. Social disruption followed, as transport networks broke down when horses starved. That same year, Mary Shelley began writing the enduringly creepy story *Frankenstein*, possibly inspired by the general sense of unease fermented by the upsets in both weather and society (see Streever, 2009, for an easy-to-read account of these events).

It is almost universally accepted by the scientific community that the Year Without a Summer was caused by an especially large and violent eruption of a volcano called Tambora, in Indonesia, the previous autumn. Tambora's eruption came on the heels of several others in the preceding few years, finally pushing the climate into a dramatic response. Although the most visible signs of a volcanic eruption are the huge clouds of ash, the most enduring effects on climate come from an invisible gas, sulfur dioxide. If this gas is blasted high enough into the atmosphere that it can reach the stratosphere, it's above most weather and won't easily be washed out of the air by rain. The sulfur dioxide can then react with water to form tiny droplets of sulfuric acid, which are highly reflective. In effect, they form a sunshade, blocking some of the Sun's rays from reaching Earth's surface and making the planet cooler (*The Economist*, 2015, has a good summary of the science of volcanically induced climate change).

Big volcanic eruptions like Tambora's change the balance between incoming and outgoing energy at Earth's surface. Together with how energy is redistributed across the planet and into different pieces of the climate system, this energy balance is ultimately responsible for the world's climate phenomena. The sulfuric acid droplets in the stratosphere cut the incoming energy, shifting the balance in favor of the outgoing energy, causing a drop in temperatures. Because a cooler world means less evaporation, reduced rainfall accompanies the drop in temperatures.

Such changes in the Earth's energy balance are known as climate *forcings*, because they push, or force, the climate into a different state: colder or warmer, drier or wetter. Much of the study of Earth's past climates is about identifying how the climates of the past were different from today, and figuring out the climate forcings that caused the differences.

Climate forcings, and the resulting climate changes, occur at many different timescales. Volcanic eruptions are among the shortest-term changes, often amounting to climate variability rather than true climate change (see question 7). However, one of the great triumphs of climate science in the 20th century was identifying the cause of much longer-term climate changes: the shifts between cold conditions known as glacial periods—sometimes popularly referred to as ice ages—and the warm periods in between known as interglacials.

After decades of gathering evidence and refining the explanations, it's now understood that global climate slides between glacial and interglacial conditions on a roughly 100,000-year cycle because of wobbles in Earth's orbit around the Sun. These wobbles, known as Milankovitch cycles for the scientist most closely associated with the theory, alter the timing and distribution of sunlight over the Earth's surface, affecting the strength of the seasons. In the Northern Hemisphere, year after year of cool summers allows snow to build up from one winter to the next, ultimately growing into huge ice sheets.

A large body of evidence indicates that these 100,000-year glacial–interglacial cycles have been persistent features of Earth's climate for about the past two million years, and the evidence also tells us when the cold and warm periods happened. The timing closely matches the predictions of Milankovitch's theory of orbital wobbles (Spencer Weart's 2008 book, and associated website, *The Discovery of Global Warming*, has more details on the development of the orbital theory of climate change). As with volcanic eruptions, the orbital wobbles affect Earth's energy balance and thus constitute a climate forcing. Across timescales both short and long, climate doesn't just change: it changes for a reason.

As research on the glacial–interglacial cycles continued, however, it became clear that Milankovitch's orbital forcing idea could not explain some important features appearing in the evidence about past climate changes. One of these challenges is that the size of the forcing from the orbital wobbles seems to be too small to bring about the climate changes that the data tell us must have happened. Something must have amplified the orbital forcing—but what?

In the 1990s, highly detailed records of past climate were retrieved from the ice sheets of Greenland and Antarctica. Scientists extracted ancient ice from deep below the surface that contained tiny bubbles, little capsules of air from around the time the ice was formed. Those bubbles showed that carbon dioxide had fluctuated up and down in time with the interglacial and glacial periods (see Figure 2.1 and the National Oceanic and Atmospheric Administration's [2014] animated depiction of this phenomenon). Since carbon dioxide is a heat-trapping gas, the obvious conclusion was that natural fluctuations in carbon dioxide were amplifying the effects of the orbital wobbles (see Richard Alley's [2014] *The Two-Mile Time Machine* for a thorough description).

A more complete explanation for the glacial–interglacial cycles was emerging, but one that still depended on the concept of changing the balance between inputs and outputs of energy: orbital wobbles trigger an initial small climate change, which in turn causes the amount of carbon dioxide in the atmosphere to go up (for an interglacial) or down (for a glacial), trapping more heat for an interglacial, or less heat for a glacial, period. Again, climate doesn't just change: it changes in response to forcings.

Given the forcing effect of carbon dioxide in the past, it should not be a surprise that climate scientists think of today's high levels of carbon dioxide as a climate forcing in the present. Carbon dioxide is currently at around 400 parts per million, as measured at the top of Mauna Loa in Hawaii, in the middle of the Pacific Ocean, well away from any local pollution sources. The data from the ice sheets tell us that this is the highest level in at least the past 800,000 years, possibly much longer

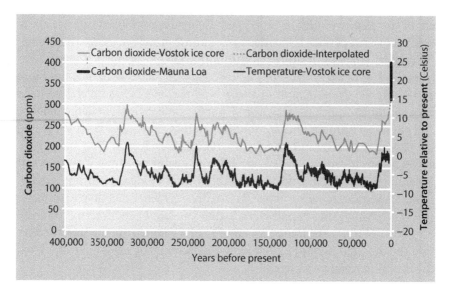

Figure 2.1 Temperature and carbon dioxide for the past 400,000 years from the Vostok ice core, Antarctica, and since 1958 from the Mauna Loa observatory in Hawaii. Temperature is reconstructed using the ratio of lighter and heavier isotopes of hydrogen that make up the ice; carbon dioxide is measured directly from air bubbles trapped in the ice.

Source: Data for the Vostok ice core from Petit et al. (1999), available from the NOAA National Centers for Environmental Information, https://www.ncdc .noaa.gov/paleo/study/2453. Accessed April 21, 2015. Data for the Mauna Loa observatory from Dr. Pieter Tans, NOAA/ESRL (www.esrl.noaa.gov/gmd/ccgg/ trends/), and Dr. Ralph Keeling, Scripps Institution of Oceanography (scripps-co2.ucsd.edu/), available at http://www.esrl.noaa.gov/gmd/ccgg/trends/index .html. Accessed May 4, 2015.

(fossilized leaves indicate that this is the highest level in around 20 million years, but the evidence is a bit less definitive). Because of carbon dioxide's heat-trapping properties, there is every reason to expect these very high levels to push the climate into a warmer state—just as it seems to have done on several occasions in the past. As question 18 will discuss, today's high level of carbon dioxide comes from burning fossil fuels, not natural sources. And as discussed in questions 4 and 5, the global average temperature is rising.

Human activity—in the form of burning fossil fuels, as well as other effects on the balance of energy—is therefore a climate forcing in its own right. Climate change forced by greenhouse gas warming should show certain telltale patterns. For example, a distinct "human fingerprint" of greenhouse warming is a cooling upper atmosphere at the same time that the lower atmosphere warms. Another distinct greenhouse pattern is winters warming faster than summers. Many of these human fingerprints have already been observed, confirming human causation of modern climate change as well as ruling out natural drivers.

We can also see the effects of these *anthropogenic* (human in origin) forcings in computer simulations of Earth's climate. When given information on all the natural climate forcings we know of, such as cyclical changes in the Sun's strength, the computer models do a poor job of reproducing the observed pattern of temperature change over the 20th century—but when given both the natural and the anthropogenic forcings together, the models simulate the past 100 years of warming quite well.

Thus, while climate clearly has changed naturally in the past, it's done so in response to forcings—and the scale of human influence on Earth's energy balance, especially from adding carbon dioxide and other heat-trapping gases to the atmosphere, means human activity itself is now a climate forcing. Natural changes in the past do not alter this fact. Suggesting otherwise is a little like saying that humans have died of natural causes in the past, so people don't get murdered today.

Despite the obvious logical fallacy here, the idea that the natural origins of past climate changes rule out an anthropogenic cause of today's climate changes seems to be at the heart of at least three books on the subject. In *Unstoppable Global Warming: Every 1500 Years*, Fred Singer and Dennis Avery (2008) write: "We know from physical evidence that our planet's climate is always cycling, warmer or cooler. . . . No one has been able to distinguish natural from man-made warming except in terms of its timing" (p. 254). Singer and Avery's book is deeply skeptical that humans are causing warming, pointing to other, natural forcings as alternatives—but as we've seen, human activities are now on a par with many natural climate forcings. Steve Goreham's (2013) *The Mad, Mad, Mad World of Climatism* relies on Singer and Avery's book, among other sources, to claim that "short-term cycles explain modern warming" (p. 66). And Ian Plimer (2009), in his book *Heaven and Earth*, writes, "Climate has always changed. It always has and always will. . . . If we humans are warming the planet now, how do we explain alternating cool and warm periods during the current post-glacial warming?" (p. 10).

The authors of these books seem to be arguing that because climate has changed in response to natural forcings in the past, we can't tell if it's changing in response to anthropogenic forcings today. Given the scale of carbon dioxide's increasing concentration in the atmosphere, its basic physics as a heat-trapping gas, its contributions to climate changes in the past, the many human fingerprints currently being observed, and climate models' inability to replicate the 20th century's observed warming without it, that position does not seem plausible. People die of natural causes all the time, but if you find a dead body with a murder weapon, DNA evidence and fingerprints all over the crime scene, there's good reason to expect foul play.

FURTHER READING

Alley, R. B. (2014). *The Two-Mile Time Machine: Ice Cores, Abrupt Climate Change, and Our Future*. Princeton University Press.

Bindoff, N. L., Stott, P. A., Achuta Rao, K. M., Allen, M. R., Gillett, N., Gutzler, D., Hansingo, K., Hegerl, G., Hu, Y., Jain, S., Mokhov, I. I., Overland, J., Perlwitz, J., Sebbari, R., and Zhang, X. (2013). Detection and Attribution of Climate Change: from Global to Regional. In *Climate Change 2013: The Physical Science Basis. Contribution of Working Group I to the Fifth Assessment Report of the Intergovernmental Panel on Climate Change*, T. F. Stocker, D. Qin, G.-K. Plattner, M. Tignor, S. K. Allen, J. Boschung, A. Nauels, Y. Xia, V. Bex, and P. M. Midgley (eds.). Cambridge University Press, Cambridge, United Kingdom and New York, NY, pp. 867–952, doi:10.1017/CBO9781107415324.022, available at http://www.climatechange2013.org/report/. Accessed April 21, 2015.

The Economist. (2015). Volcanoes and Climate: After Tambora. April 11, 2015, 21–24. Available at http://www.economist.com/news/briefing/21647958-two-hundred-years-ago-most-powerful-eruption-modern-history-made-itself-felt-around. Accessed April 21, 2015.

Goreham, S. (2013). *The Mad, Mad, Mad World of Climatism: Mankind and Climate Change Mania*. New Lenox Books.

National Oceanic and Atmospheric Administration, Environmental System Research Laboratory. (2014). History of Atmospheric Carbon Dioxide from 800,000 Years Ago until January 2014. Available at http://www.esrl.noaa.gov/gmd/ccgg/trends/history.html. Accessed April 21, 2015.

Petit, J. R., Jouzel, J., Raynaud, D., Barkov, N. I., Barnola, J. M., Basile, I., Bender, M., Chappellaz, J., Davis, J., Delaygue, G., Delmotte, M., Kotlyakov, V. M., Legrand, M., Lipenkov, V., Lorius, C., Pépin, L., Ritz, C., Saltzman, E., and Stievenard, M. (1999). Climate and atmospheric history of the past 420,000 years from the Vostok Ice Core, Antarctica. *Nature* 399, 429–436.

Plimer, I. R. (2009). *Heaven and Earth*. Taylor Trade.
Singer, S. F., and Avery, D. T. (2008). *Unstoppable Global Warming: Every 1500 Years*. Updated and expanded edition. Rowman & Littlefield.
Streever, B. (2009). *Cold: Adventures in the World's Frozen Places*. Little, Brown.
Weart, S. R. (2008). *The Discovery of Global Warming*. Second edition. Harvard University Press.
Weart, S. R. (2015). The Discovery of Global Warming: A Hypertext History of How Scientists Came to (Partly) Understand What People Are Doing to Cause Climate Change. Available at http://www.aip.org/history/climate/index.htm. Accessed April 21, 2015.

Q10. HOW DOES MODERN GLOBAL WARMING COMPARE TO THE SO-CALLED MEDIEVAL WARM PERIOD?

Answer: The world is probably warmer today than at any time in the past 1,400 years, according to the most recent, most comprehensive research. The Medieval Climate Anomaly was a time when the world's climate was abnormal, but in different ways in different places.

The Facts: As we saw in question 8, scientists are professional skeptics. That skeptical attitude is formalized by the processes of science, notably the peer review that new research undergoes before being published in a reputable journal, and the efforts of other scientists to replicate or improve upon findings once they've been published. One of the consequences of this process of testing and re-testing is that the peer-reviewed scientific literature sometimes contains multiple studies of the same issue, with each study taking a different approach and analyzing the problem from a different angle. If those multiple different studies find essentially the same results, then we can be more confident that the finding is correct. This is the idea of a *scientific consensus*, which we touched on in question 8 and which we'll return to in more detail in question 26, but one of the other consequences of testing and re-testing is that sometimes the later tests find problems with the original research. When this happens, the older ideas are modified to account for the new findings, or, sometimes, rejected altogether. It can be harsh, but this is how scientific knowledge progresses, and we've seen several examples in this book already. For example, question 5 examined revisions to how the satellite measurements of air temperature are calculated, and question 9 mentioned improvements to the

Milankovitch "orbital wobble" theory of the glacial and interglacial cycle to include the amplifying effects of carbon dioxide.

In this question, we focus on another example, that of our understanding of how climate has changed over the past dozen or so centuries, and in particular the climate between roughly 1,100 and 700 years ago, a time coinciding with the Medieval period of European history. Climate scientists currently understand this period to have been generally cooler than today's climate, but warm in comparison to the centuries before and after it. This understanding is based on reconstructions of global temperature using combinations of measurements that serve as stand-ins, or proxies, for temperature. We looked at these *proxy measurements* in question 8, and there are many different kinds, from the width of the growth rings of certain tree species to the chemistry of stalagmites, and many others besides. Each has its own particular strengths, weaknesses, and quirks, so combining many different proxy measures to give a single temperature signal is a demanding technical challenge.

As discussed in question 8, the first rigorous effort to do this was undertaken in 1998, by Michael Mann, Ray Bradley and Malcolm Hughes. Since then, many other scientists from all over the world have studied the issue. Different teams have found somewhat different temperatures for the Medieval period, but there is widespread agreement that today's temperatures are probably warmer. As we noted earlier, the fact that so many different teams, using different approaches and in some cases different data, all converge on this result gives us confidence that it's probably right.

The most recent effort in this area, known as the PAGES 2k project, represents the work of 78 scientists from 60 different scientific institutions around the world (Ahmed et al., 2013). Although a few pioneering scientists have looked at the Southern Hemisphere (Mann et al., 2008, 2009), most studies thus far have tended to emphasize the Northern Hemisphere, because there are many more proxy data sets available than for the Southern Hemisphere. With PAGES 2k, that changed. Their work brought in many more temperature proxies from the Southern Hemisphere than had been analyzed previously, making their results much more of a truly global picture. That picture indicates that some places were probably warmer than today during the Medieval period, while other places were probably cooler. Because of this variation from place to place, with no single clear signal of warming or cooling for the world as a whole, the period between the 9th and 14th centuries CE has become known as the Medieval Climate Anomaly. The climate was unusual—anomalous—but in different ways in different places, with no clear signal of global Medieval warmth.

Thirty to forty years ago, however, our understanding of Medieval climate was somewhat different. Our current thinking is the result of many years of refinements and improvements, by many scientists, testing and re-testing each other's ideas and making use of new data and new analytical techniques as they became available. In the 1970s and 1980s, the prevailing view was not of a Medieval Climate Anomaly but of a Medieval Warm Period. This view was shaped by the data and methods available at the time, which relied extensively on written historical records, with only a few proxy sources. Ingenious analysis of these records could extract information about the climate of the past, utilizing, for example, evidence of grape harvests, or market prices for wheat. At the time, this work was cutting edge and suggested that the Medieval period may have been warmer than today.

However, this work suffered from a bias: places with extensive written records were overrepresented, at the expense of places with few, if any, written records. In practice, this meant the Northern Hemisphere, especially Europe and China, had disproportionate weight in the reconstructions. Because some of these places probably were warmer in Medieval times than today, the perception developed that the whole world was warmer than today. Climate at the local level was mistaken for climate at the global level.

As new technology, more data, and the skeptical instincts of scientists chipped away at the idea of the Medieval Warm Period, serious questions began to be asked about whether this was a truly global event. These questions began over 20 years ago (e.g., Hughes and Diaz, 1994) and ushered in a new series of efforts to build the scale of our understanding of climate over the past 1,000–1,300 years, from a regional picture dominated by Europe and Asia to a picture of the entire Northern Hemisphere, and, most recently, the entire globe, using multi-proxy studies. These reconstructions find the climate of the Medieval period to have been somewhat less warm than we used to think—slightly cooler, in fact, than today's global average temperature. Scientists are a lot more confident that this is true for the Northern Hemisphere than for the entire globe, but the results of recent studies have also boosted scientific confidence that the world as a whole was not as warm as it is today.

Several sources, however, either are unaware of or disregard recent scientific research in this area, and they continue to insist that Medieval times globally were warmer than today. These sources include Fred Singer and Dennis Avery's (2008) *Unstoppable Global Warming: Every 1500 Years*, Ian Plimer's (2009) *Heaven and Earth*, Sen. James Inhofe's (2012) *The Greatest Hoax*, and Steve Goreham's (2013) *The Mad, Mad, Mad World of*

Climatism. These books all identify individual locations around the world where some research indicates warmer conditions during the Medieval period than today. This by itself is not problematic, but the books then go on to claim that these individual locations add up to a global-scale warm period.

This selective use of data does not provide an accurate picture of climate change at the global level. What matters is not so much *whether* some places outside Europe were warmer 1,000 years ago, but by *how much*, and which places were *cooler*, and by how much—in other words, a comprehensive picture of hemispheric and global temperatures. This is the perspective afforded by numerous studies of the Northern Hemisphere, and several studies for the entire globe, most recently the PAGES 2k project. The strong consensus of this body of work is that temperatures in the Northern Hemisphere are very likely warmer today than they were in Medieval times (see Masson-Delmotte et al., 2013, for a fairly technical summary), and this probably also holds true for the world as a whole (Mann et al., 2008; Ahmed et al., 2013).

The explicit reasoning behind claims to the contrary is the erroneous argument that if it was as warm or warmer in the past, due to natural variations, then today's warmth is really no different and could just as easily be due to natural causes. However, as we saw in question 9, previous natural climate change does not preclude today's climate change being due to human activities. We know that today's high levels of carbon dioxide in the atmosphere constitute a climate forcing, and it's different from the forcings that produced the Medieval Climate Anomaly. Current research suggests the Medieval Climate Anomaly was driven by a slight increase in the strength of the Sun, combined with relatively few cooling volcanic eruptions, along with the Earth's natural internal climate variability—a set of forcings fundamentally different from today's (see, e.g., Goosse et al., 2012).

Some books and blogs add a hint of conspiracy to their arguments. These sources suggest that the Medieval Warm Period has been airbrushed out of climate history, not because more recent science has provided a more comprehensive picture but because it is somehow inconvenient to the case that recent warming is attributable to human activity. This claim often takes the form of references to the reports of the Intergovernmental Panel on Climate Change (IPCC), an international body charged by the United Nations and the World Meteorological Organization with summarizing the state of climate change science every few years. The IPCC's First Assessment Report, released in 1990, mentioned the Medieval Warm Period but used the typically cautious language of science, stating that it "may not have been global" (Folland et al., 1990, p. 199). However, both Steve Goreham's and Senator Inhofe's books claim that the IPCC report indicates a much greater level of certainty. Many blogs follow the same reasoning. One example is a website called A Sceptical Mind, which states, "Until about the mid-1990s the Medieval Warm Period was for climate researchers an undisputed fact. The existence of the Medieval Warm Period was accepted without question and noted in the first progress report of the IPCC from 1990." This misrepresents the state of scientific understanding at the time by ignoring the important caveat clearly stated in the IPCC's 1990 report, that the Medieval Warm Period may not have been global. But by overstating the change in scientific consensus on this issue, climate change denialists have sought to cast suspicion on growing scientific acceptance of the more nuanced Medieval Climate Anomaly terminology.

At any rate, as climate scientist Richard Alley (2011, p. 167) points out, it would be better for the arguments of those dismissive of human-caused climate change if Medieval climate *wasn't* warmer than today. If Medieval climate was especially warm, this would suggest a global climate that is highly sensitive to external forcings, with small pushes resulting in large changes in temperature. If the Earth warmed up substantially in response to the joint forcings of a slightly stronger Sun and fewer volcanic eruptions, then it should warm up even more substantially in response to today's high levels of carbon dioxide in the atmosphere. Such a finding would lead logically to serious concern about climate change in the coming decades.

FURTHER READING

A Sceptical Mind. (n.d.). The Rise and Fall of the Hockey Stick. Available at http://a-sceptical-mind.com/the-rise-and-fall-of-the-hockey-stick. Accessed May 4, 2015.

Ahmed, M., Anchukaitis, K., Asrat, A., Borgoankar, H. P., Braida, M., Buckley, B. M., Büntgen, U., Chase, B. M., Christie, D. A., Cook, E. R., Curran, M.A.J., Diaz, H. F., Esper, J., Fan, Z.-X., Gaire, N. P., Ge, Q., Gergis, J., González-Rouco, J. F., Goosse, H., Grab, S. W., Graham, N., Graham, R., Grosjean, M., Hanhijärvi, S. T., Kaufman, D. S., Kiefer, D., Kimura, K., Korhola, A. A., Krusic, P. J., Lara, A., Lézine, A.-M., Ljungqvist, F. C., Lorrey, A. M., Luterbacher, J., Masson-Delmotte, V., McCarroll, D., McConnell, J. R., McKay, N. P., Morales, M. S., Moy, A. D., Mulvaney, R., Mundo, I., Nakatsuka, T., Nash, D. J., Neukom, R., Nicholson, S. R., Oerter, H., Palmer, J. G., Phipps, S. J., Prieto, M. R.,

Rivera, A., Sano, M., Severi, M., Steig, E. J., Stenni, B., Thamban, M., Trouet, V., Turney, C.S.M., Umer, M., van Ommen, T., Verschuren, D., Viau, A. E., Villalba, R., Vinther, B. M., von Gunten, L., Wagner, S., Wahl, E. R., Wanner, H., Werner, J. P., White, J.W.C., Yasue, K., and Zorita, E. (2013). Continental-scale temperature variability during the past two millennia. *Nature Geoscience*, 6(5), 339–346.

Alley, R.B. (2011). *Earth: The Operators' Manual*. W.W. Norton & Company.

Folland, C. K., Karl, T. R., and Vinnikov, K. Ya. (1990). Observed climate variations and change. In Houghton, J. T., Jenkins, G. J., and Ephraums, J. J. (eds.) *Climate Change: The IPCC Scientific Assessment*. Cambridge University Press, Cambridge, United Kingdom and New York, NY, available at http://www.ipcc.ch/ipccreports/far/wg_I/ipcc_far_wg_I_chapter_07.pdf. Accessed May 4, 2015.

Goosse, H., Crespin, E., Dubinkina, S., Loutre, M. F., Mann, M. E., Renssen, H., Sallaz-Damaz, Y., and Shindell, D. (2012). The role of forcing and internal dynamics in explaining the "Medieval Climate Anomaly." *Climate Dynamics*, 39(12), 2847–2866.

Goreham, S. (2013). *The Mad, Mad, Mad World of Climatism: Mankind and Climate Change Mania*. New Lenox Books.

Hughes, M.K., and Diaz, H.F. (1994). Was there a "Medieval Warm Period," and if so, where and when? *Climatic Change*, 26(2–3), 109–142.

Inhofe, J.M. (2012). *The Greatest Hoax: How the Global Warming Conspiracy Threatens Your Future*. WND Books, Washington, DC.

Mann, M.E., Zhang, Z., Hughes, M.K., Bradley, R.S., Miller, S.K., Rutherford, S., and Ni, F. (2008). Proxy-based reconstructions of hemispheric and global surface temperature variations over the past two millennia. *Proceedings of the National Academy of Sciences*, 105(36), 13252–13257.

Mann, M.E., Zhang, Z., Rutherford, S., Bradley, R.S., Hughes, M.K., Shindell, D., Amman, C., Faluvegi, G., and Ni, F. (2009). Global signatures and dynamical origins of the Little Ice Age and Medieval Climate Anomaly. *Science*, 326(5957), 1256–1260.

Masson-Delmotte, V., Schulz, M., Abe-Ouchi, A., Beer, J., Ganopolski, A., González Rouco, J. F., Jansen, E., Lambeck, K., Luterbacher, J., Naish, T., Osborn, T., Otto-Bliesner, B., Quinn, T., Ramesh, R., Rojas, M., Shao, X., and Timmermann, A. (2013). Information from Paleoclimate Archives. In *Climate Change 2013: The Physical Science Basis. Contribution of Working Group I to the Fifth Assessment Report of the Intergovernmental Panel on Climate Change*, T. F. Stocker, D. Qin, G.-K. Plattner, M. Tignor, S. K. Allen, J. Boschung, A. Nauels, Y. Xia,

V. Bex, and P. M. Midgley (eds.). Cambridge University Press, Cambridge, United Kingdom and New York, NY, available at http://www
.climatechange2013.org/images/report/WG1AR5_Chapter05_FINAL.
pdf. Accessed May 4, 2015.
Plimer, I. R. (2009). *Heaven and Earth*. Taylor Trade.
Singer, S. F. and Avery, D. T. (2008). *Unstoppable Global Warming: Every
1500 Years*. Updated and expanded edition. Rowman & Littlefield.

Q11. WHAT IS THE "HOCKEY STICK" AND HOW ACCURATE A PICTURE DOES IT PROVIDE OF GLOBAL CLIMATE CHANGE?

Answer: Many independent studies have confirmed that, for the past 1,000 years or more, the world was gradually cooling—but in the mid-20th century, temperatures began to rise rapidly. The pattern of long, gradual cooling followed by recent rapid warming forms the shape of a hockey stick.

The Facts: The "hockey stick" is a term that describes the pattern of temperature change over the past several centuries: a gradual, steady cooling followed, in the mid-20th century, by a sharp warming. When presented in graph form, the overall effect resembles a long hockey stick with an upturned blade at the end.

This pattern emerged from the first serious efforts in what are known as *multi-proxy* temperature reconstructions, and has been confirmed many times over. Recall from earlier questions that reconstructing the climate of the past—*paleoclimate*—depends on the use of indirect measurements of climate features such as rainfall or temperature. Because we don't have rain gauge or thermometer records from a 1,000 years ago (or even rain gauges or thermometers), paleoclimatologists rely on substitutes, proxy measures, that are influenced by the climate feature in question. Temperature can be estimated indirectly by looking at many different features of the natural world: the width of the growth rings of certain tree species, the chemistry of the snow that falls at the poles and in high mountains that is compressed into ice, the chemistry of the limestone deposited drop by drop, year by year, to form stalagmites in caves, the pollen collected in bogs to form a record of the plants that lived there over time, and many others. These proxy measures record temperature, but they are influenced by other things as well, so determining exactly how a change in any given proxy actually translates to a change in temperature can be difficult.

Because of these challenges, expertise tended to be proxy-specific: scientists were experts in interpreting tree rings, or stalagmites, but not ice cores or pollen. Consequently, proxy records of paleoclimate tended to be viewed in isolation, forming a set of fragments that were viewed as only applying to the place they were collected from. This made it difficult for scientists to say much about how climate had changed over larger scales, such as the Northern Hemisphere or the entire world. It was as if scientists had a set of individual pieces of a jigsaw puzzle scattered across a table, and no way to put them together into a bigger picture.

In 1998, the first serious effort to assemble the jigsaw puzzle was undertaken by paleoclimatologists Ray Bradley and Malcolm Hughes in collaboration with climate scientist Michael Mann, who served as lead author. Their paper combined 22 different proxy measures of temperature that stretched back to the year 1400, as well as others that went less far back in time, to produce a comprehensive picture of temperature change for the Northern Hemisphere over the past 600 years. This groundbreaking work resulted in a view of temperature change over time that was both broader in geographical scope and of greater length than any single proxy record was able to provide. The whole was more than the sum of the parts.

The following year, the same team extended their Northern Hemisphere temperature reconstruction back to the year 1000. The clear hockey stick pattern from that study was featured prominently in the IPCC's Third Assessment Report, published in 2001, notably the influential Summary for Policymakers (IPCC, 2001). The groundbreaking nature of the research, combined with the compelling story told by the graph, prompted considerable scrutiny from scientists, politicians, and interested members of the public. Some of this scrutiny was conducted through the scientific processes of peer review discussed earlier, and was entirely appropriate. Discussions of some of the other, less appropriate ways in which the hockey stick research was examined, including political hearings, are provided separately by two of the scientists involved (Bradley, 2011; Mann, 2012). The remainder of this entry is concerned with the scientific discussions of the hockey stick.

Although much argument about the validity of the hockey stick work occurred on websites, the relevant scientific scrutiny took place in the peer-reviewed literature. For several years, an extensive back-and-forth debate took place in leading journals on the merits of various statistical techniques and their application or misapplication in different situations. A thorough overview was provided by the National Academy of Sciences, which in 2006 issued a report finding that the hockey stick was basically an accurate representation of Northern Hemisphere temperature over the past 600 years, though it was harder to tell what was happening further back in time, and in some technical aspects the original hockey stick work could be improved. (A reasonably readable account of some of the technical issues is provided in a RealClimate blog post by Tamino, 2010.)

This, of course, is exactly how science is supposed to work: an important scientific challenge is met with a bold new approach; criticisms are leveled, rejected, or confirmed; and the science is improved. In the wake of the critiques of Mann, Bradley, and Hughes's important work, many new studies were launched into both Northern Hemisphere and global temperature over the past 1,000 or more years. These studies used different statistical techniques and sometimes different collections of proxies. Although the results differ in a few details—some found a warmer Medieval period than others, for example—their broad conclusions are all that temperatures were cooling steadily until the mid-20th century, when rapid warming kicked in. In other words, they all show a hockey stick pattern. Thus, whatever the merits of the various technical objections to Mann, Bradley, and Hughes's original work, the science on this issue has moved on. Many critics, however, have not. A recurring theme in some blogs and books on climate change is that the hockey stick is broken, or flawed in some way. These criticisms tend to focus on the situation 10 or more years ago, often without acknowledging the complexity of the scientific debate and sometimes neglecting to mention that climate scientists have used their research to create not just one hockey stick but many independently re-created hockey sticks. Steve Goreham (2013), for example, emphasizes a criticism raised in 2005 in the peer-reviewed literature by Steve McIntyre and Ross McKitrick, without mentioning that this criticism was itself subject to considerable debate about how strongly it affected the final result. Fred Singer and Dennis Avery (2008, pp. 127–135) focus on Mann et al.'s work and the subsequent scientific debate, but cite no peer-reviewed work on the matter published after 2003, thus missing many important studies that confirm the hockey stick result. The blog A Sceptical Mind claims that the hockey stick has been disproved, focusing only on the original Mann et al. work and its subsequent criticism, without mentioning the numerous follow-up studies that demonstrate its basic accuracy.

One other important point about the claim that the hockey stick is "broken" is that even if that were true, it does not address other evidence of human-caused climate change. The idea that humans are changing the climate does not hang by a single thread of evidence, but by many threads woven into a strong cable (a metaphor borrowed from Richard Alley, 2011, pp. 168–169). The hockey stick pattern of temperature change has been confirmed by many separate studies, but in many respects, the hockey stick is a side issue—an interesting and important one, but nevertheless, a side issue—and technical arguments about its validity are a distraction.

FURTHER READING

Alley, R. B. (2011). *Earth: The Operators' Manual.* W.W. Norton & Company.

Arbesman, S. (2012). *The Half-Life of Facts: Why Everything We Know Has an Expiration Date.* Penguin.

Bradley, R. S. (2011). *Global Warming and Political Intimidation: How Politicians Cracked Down on Scientists as the Earth Heated Up.* University of Massachusetts Press, Amherst and Boston.

The Economist. (2013). Unreliable Research: Trouble at the Lab. October 19, 2013. Available at http://www.economist.com/news/briefing/21588057-scientists-think-science-self-correcting-alarming-degree-it-not-trouble. Accessed May 7, 2015.

Goreham, S. (2013). *The Mad, Mad, Mad World of Climatism: Mankind and Climate Change Mania.* New Lenox Books.

IPCC. (2001). Summary for Policymakers. In IPCC (2001). *Climate Change 2001: The Scientific Basis. Contribution of Working Group I to the Third Assessment Report of the Intergovernmental Panel on Climate Change,* J. T. Houghton, Y. Ding, D. J. Griggs, M. Noguer, P. J. van der Linden, X. Dai, K. Maskell, and C. A. Johnson (eds.). Cambridge University Press, Cambridge, United Kingdom, and New York, NY, pp. 1–20, available at http://www.grida.no/climate/ipcc_tar/wg1/pdf/WG1_TAR-FRONT.pdf. Accessed May 7, 2015.

Mann, M. E. (2012). *The Hockey Stick and the Climate Wars: Dispatches from the Front Lines.* Columbia University Press, New York.

Mann, M. E., Bradley, R. S., and Hughes, M. K. (1998). Global-scale temperature patterns and climate forcing over the past six centuries. *Nature, 392*(6678), 779–787.

Mann, M. E., Bradley, R. S., and Hughes, M. K. (1999). Northern hemisphere temperatures during the past millennium: inferences, uncertainties, and limitations. *Geophysical Research Letters, 26*(6), 759–762.

Masson-Delmotte, V., Schulz, M., Abe-Ouchi, A., Beer, J., Ganopolski, A., González Rouco, J. F., Jansen, E., Lambeck, K., Luterbacher, J., Naish, T., Osborn, T., Otto-Bliesner, B., Quinn, T., Ramesh, R., Rojas, M., Shao, X., and Timmermann, A. (2013). Information from Paleoclimate Archives. In *Climate Change 2013: The Physical Science Basis. Contribution of Working Group I to the Fifth Assessment Report of the Intergovernmental Panel on Climate Change,* T. F. Stocker, D. Qin,

G.-K. Plattner, M. Tignor, S. K. Allen, J. Boschung, A. Nauels, Y. Xia, V. Bex, and P. M. Midgley (eds.). Cambridge University Press, Cambridge, United Kingdom, and New York, NY, available at http://www .climatechange2013.org/images/report/WG1AR5_Chapter05_FINAL. pdf. Accessed May 4, 2015.

McIntyre, S., and McKitrick, R. (2005). Hockey sticks, principal components, and spurious significance. *Geophysical Research Letters*, 32(3), DOI: 10.1029/2004GL021750.

A Sceptical Mind. (n.d.). The Rise and Fall of the Hockey Stick. Available at http://a-sceptical-mind.com/the-rise-and-fall-of-the-hockey-stick. Accessed May 4, 2015.

Singer, S. F., and Avery, D. T. (2008). *Unstoppable Global Warming: Every 1500 Years*. Updated and expanded edition. Rowman & Littlefield.

Tamino. (2010). The Montford Delusion. Posted to RealClimate.org, July 22, 2010, available at http://www.realclimate.org/index.php/ archives/2010/07/the-montford-delusion/. Accessed May 7, 2015.

Q12. WHAT ROLE DOES THE SUN PLAY IN GLOBAL TEMPERATURE RISE?

Answer: Observed climate patterns confirm greenhouse warming, and rule out the Sun, as the primary driver of recent global warming. In fact, measurements of solar behavior show a cooling Sun in recent decades, even as global temperatures have warmed.

The Facts: Climate scientists have long been aware of the central role of the Sun in explaining numerous basic aspects of Earth's climate. For example, the curvature of Earth's surface means the Sun's rays strike at a progressively shallower angle closer to the poles, making them less focused and therefore less powerful, and explaining why the equator is hot and the poles are cold. The resulting energy imbalance between the equator and poles drives much of the large-scale movement of the atmosphere and oceans. Another example: winter and summer occur because the tilt of the Earth's axis of rotation causes the Northern and Southern Hemispheres to receive greater and lesser amounts of sunlight at different times of the year.

The central role assigned by climate scientists to the Sun is clear from the U.S. Global Change Research Program's (2009) guide to the essential principles of climate science: principle #1 states that "the Sun is the primary source of energy for Earth's climate system" (p. 10).

There's no question, then, that the Sun is a major player in Earth's present-day climate. The same can be said of changes in Earth's climate in the past, many of which can be explained at least in part by changes in the amount or distribution of sunlight received. We've already seen several examples over a range of timescales, from the short-term year-to-year effects of volcanic eruptions, like 1815's Tambora eruption and 1816's Year Without a Summer, to the longer-term glacial and interglacial periods, swinging from warm to cold and back again over a 100,000 years as the orbital wobbles of Milankovitch theory drive changes in the distribution of sunlight. We looked at both of these examples in question 9.

These climate changes are a result of characteristics of the Earth: wobbles in its orbit, or changes in how clear or reflective its atmosphere is. But there's a large body of evidence that tells us there are also changes in the characteristics of the Sun, specifically, how active it is, and, as a result, how much solar radiation reaches the Earth. There are several manifestations of solar activity, but they all follow a roughly 11-year cycle of increases and decreases (Figure 2.2). The amount of solar radiation reaching the Earth—the total solar irradiance, or TSI—has been

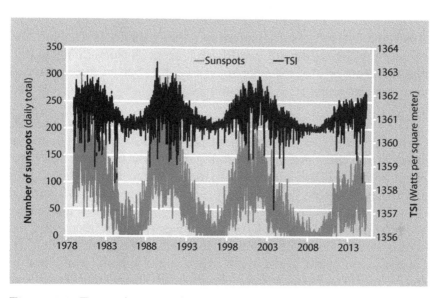

Figure 2.2 Two indicators of solar activity, daily sunspot numbers and daily total solar irradiance (TSI) since 1978. Both indicators rise and fall on a roughly 11-year cycle.

Source: Sunspot data from WDC-SILSO (2015); TSI data from PMOD/WRC (2015). See also Fröhlich (2006).

measured directly since 1978 using satellites. Indirect proxy measures have allowed TSI to be estimated as far back as 1,000 years ago, much like the temperature reconstructions using proxy measures that we examined in questions 8, 10, and 11. From these reconstructions, it's clear that there were times in the past when the Sun was more active, bathing the Earth in more sunlight, and times when it was less so. Solar activity mostly still follows the 11-year up-and-down cycle, but the peaks are higher at some times and lower at others. (Solar physics expert Judith Lean, 2010, provides a fairly readable summary.)

These variations in TSI help to explain some of the climate changes evident in the proxy temperature reconstructions. For example, in question 10 we examined the Medieval Climate Anomaly and saw that its warmth, while less than today's, could be explained by slightly higher TSI, somewhat fewer volcanic eruptions, and the internal variability of the climate system. Several hundred years later, a more obviously worldwide cooling event seems to have occurred, known as the Little Ice Age, running roughly between 1450 and 1850. This corresponds with somewhat lower TSI.

How does this relate to today's changing climate? We know from numerous indicators, both direct and indirect, that the Earth is getting warmer (see questions 1 and 3–5). Given the relationship that we've seen for earlier climate changes in Earth's history, we would expect TSI to be going up. However, satellite measurements and reconstructions show that the Earth has been receiving slightly *less* solar radiation in recent decades, not more. Figure 2.3 shows that sunspots and global average temperatures track quite closely up until the late 1950s. At this point, the Sun started to become slightly less bright—but global average temperatures continued to climb. In fact, numerous peer-reviewed studies show that the Sun can explain no more than a small fraction of the Earth's recent warming, if any—and several studies indicate that, since 1979, the less-bright Sun should have resulted in global average cooling, instead of the warming that we've actually seen (a thorough list of publications is provided at SkepticalScience.com).

The mismatch between the behavior of the Sun and the behavior of global average temperature illustrates two important points about climate change. First, it's a strong indication that something other than the Sun must be driving the current warming. The most obvious candidate is the very high levels of heat-trapping gases currently in the atmosphere: more carbon dioxide today, for example, than at any time in the past 800,000 years, as we saw in question 9.

Second, however, it's important to recognize that the climate system is rarely, if ever, affected by only one influence at a time. Recall from

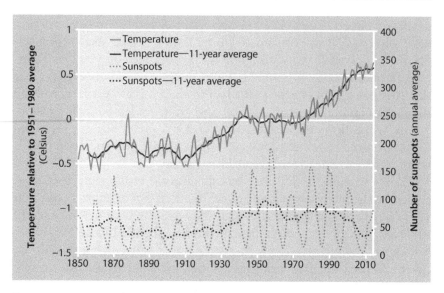

Figure 2.3 Annual average number of sunspots and global average temperature. Note that sunspots and temperature are closely related until the late 1950s, when sunspots begin to fall but temperature continues to rise. Sunspots are a good indicator of TSI, as shown in Figure 2.2. Temperature is shown as difference relative to 1951–1980 average, in Celsius. Eleven-year averages are shown to smooth out short-term variations, bringing the patterns into focus.

Source: Temperature data from Berkeley Earth (2015); sunspot data from WDC-SILSO (2015).

question 9 the concept of climate *forcings*, the pushes and pulls on climate that result from orbital wobbles, for example, or volcanic eruptions—or changes in the strength of the Sun. There are many different climate forcings, sometimes reinforcing each other, sometimes working against each other, and the end result in terms of climate change is the sum of all the pushes and pulls. It's a bit like driving a car, but forgetting to take the parking brake off: if the engine is powerful enough, and you rev it hard enough, the car will move forward, but if the brakes are strong, or the engine is weak, the car won't move.

This balancing act shows up in the climate changes of the past. The Medieval Climate Anomaly, for example, can be explained partly by a slightly stronger Sun but also by a period of relatively few cooling volcanic eruptions. Here, the forcings acted together to warm up the Earth slightly. The glacial and interglacial periods can be explained fully only if the reinforcing effect of carbon dioxide is included, as discussed in question 9. Today, the forcing from the Sun is running against the forcing from carbon dioxide, helping to make the warming somewhat less than we might otherwise expect. In other words, the Sun is well understood to be one of the drivers of Earth's climate—but it's not the only one. This concept of multiple climate forcings sometimes working together and sometimes working against each other is an important one, and we'll return to it in several later questions.

Just as there are many potential drivers of climate, many of these climate drivers have distinctive patterns that we can look for to rule out or confirm their contributions. In some cases, the patterns from solar-induced warming versus greenhouse warming are opposite in nature. This provides a handy way to independently check what is the main driver of recent global warming.

For example, one pattern of greenhouse warming is that the upper atmosphere (or stratosphere) should show cooling at the same time that the lower atmosphere (or troposphere) is warming, as discussed in question 2. This occurs in part because greenhouse gases are trapping heat in the lower atmosphere. In contrast, if the Sun was causing recent global warming, warming would be taking place in both the upper and lower atmosphere. Observations indeed show a cooling upper atmosphere and warming lower atmosphere. This is another line of evidence for greenhouse warming, as well as ruling out the Sun as a major driver of global warming.

One of the earliest predicted patterns of greenhouse warming was made in 1861 by John Tyndall, who expected greenhouse warming to result in winters warming faster than summers. This is because greenhouse gases slow down cooling out to space, so that winters will cool less with more greenhouse gases in the atmosphere. This pattern is the opposite of that expected from solar-induced warming, which should cause summers to warm faster than winters. Observations show that winters have been warming faster, again confirming greenhouse warming and ruling out the Sun.

Despite the strong evidence that the Sun is not a primary cause of global warming, that theory continues to be advanced. Steve Goreham's (2013) *The Mad, Mad, Mad World of Climatism* argues that the Sun is the main driver of recent warming. According to Goreham, "Solar activity better explains both twentieth century and millennial temperature variations than does atmospheric carbon dioxide" (p. 99). He also asserts that mainstream climate science, which he refers to as Climatism, has erroneously concluded that the "sun is an insignificant factor in climate change"

(p. 91). Actually, however, mainstream climate scientists have not made any such conclusion. The Sun helps explain the Medieval Climate Anomaly and the Little Ice Age, among other features of Earth's climate history, so the statement that solar activity helps explain temperature variations over the past 1,000 years (millennial temperature variations) is therefore broadly accurate. However, the observed behavior of the Sun rules it out as the primary cause of the *current*, late 20th- and early 21st-century climate change.

Goreham does not claim that solar activity directly causes changes in temperature, acknowledging that recent variations are too small by themselves to produce much in the way of climate change. But like some other works by climate change skeptics, including Fred Singer and Dennis Avery's (2008) *Unstoppable Global Warming: Every 1500 Years*, and Roy Spencer's (2007) *Climate Confusion*, Goreham's book argues that an amplifying mechanism exists, in the form of galactic cosmic rays. These are a real phenomenon, and the proposed mechanism has a limited amount of evidence supporting it (and some evidence that does not support it).

The idea is that cosmic rays, originating from outside of our solar system, may help form more low clouds, which reflect sunlight and cool the Earth. A more active Sun makes for a stronger solar wind, which reduces the number of cosmic rays reaching our atmosphere—so a more active Sun means fewer cosmic rays, fewer low clouds, and more warming, while a less active Sun means the opposite. Roy Spencer accurately refers to this as "a rather controversial theory" (p. 74).

However, even if this idea were correct, the mechanism only amplifies the warming or cooling associated with a more or a less active Sun—and the evidence is clear that the Sun has been getting less active in recent years. This should make for even stronger cooling than mainstream science suggests, and yet the Earth is very clearly getting warmer, not cooler. Curiously, in support of the view that the Sun might be driving the recent warming, Roy Spencer (2007) states that "sunspot activity is now at an historical high" (p. 74), despite the clear evidence to the contrary.

According to the World Data Center for the Sunspot Index and Long-Term Solar Observations (WDC-SILSO, 2015), which is the official source for the international sunspot number, the highest number of sunspots since their records began in 1818 was on December 24, 1957, measuring 355 sunspots. The peaks of all the following sunspot cycles were lower: 215 in 1969, 302 in 1979, 295 in 1990, 246 in 2000, and 154 in 2014 (see Figure 2.3). Sunspot activity is not at an historical high.

FURTHER READING

Berkeley Earth. (2015). Land + Ocean Data. Available at http://berkeley earth.org/land-and-ocean-data/. Accessed March 27, 2015.

Fröhlich, C. (2006). Solar irradiance variability since 1978. *Space Science Reviews*, *125*(1–4), 53–65.

Goreham, S. (2013). *The Mad, Mad, Mad World of Climatism: Mankind and Climate Change Mania*. New Lenox Books.

Lean, J. L. (2010). Cycles and trends in solar irradiance and climate. *Wiley Interdisciplinary Reviews: Climate Change*, *1*(1), 111–122.

PMOD/WRC (Physical Meteorological Observatory Davos/World Radiation Center). (2015). Total Solar Irradiance Composite Data Version 42_64_1504. Available at ftp://ftp.pmodwrc.ch/pub/data/irradiance/composite/DataPlots/composite_42_64_1504.dat. Accessed May 6, 2015.

A Sceptical Mind. (n.d.). The Rise and Fall of the Hockey Stick. Available at http://a-sceptical-mind.com/the-rise-and-fall-of-the-hockey-stick. Accessed May 4, 2015.

Singer, S. F., and Avery, D. T. (2008). *Unstoppable Global Warming: Every 1500 Years*. Updated and expanded edition. Rowman & Littlefield.

WDC-SILSO, Royal Observatory of Belgium. (2015). Daily Total Sunspot Number. Available at http://sidc.be/silso/datafiles. Accessed May 6, 2015.

Q13. HOW HAS CLIMATE BEEN CHANGING ON MARS AND OTHER PLANETS?

Answer: Scientists have found no evidence for planet-wide warming on Mars or other planets in Earth's solar system. The solar system doesn't tell us much about global warming on Earth, as the Sun has shown little change in recent decades other than slight cooling.

The Facts: Studying other planets is a scientifically rewarding undertaking. Besides satisfying fundamental human curiosity, it helps us learn about how the solar system formed, which can help us learn more about the Earth. It can also shed light on the fundamental physics of key planetary characteristics, like climate. For example, we can see how the levels of heat-trapping gases in the atmosphere can make a planet warm or cold by studying Earth and its nearest neighbors, super-hot Venus and chilly Mars.

Of the three planets, Venus is the closest to the Sun, so it basks in more sunlight—but this alone can't explain why Venus is so hot (temperatures at the surface are hot enough to melt lead). In fact, Venus actually absorbs *less* sunlight than Earth does, because Venus's atmosphere is so dense and so full of thick clouds that reflect much of the sunlight away. So why is Venus so hot? Although it absorbs surprisingly little sunlight, that thick, reflective atmosphere also prevents what energy it does absorb from escaping to space. In a sense, Venus wears a very, very thick overcoat. Venus is hot not because of sunlight but because of its dense, heat-trapping atmosphere. Mars, by contrast, has a very thin atmosphere, which traps very little heat, helping to make it very cold. Earth is the Goldilocks planet, neither too hot nor too cold, but just right (see Zalasiewicz and Williams, 2012).

As this example shows, comparisons between planets can be useful. But they can be tricky, because other planets are a very long way away, and we know a lot less about them than we do about Earth. This can make it difficult to put new findings from other planets into context. Mars is probably the best known of the other planets in the solar system, partly because it's relatively close and partly because it has a thin, relatively cloud-free atmosphere (though it does get obscured by giant dust storms from time to time, as we'll see later). Even so, it's still never closer than 55.7 million kilometers (34.6 million miles) away, and it's usually a lot further (NASA, 2014)—and although it's been visited by several spacecraft, including high-profile missions like the NASA rovers Spirit, Opportunity, and Curiosity, the data they have sent back are still only a tiny fraction of the mountains of information we have for Earth. Caution is therefore warranted in interpreting observations from other planets.

In fact, the history of Mars studies shows how easy it is to jump to the wrong conclusions. In the late 1800s, telescope observations of Mars appeared to show a network of dark lines on the planet's surface. More recent observations show no such features, and they are now understood to have been optical illusions brought about by the low-quality telescopes being used. However, at the time, many observers were convinced not only that the dark lines were real but also that they were artificial features, canals, that were evidence of intelligent life. This view was by no means universally accepted among scientists, but it took hold in the popular imagination despite being wildly wrong. When interpreting sparse data from a long way away, it's worth being careful before reaching a final decision.

This doesn't mean that we can't say *anything* about Mars or other planets. For example, the fact that the planets are so different from Earth allows us to test our understanding of the fundamental physics of weather and climate. Mars lacks oceans, so it lacks the huge storehouse for heat that Earth has (recall from question 8 that about 90% of the heat accumulating due to global warming is going into the oceans). This makes it highly responsive to changes in external forcings on its climate system, much more so than Earth (remember the idea of climate forcings from questions 9 and 12). In a sense, Mars is the drama queen of the solar system—a little disturbance causes a big response.

Mars also has a much more stretched-out oval of an orbit than Earth does. All the planets have elliptical, oval-shaped orbits, but some are more like circles than others. Mars's orbit is very elliptical, so it gets a lot more sunlight at the point on its orbit when it's closest to the Sun compared with when it's farthest away (about 40% more, compared with Earth's 7% more). This big increase in sunlight gives drama-queen Mars plenty to respond to when it's closest to the Sun, especially in the Southern Hemisphere, where summer coincides with the closest pass to the Sun. (Winter and summer are caused by the tilt of a planet's axis of rotation, not by distance from the Sun, so winter and summer do not always coincide with furthest and closest to the Sun—but for Mars's Southern Hemisphere, they do.) The dramatic changes in temperature that result seem to play a role in generating very large dust storms, some of which can grow to cover the entire planet. NASA's Mariner 9 spacecraft could see disappointingly little of the surface when it first arrived near Mars in 1971, because of a huge dust storm blocking the view.

These dust storms themselves may further affect Mars's temperature. They seem to move shiny, reflective dust onto darker surfaces, temporarily brightening them and reflecting more sunlight, which can cool the planet. The dust is gradually shifted by gentler winds after the dust storm subsides, and the effect disappears after a year or so, bringing the temperature back up again. Fenton et al. (2007) looked at satellite images of Mars in 1977 and 1999, finding 1999 to be less reflective. They went on to calculate that the change should have caused Mars to warm by about 0.65°C (1.2°F) over the 22-year interval.

The key point about this research is that it was an investigation of the effects on Mars's temperature of changes in reflection because of dust storms, an effect unique to Mars. However, in a 2010 post, the Hockey Schtick blog mixed up units of Fahrenheit and Celsius to claim that, because Earth had warmed by about 0.4°C over the same time frame, Mars was warming four times faster than Earth. The post also suggested that the warming on the two planets might have a common cause, asking "Could it be the sun?" This misrepresents Fenton et al.'s work, as their paper very clearly states their proposed warming mechanism for Mars as dust storms and the associated reflection changes.

Misinterpretation of Mars research is not limited to Fenton et al.'s paper. When NASA announced in 2005 that Mars's southern polar ice-cap was melting rapidly, the news was quickly taken as evidence that Mars as a whole was warming. This is what scientists call "going beyond the data"—essentially, jumping to conclusions that say more than the evidence can actually support. While a large body of evidence tells us that ice is melting not just in one location on Earth, but all over the planet, and numerous independent measurements confirm that global average temperatures are rising, no such comparable body of evidence exists for Mars. We have a very geographically limited set of observations, for only a very short time period, and while Mars as a whole might be warming up, the melting of the southern polar icecap might also be only a regional phenomenon. It's unwise to go beyond the data to claim definitively that Mars is warming globally.

Nevertheless, James Taylor, writing at the Heartland Institute's website in 2005, stated: "The planet Mars is undergoing significant global warming, new data from . . . NASA show, lending support to many climatologists' claims that the Earth's modest warming during the past century is due primarily to a recent upsurge in solar energy." First, as noted earlier, there is no clear evidence of a global-scale warming trend on Mars. Second, we saw in question 12 that there has been no recent upsurge in solar energy; rather, the Sun has shown a slight cooling trend. Third, a number of observed climate patterns have ruled out solar-induced global warming (again, examined in question 12) while confirming human-caused global warming. Finally, a 2007 story at National Geographic.com News by Kate Ravilious was able to find only one climatologist claiming that warming was induced by the Sun, not many.

Still, Ravilious's article served as the basis for a nationally syndicated cartoon, Mallard Fillmore by Bruce Tinsley, who wrote in January 2011, lampooning college professors: "I teach in elite seminars/That the Earth's warmed by people and cars./I resolve this is so, even though we now know/That they've found global warming on Mars." The reasoning seems to be that if Mars is warming, the absence of people there means that it must be due to natural causes, which could therefore be behind Earth's warming as well. The assumption behind Tinsley's cartoon is that Mars really is warming, which we've seen is a conclusion that goes beyond the data. However, even if it were true, the reasoning commits the logical fallacy of jumping to conclusions. In the same way that natural climate changes in Earth's past do not preclude human-caused climate changes in the present, as discussed in question 9, so natural climate changes on Mars do not preclude human-caused climate changes on Earth.

Interesting climate phenomena have also been observed in recent years elsewhere in the solar system, including Jupiter, Neptune and its moon Triton, and Pluto. However, we know even less about these planets and moons than we do about Mars. For example, Pluto was discovered only in 1930, and astronomers are still arguing about whether it's even a planet or not (the International Astronomical Union ruled in 2006 that it was not, but debate continues—see Chang, 2015). Pluto takes almost 248 years to orbit the Sun, so we've only known about its existence, let alone been able to make detailed observations, for about a third of its year. This does not provide a strong background from which to say whether recent observed events constitute the normal shift from winter to summer, or whether they constitute a longer-term change.

Many blogs try to claim otherwise, though, and suggest that climate phenomena on these planets are evidence of a solar system-wide warming driven by the Sun (e.g., Watson, 2006; Gunter, 2007; The Critical Thinker, 2008). Besides the facts that the Sun is getting less, not more, active, and many other planets and moons in the solar system show no signs of warming, the data from Jupiter, Neptune, Triton, and Pluto are hard to interpret. But humans are pattern-seeking creatures, and for thousands of years we've told each other stories based on the shapes we saw, or thought we saw, in the night sky. We're all prone to finding patterns, whether they are real or, as in the case of alleged solar system-wide warming, not real. This is why science and its related processes, such as peer review, are so important: they help weed out the real patterns from the ones we simply want to see. In comparison to peer-reviewed publications, blog posts should be interpreted with caution—just like temperature data from Mars.

FURTHER READING

Chang, K. (2015). NASA spacecraft closing in on dwarf planets Pluto and Ceres. *The New York Times*, January 19, 2015, available at http://www.nytimes.com/2015/01/20/science/nasa-spacecraft-get-a-closer-look-at-pluto-and-ceres-whatever-they-may-be.html?_r=0. Accessed May 7, 2015.

The Critical Thinker. (2008). Climate change felt on other planets. Posted to The Critical Thinker blog, November 1, 2008, available at https://thecriticalthinker.wordpress.com/2008/11/01/climate-change-felt-on-other-planets/. Accessed May 7, 2015.

Fenton, L. K., Geissler, P. E., and Haberle, R. M. (2007). Global warming and climate forcing by recent albedo changes on Mars. *Nature, 446*(7136), 646–649.

Fröhlich, C. (2006). Solar irradiance variability since 1978. *Space Science Reviews, 125*(1–4), 53–65.

Gunter, L. (2007). Breaking: warming on Jupiter, Mars, Pluto, Neptune's Moon and Earth linked to increased solar activity, scientists say. Posted to Canada Free Press.com, March 13, 2007, available at http://canadafreepress.com/2007/global-warming031307.htm. Accessed May 7, 2015.

The Hockey Schtick. (2010). Mars has warmed 4 times more than Earth over last 20 years. Posted to hockeyschtick.blogspot.com, May 8, 2010, available at http://hockeyschtick.blogspot.com/2010/05/whoopsmars-has-warmed-4-times-more-than.html. Accessed May 7, 2015.

NASA. (2014). Mars Fact Sheet. NASA Space Sciences Coordinated Data Archive. Available at http://nssdc.gsfc.nasa.gov/planetary/factsheet/marsfact.html. Accessed May 7, 2015.

Ravilious, K. (2007). Mars melt hints at solar, not human, cause for warming, scientist says. Posted to National Geographic News website, February 28, 2007, available at http://news.nationalgeographic.com/news/2007/02/070228-mars-warming.html. Accessed May 7, 2015.

Taylor, J. (2005). Mars is warming, NASA Scientists Report. Posted November 1, 2005, to heartland.org, available at http://news.heartland.org/newspaper-article/2005/11/01/mars-warming-nasa-scientists-report. Accessed May 7, 2015.

Tinsley, B. (2011). Mallard Fillmore, January 15, 2011. Available at http://www.thecomicstrips.com/store/add.php?iid=56059. Accessed May 7, 2015.

Watson, P. J. (2006). SUV's on Jupiter?—solar system warming. Posted to Red Ice Creations website, November 11, 2006, available at http://www.redicecreations.com/specialreports/2006/11nov/solarsystem-warming.html. Accessed May 7, 2015.

Zalasiewicz, J., and Williams, M. (2012). *The Goldilocks Planet: The 4 Billion Year Story of Earth's Climate.* Oxford University Press.

Q14. IS THE OZONE HOLE A FACTOR IN GLOBAL WARMING?

Answer: Global warming is caused by an ever-thickening blanket of heat-trapping gases in Earth's atmosphere. This has nothing to do with the hole in the ozone layer, which is a separate phenomenon.

The Facts: As earlier sections of this book have documented, global climate change is a real phenomenon. The average temperature of the Earth at and near the surface is rising, according to a host of indicators, and the warming that we're experiencing is highly unusual, perhaps even unprecedented in the past 1,000 or more years. In this question, and several that follow, we'll examine the evidence that this warming is being caused by human emissions of heat-trapping gases into the atmosphere. In particular, the focus of this question is the workings of the *greenhouse effect*. Although this is sometimes confused with the ozone hole, the two phenomena are fundamentally different.

The greenhouse effect has, at this point in history, been thoroughly studied and is now well understood. The comparisons between Venus, Earth, and Mars in the previous question showed how important it is for understanding climate. Recall that Venus is extremely hot because its atmosphere traps a lot of heat. That's the greenhouse effect at work.

The existence of the greenhouse effect was first proposed by the now-legendary mathematician Joseph Fourier in 1824 (Fourier's original article and many other foundational papers in the study of climate change have been collected by David Archer and Raymond Pierrehumbert in *The Warming Papers*). By estimating the amount of energy Earth receives from the Sun, Fourier concluded that the planet was warmer than it should be. Something else must be keeping us warm, he thought, and a likely candidate was the atmosphere trapping some of the energy from the Sun. Sunlight warms up the surface of the Earth, and a walk across a large parking lot at the end of a sunny day shows this plainly enough. But what happens to the heat that is in turn radiated away from the surface? If the atmosphere allows sunlight in, but does not allow all of the heat back out, the Earth would be warmer than you'd expect based on the amount of sunlight alone.

Fourier's idea was later shown to be right, by experiments reported first by Irish scientist John Tyndall in 1861. Tyndall found that certain gases worked as Fourier had suggested, absorbing infrared radiation from the Earth's surface, but letting sunlight pass through unhindered. These heat-trapping gases are known as greenhouse gases and include water vapor, carbon dioxide, methane, and nitrous oxide. Although the analogy is not completely accurate, the atmosphere is sometimes likened to the glass in a greenhouse, allowing sunlight in but blocking the escape of heat—hence the name, the greenhouse effect. (The University of Colorado's PhET science animations website has a nice illustration of the greenhouse effect. The history of the science underpinning the greenhouse effect is nicely described by Weart, 2008, and Kolbert, 2006.)

Considerably more research was conducted on greenhouse gases by the U.S. Air Force soon after World War II, as part of a program to develop heat-seeking anti-aircraft missiles. To make sure the missiles would work, the Air Force needed to know exactly how greenhouse gases trapped heat. If their missiles were tuned to home in on the particular wavelengths absorbed by water vapor or carbon dioxide, the heat from an enemy's jet engine would be blocked long before the missile could pick it up, and the missile wouldn't be able to "see" very far (see Alley, 2011, and Haines-Stiles and Alley, 2011). As a result of this missile research, scientists and engineers now know a lot about the detailed workings of the greenhouse effect. And starting in the 1970s, satellite measurements of energy being radiated out to space from the Earth have confirmed the U.S. Air Force's research—and John Tyndall's.

The fundamental physics of the greenhouse effect is therefore well understood. And from everything we know, and everything we've observed, more heat-trapping gases in the atmosphere cause more heat to be trapped. This is supported by evidence from earlier climate changes in Earth's history, as we saw in question 9—recall that the glacial and interglacial periods cannot be explained by orbital wobbles alone, but need changes in carbon dioxide to amplify them. While changes in greenhouse gas levels are not the only things that can drive temperature changes, the evidence tells us that increases and decreases in greenhouse gases cause increases and decreases in temperature.

Direct measurements of the atmosphere also tell us, clearly and resoundingly, that levels of atmospheric greenhouse gases are going up. Measurements of atmospheric carbon dioxide have been made at the Mauna Loa Observatory in Hawaii since 1958, and elsewhere around the world at various times since then. The measurements show that carbon dioxide concentrations have gone from just under 316 parts per million in March 1958 to around 404 parts per million in early May 2015. (See data from NOAA's Earth System Research Laboratory, 2015, shown in Figure 2.4. *The New York Times* reporter Justin Gillis wrote an excellent article about the measurements in 2010.) Levels of other greenhouse gases, such as methane and nitrous oxide are rising, too. More heat-trapping gases result in more heat trapped—and measurements from satellites confirm that less heat is escaping to space. It's a bit like coming home to find the house cold, because someone left all the windows open. The first thing you'd do is close all the windows to stop heat leaving the house. The increasing levels of greenhouse gases mean that we are now rapidly closing windows, keeping more heat inside.

So far in this discussion, we've seen that the scientific evidence telling us how increased greenhouse gases should cause an increased greenhouse effect is overwhelming and spans over a century of research. This solid

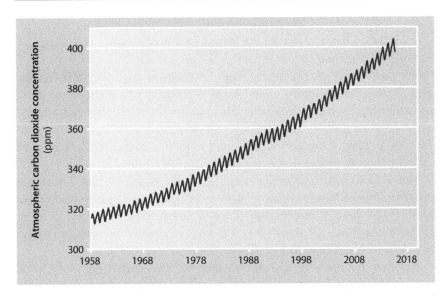

Figure 2.4 Carbon dioxide concentration in the atmosphere, measured at the Mauna Loa Observatory in Hawaii.
Source: NOAA ESRL.

foundation is an important reason why scientists are confident that the warming we've seen happening over the past several decades is mainly due to the increase in atmospheric carbon dioxide and other greenhouse gases. According to research on people's understanding of climate change, however, it seems that many people are mixed up about why the world is getting warmer. One study, by a team from the Yale Project on Climate Change Communication (Leiserowitz et al., 2010), found that, in the United States, at least, people generally have a fairly shaky understanding of the science, with a basic test of climate science knowledge yielding only 1% of people scoring an A (90% or better on the test) and 77% scoring a D or an F (69% or less on the test). One common mistake was to confuse the greenhouse effect with a different issue, the hole in the ozone layer.

The ozone hole is an important problem, but it's fundamentally different from global warming. The ozone hole is caused by chlorine from industrial chemicals breaking down ozone in the stratosphere. Ozone occurs naturally at high altitudes and forms the ozone layer, an important protective shield against harmful ultraviolet rays from the Sun, acting like a planet-wide sunscreen. So when it was discovered in 1985 that industrial chlorine was decimating the ozone layer over Antarctica, the world was alarmed. The production of the industrial chemicals that were the source of the chlorine has now been banned by international treaty. The ozone hole is clearly a serious environmental problem—but it's different from global warming.

Why do people get them mixed up? One reason might be the language used to describe the ozone hole. We're concerned about the ozone hole and took steps to fix it, because it lets in more ultraviolet rays, which can cause sunburn and skin cancer. The obvious mental image is a hole in the roof, letting in more sunlight. From here, it's easy to think that more sunlight coming in causes more warming.

Unfortunately, this misunderstands the basic physics. Global warming is happening because a thicker blanket of greenhouse gases means less heat is being let out, not because more sunlight is being let in. The more accurate image for global warming is that we're closing the windows in the house, preventing heat from escaping.

Another reason why it's easy to mix up the ozone hole and global warming is that, despite their fundamental differences, the two problems are related in certain ways. The ozone hole over Antarctica is a result of chlorine breaking down the ozone layer. The chlorine comes from industrial chemicals called chlorofluorocarbons (CFCs)—so named because they're built from chlorine, fluorine, and carbon, among other elements. CFCs were invented in 1928 and went into large-scale production a few years later, although, as mentioned earlier, they're now banned. But in addition to destroying ozone, CFCs are powerful greenhouse gases, each CFC molecule trapping several thousand times as much heat as a molecule of carbon dioxide. (Although there are several different CFCs, they share this heat-trapping power; see Blasing, 2014.) There's about a million times more carbon dioxide in the atmosphere than the various individual CFCs, though, so while CFCs are the villain of the piece when it comes to the ozone hole, they're much, much less important than carbon dioxide when it comes to global warming. But they do trap heat, so they contribute a small amount to global warming, as well as breaking down the ozone layer.

At the same time, the complex chemistry involved in exactly how chlorine breaks down the ozone layer works more effectively when it's very, very cold. This is why the ozone hole is most fully developed over the South Pole (the North Pole, which isn't as cold, has a smaller "ozone dimple"). As discussed in question 5, the increasing concentrations of greenhouse gases are warming the lower atmosphere, the troposphere, but they're cooling the upper atmosphere, the stratosphere—and the stratosphere is where the ozone breakdown happens. Given that colder conditions help the process along, it's reasonable to worry that a colder stratosphere could accelerate the breakdown of the ozone layer, even as the supply of chlorine has been cut off by the ban on CFCs. This is a second way in which the ozone hole, while a fundamentally different problem, is related to global warming.

Given these two connections with global warming, and the mental image that the name "ozone hole" suggests, it's easy to see why people get the two problems mixed up. But the fundamental science underlying the two issues is very different, and global warming is not caused by the ozone hole. Instead, it's caused by the ever-thickening blanket of greenhouse gases building up in our atmosphere. This traps heat, making the Earth warmer. We're closing the windows, not letting more light in through the roof.

FURTHER READING

Alley, R. B. (2011). *Earth: The Operators' Manual*. W.W. Norton & Company.

Archer, D., and Pierrehumbert, R. (Eds.). (2011). *The Warming Papers*. John Wiley & Sons.

Blasing, T. J. (2014). Recent Greenhouse Gas Concentrations. U.S. Department of Energy Carbon Dioxide Information Analysis Center. Available at http://cdiac.ornl.gov/pns/current_ghg.html. Accessed May 9, 2015.

Gillis, J. (2010). A scientist, his work and a climate reckoning. *The New York Times*, December 2010, available at http://www.nytimes .com/2010/12/22/science/earth/22carbon.html?scp=1&sq=a%20scie ntist%20his%20work%20and%20a%20climate%20reckoning&st=cse. Accessed May 9, 2015.

Haines-Stiles, G. (writer, producer, director), and Alley, R. B. (host). 2011. *Earth: The Operators' Manual*, program 1 in *Earth: The Operators' Manual* (series), PBS, 2011 and 2012, available at http://earththe operatorsmanual.com/feature-video/earth-the-operators-manual. Accessed May 8, 2015.

Kolbert, E. (2006). *Field Notes from a Catastrophe: Man, Nature, and Climate Change*. Bloomsbury Publishing USA.

Leiserowitz, A., Smith, N., and Marlon, J. R. (2010). *Americans' Knowledge of Climate Change*. Yale University. New Haven, CT: Yale Project on Climate Change Communication, available at http://environment .yale.edu/climate/files/ClimateChangeKnowledge2010.pdf. Accessed May 9, 2015.

National Oceanic and Atmospheric Administration (NOAA), Environmental System Research Laboratory. (2014). History of Atmospheric Carbon Dioxide from 800,000 Years Ago until January 2014. Available at http://www.esrl.noaa.gov/gmd/ccgg/trends/history.html. Accessed April 21, 2015.

NOAA, Environmental System Research Laboratory. (2015). Trends in Atmospheric Carbon Dioxide. Available at http://www.esrl.noaa.gov/gmd/ccgg/trends/weekly.html. Accessed May 9, 2015.

Schmidt, G. (2010). Science Briefs—Taking the Measure of the Greenhouse Effect. NASA Goddard Institute for Space Studies, October 2010. Available at http://www.giss.nasa.gov/research/briefs/schmidt_05/. Accessed May 9, 2015.

University of Colorado. (2015). PhET: The Greenhouse Effect. Available at https://phet.colorado.edu/en/simulation/greenhouse. Accessed May 8, 2015.

Weart, S.R. (2008). *The Discovery of Global Warming: Revised and Expanded Edition.* Harvard University Press.

Q15. CARBON DIOXIDE IS A SMALL FRACTION OF THE ATMOSPHERE, SO WHY IS IT SO IMPORTANT FOR CLIMATE CHANGE?

Answer: Scientists cite carbon dioxide as a major contributor to the greenhouse effect, despite the fact that it comprises a small percentage of the atmosphere. How much of a gas there is in the atmosphere is not necessarily a good indicator of how important it is.

The Facts: The expression "size isn't everything" applies to many things in life. It's certainly true for the atmosphere, and how weather and climate processes work. The atmosphere is made up of several different gases, in differing amounts—but how much of any particular gas there is in the atmosphere is a poor guide to its importance.

Water vapor is a good example. From the standpoint of weather and climate, it's an extremely important gas. It's a key component of the water cycle, which moves water from oceans to atmosphere to land, and back to oceans via rivers. When water vapor condenses, it forms fog, clouds, and the various things that can fall out of clouds, like rain, snow, and hail. The condensation process releases energy (latent heat) that can fuel thunderstorms, tornadoes, and hurricanes.

Given all this, it would defy reason for anyone to suggest that water vapor is not important—yet it makes up only a small percentage of the atmosphere. The exact amount varies, depending on whether you're in a desert or a rainforest, but it's never more than about 4% of the atmosphere by volume for the most humid of places. As an example, a place we might think of as really humid is New Orleans in July, but even there the atmosphere is typically only about 2.6% water vapor by volume. Water vapor may not make up much of the atmosphere, but it wields outsize influence on weather and climate.

Other gases similarly punch far above their weight. We've already seen how chlorofluorocarbons (CFCs) caused the Antarctic ozone hole, but they make up only a tiny fraction of the atmosphere, measured in parts per trillion (current concentrations of CFCs are available from the U.S. Department of Energy's Carbon Dioxide Information Analysis Center—see Blasing, 2014). Conversely, nitrogen makes up about 78% of the dry atmosphere (i.e., not counting water vapor). But its role in weather and climate processes is quite limited, serving mainly to add mass to the atmosphere, thereby boosting atmospheric pressure to the point where it can sustain life, and diluting oxygen, which makes up 21% of the dry atmosphere and is a far more reactive gas. These examples all point to the idea that the amount of a gas in the atmosphere is not a good indicator of its importance.

Like water vapor and CFCs, carbon dioxide is only a small percentage of the atmosphere by volume, currently just over 400 parts per million, or about 0.04%. But also like water vapor and CFCs, this number belies carbon dioxide's importance. It contributes about 20% of the total greenhouse effect, according to research by NASA scientists (see Hansen, 2010, for a short summary of the research, or papers by Schmidt et al., 2010, and Lacis et al., 2010, for the technical details). This shows, once again, that looking only at how much of a gas there is, instead of what the gas actually does, is not a good way to determine its importance.

And carbon dioxide is actually more important than even these numbers suggest. The biggest single contributor to Earth's greenhouse effect is water vapor, which provides about half of the total. But unlike carbon dioxide, there's a limit to how much water vapor the air can hold. Add enough moisture to the air, and eventually the water vapor will condense out as clouds or fog. (The same thing happens when air cools down, which is why rising air, which cools as it rises, forms clouds.) This is why the amount of water vapor in the air never exceeds about 4% by volume, even in the most humid places: after a certain point, adding more water vapor to the atmosphere simply causes more condensation, rather than an increase in the amount of water vapor in the air.

In contrast, carbon dioxide does not condense out of the atmosphere, and there is therefore no upper limit on the amount that can be squeezed into the atmosphere. Other greenhouse gases, such as methane and CFCs, behave in a similar way. These gases are known as the non-condensing greenhouse gases, and carbon dioxide contributes about 80% of the greenhouse effect from the non-condensing greenhouse gases.

In addition, when carbon dioxide causes some warming, it increases the atmosphere's ability to retain more water vapor. As water vapor is also a greenhouse gas, this causes further warming. This reinforcing feedback is another way that carbon dioxide causes further warming on top of the direct warming from the heat it traps. It's important for explaining the large temperature swings of the glacial and interglacial periods in the past, and is an important element in computer simulations of Earth's future climate.

We'll return to the concept of condensing and non-condensing greenhouse gases in question 20, particularly the relationship between carbon dioxide and water vapor, but for now it's clear that, once again, looking only at carbon dioxide as 0.04% of the atmosphere misses the significance of this important non-condensing greenhouse gas.

Some arguments about climate change, however, do exactly this. Atmospheric carbon dioxide concentrations measured at Mauna Loa have risen from just over 315 parts per million in March 1958, when records began at that site, to just over 404 parts per million in April 2015, an increase of nearly 28%. Compared with an estimated level of carbon dioxide from before the Industrial Revolution, of around 280 parts per million, the increase to April 2015 is around 44% (see NOAA Environmental System Research Laboratory, 2015, for the data). Steve Goreham's (2013) *The Mad, Mad, Mad World of Climatism*, however, prefers to express this marked increase in an important greenhouse gas in terms of carbon dioxide's percentage of the total atmosphere. When expressed this way, carbon dioxide increased from 0.03% of the atmosphere to 0.04% of the atmosphere.

This looks like a negligible increase when framed this way, but, of course, misses the point. Carbon dioxide wields outsize power with regard to the greenhouse effect, as the NASA research mentioned earlier shows. The late Michael Crichton, in his 2004 novel *State of Fear*, makes the same point, though with a more metaphorical flair: "That's how much CO_2 we have in our atmosphere. One inch in a hundred-yard football field" (p. 387). Crichton's football-field metaphor, which has been repeated in the blogosphere, too (see, e.g., Wagner, 2009), essentially asserts that carbon dioxide is such a tiny part of the atmosphere that it's surely unreasonable to think it can affect the climate. But as we've seen, the amount of a gas that there is in the atmosphere does not necessarily correlate with its importance or impact. With the atmosphere, as with many things in life, size isn't everything.

FURTHER READING

Blasing, T. J. (2014). Recent Greenhouse Gas Concentrations. U.S. Department of Energy Carbon Dioxide Information Analysis Center. Available at http://cdiac.ornl.gov/pns/current_ghg.html. Accessed May 9, 2015.

Crichton, M. (2004). *State of Fear*. HarperCollins, New York, New York.

Hansen, K. (2010). Carbon dioxide controls Earth's temperature. Posted to NASA's Earth Science News website, October 14, 2010, available at http://www.nasa.gov/topics/earth/features/co2-temperature.html. Accessed May 9, 2015.

Lacis, A. A., Schmidt, G. A., Rind, D., and Ruedy, R. A. (2010). Atmospheric CO_2: principal control knob governing Earth's temperature. *Science*, 330(6002), 356–359.

NOAA, Environmental System Research Laboratory. (2015). Trends in Atmospheric Carbon Dioxide. Available at http://www.esrl.noaa.gov/gmd/ccgg/trends/weekly.html. Accessed May 9, 2015.

Schmidt, G. A., Ruedy, R. A., Miller, R. L., and Lacis, A. A. (2010). Attribution of the present-day total greenhouse effect. *Journal of Geophysical Research: Atmospheres (1984–2012)*, 115(D20), DOI: 10.1029/2010JD014287.

Wagner, C. (2009). Dip into *State of Fear* for global warming answers. Posted to website The Next Ice Age—Now on May 1, 2009, available at http://www.iceagenow.com/Dip_into_State_of_Fear_for_global_warming_answers.htm. Accessed May 11, 2015.

Q16. DOES A HISTORICAL CORRELATION EXIST BETWEEN CHANGES IN CARBON DIOXIDE LEVELS AND TEMPERATURE?

Answer: Climate scientists have found that carbon dioxide and temperature track each other very closely over the past 800,000 years.

The Facts: Richard Muller is an accomplished physicist at the University of California-Berkeley, who for many years doubted that the Earth was warming up. He put together his own team to investigate, and they developed an independent reconstruction of global average temperature stretching back to the year 1750. The new reconstruction closely matched the existing ones from government agencies such as NASA and NOAA, providing further evidence that they had been assembled correctly. Muller and his Berkeley Earth team found about 1.5°C of warming over the past 250 years, a rate very similar to what other teams had found (see Berkeley Earth's Summary of Findings). To his credit, Muller was prepared to admit that the data showed he had been wrong: the world really was getting warmer. Furthermore, he had concluded that the warming was almost entirely due to human emissions of carbon dioxide (see Muller, 2012, and Berkeley Earth's Summary of Findings).

The reason for Muller's confidence that global warming is caused by carbon dioxide is the very close match between atmospheric CO_2 levels and temperature, shown in Figure 2.5. Direct measurements of CO_2 began at the Mauna Loa Observatory in 1958, but evidence from earlier time periods is available from bubbles of air trapped in the ice of Greenland and Antarctica, and retrieved by ice core drilling projects. Writing about Berkeley Earth's findings in *The New York Times* in 2012, Muller stated: "Our result is based simply on the close agreement between the shape of the observed temperature rise and the known greenhouse gas increase."

The close match between CO_2 and temperature is a lot more than coincidence. As discussed in question 14, carbon dioxide is a heat-trapping

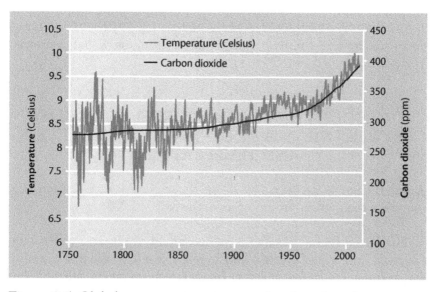

Figure 2.5 Global average temperature and carbon dioxide, as reconstructed by the Berkeley Earth project.

Source: Data from Berkeley Earth (2015), available at http://berkeleyearth.org/summary-of-findings/. Accessed May 11, 2015.

greenhouse gas, so the more of it there is in the atmosphere, the more heat will be trapped, causing temperatures to rise. This known characteristic of carbon dioxide gives a physics-based reason for why the two curves should track each other so closely.

As well as physics, we also have many direct measurements that confirm the extra heat being trapped by carbon dioxide. Satellites have measured less heat escaping to space at the very wavelengths absorbed by carbon dioxide (as well as other greenhouse gases). Surface measurements measure more heat returning to Earth, consistent with an increased greenhouse effect. In addition, a number of "human fingerprints" or patterns consistent with greenhouse warming have been observed. Winters warming faster than summers, nights warming faster than days, and a cooling upper atmosphere are all observational confirmation of the warming effect of increasing atmospheric carbon dioxide.

Furthermore, carbon dioxide and temperature dance closely together not just for the past 200 years, but much further back in time, too. As we saw in question 9, detailed ice core data now go back 800,000 years into the past, and throughout that time we see that carbon dioxide and temperature swing up and down together. Glacial and interglacial periods correspond to times of low and high CO_2, respectively, a point we'll return to in question 17.

Although it's pretty clear from Figure 2.5 that temperature and CO_2 are closely related over time, there is a misconception that they're not. This misconception arises from the technique of cherry-picking: focusing on short periods of time when temperature may have been going down briefly, even as carbon dioxide was going up. Focusing on the period 1940–1970, when global average temperatures declined somewhat, Michael Crichton has one of his fictional characters in *State of Fear* ask, "So, if rising carbon dioxide is the cause of rising temperatures, why didn't it cause temperatures to rise from 1940 to 1970?" (p. 87).

Crichton was right to say that global average temperatures cooled slightly between 1940 and 1970, but his mistake was to assume that the only thing affecting temperature is carbon dioxide. As we've seen, there are many forcings on global temperature, and although carbon dioxide is an increasingly important forcing at timescales approaching a century or so, it's not the only one. And many forcings are important at shorter timescales, such as volcanic eruptions affecting global temperatures for a year after they occur, or the fluctuations in ocean temperature brought about by El Niño and La Niña, or their bigger cousins, the Pacific Decadal and Atlantic Multidecadal Oscillations (see question 7). The period 1940–1970, in particular, is currently understood to have cooled largely because of high levels of air pollution, helped along by cool phases of the big oscillations in temperature in the Atlantic and the Pacific.

Nevertheless, this mischaracterization of the relationship between carbon dioxide and temperature is quite widespread. "If we take a closer look at the modern warming and the rise in atmospheric carbon dioxide," writes Steve Goreham (2013, p. 66), "we find that the curves don't track very well." James Taylor, writing for Forbes.com in 2013, makes the same point, again focusing on 1940–1970, as does Larry Vardiman, writing for the Institute for Creation Research website in 2008.

Claims such as these represent a confusion of short-term and long-term forcings, short-term climate *variability* confused with longer-term climate *change*, as we discussed in question 7. Identifying periods when CO_2 goes up but temperature does not is easy, because temperature wiggles up and down in response to multiple short-term forcings. Focusing on a select, short-enough period of the temperature record will produce the desired result, but such outcomes are misleading. A proper scientific approach looks at *all* the data. Doing so in this case shows very clearly that carbon dioxide and temperature move together, like two talented dancers.

FURTHER READING

Berkeley Earth. (2015). Summary of Findings. Available at http://berkeley earth.org/summary-of-findings/. Accessed May 11, 2015.

Crichton, M. (2004). *State of Fear*. HarperCollins, New York, New York.

Goreham, S. (2013). *The Mad, Mad, Mad World of Climatism: Mankind and Climate Change Mania*. New Lenox Books.

Muller, R. A. (2012). The conversion of a climate change skeptic. *The New York Times*, July 28, 2012 (published in print July 30, page A19), available at http://www.nytimes.com/2012/07/30/opinion/the-conversion-of-a-climate-change-skeptic.html?_r=0. Accessed February 25, 2015.

Taylor, J. (2013). As carbon dioxide levels continue to rise, global temperatures are not following suit. Posted to Forbes.com on March 6, 2013, available at http://www.forbes.com/sites/jamestaylor/2013/03/06/as-carbon-dioxide-levels-continue-to-rise-global-temperatures-are-not-following-suit/. Accessed May 11, 2015.

Vardiman, L. (2008). Does carbon dioxide drive global warming? *Acts & Facts*, 37(10): 10, available from the Institution for Creation Research website https://www.icr.org/article/4128. Accessed May 11, 2015.

Q17. WHAT DOES PAST CLIMATE CHANGE TELL US ABOUT THE RELATIONSHIP BETWEEN CARBON DIOXIDE AND TEMPERATURE?

Answer: When Earth's last major cold period ended 18,000 years ago, proxy records show that, for most of the planet, most of the rise in temperature followed an increase in carbon dioxide (CO_2) levels. A small initial warming seems to have been caused by orbital wobbles, which was then amplified by rising levels of carbon dioxide.

The Facts: Straightforward cause and effect relationships are easy to visualize. Study hard for a test, get a good score; skip the study sessions and go to the movies with your friends, your grades suffer. However, it can be harder to visualize a more interconnected, chicken-and-egg type of relationship, but they're surprisingly common, especially in Earth's climate system.

Imagine, for example, that you didn't study for an important test—but you got lucky. The few things you did actually study came up on the test, so you did well despite your lack of preparation. Impressed by your high test score, your friends start to say nice things about what a great student you are, and you decide to live up to their expectations. You study hard for the next test, and you ace it. Encouraged, you study hard for the next test, and ace that one, too, establishing a cycle of success. Each high test score was the result of the hard work you put into it—but you put the work in because you did well on previous tests. So which causes which, the high test scores or the hard work? The chicken, or the egg? In this case, the process started with a lucky break, doing well on that first test. But after that, success and studying worked together.

The climate system is full of relationships like this. They're known as *feedbacks*, because one thing affects another, which then returns the favor, feeding back onto the first thing again. Many of these relationships are not understood in detail, only in broad outline, but the broad outlines tell us quite a lot by themselves. A particularly important example for climate change is the feedback between carbon dioxide and temperature.

For a feedback relationship to exist, carbon dioxide must affect temperature, which must in turn affect carbon dioxide, affecting temperature again, and so on. We've already seen that carbon dioxide is a greenhouse gas and therefore affects temperature. In turn, there are several ways in which a change in temperature might lead to a change in the amount of carbon dioxide in the atmosphere. For example, a large amount of carbon dioxide is dissolved in the oceans, but carbon dioxide is more readily dissolved in cooler water. A shift toward a cooler climate should result in more carbon dioxide being dissolved in the oceans, leaving less in the atmosphere. This would weaken the greenhouse effect, making the Earth cooler still, allowing more carbon dioxide to dissolve, weakening the greenhouse effect even more, and so on. The initial temperature change would then grow and grow, amplified by the connection with carbon dioxide. The same thing would happen in reverse if the initial temperature change nudged the Earth toward warming. More carbon dioxide would be released from the oceans, strengthening the greenhouse effect, warming the Earth even more.

Scientists studying how climate has changed in the past have shown that this is probably what happened during the transitions from glacial to interglacial periods. Recall from question 9 that wobbles in Earth's orbit, the Milankovitch cycles, are the driving forces triggering the cool and warm episodes of the glacial–interglacial cycle. The wobbles are too weak by themselves to cause the large temperature changes that occurred as Earth's climate swung from frigid glacial to mild interglacial. Something must have amplified the initial change brought on by the wobbles, and the evidence points clearly to carbon dioxide.

A richer insight into the complex transition from glacial to interglacial came from an important study by a team led by Jeremy Shakun (2012), which focused on the most recent glacial–interglacial transition, from around 18,000 to around 11,000 years ago. Shakun and his team compiled a range of proxy measurements of temperature and carbon dioxide from all across the globe (recall that we discussed the concept of proxy measurements in questions 8 and 10). Their data showed that a small initial warming was followed by a large and rapid increase of carbon dioxide in the atmosphere. This was followed in turn by a much stronger warming that brought the Earth out of the last glacial and into the present-day interglacial. Their findings can be seen in Figure 2.6, where carbon dioxide levels are shown by black circles, and global temperature by the black line. It's clear that, for most of the transition from glacial to interglacial, global temperatures increased only after carbon dioxide had gone up. The only exception is right at the beginning of the transition, where a barely noticeable increase in temperature was triggered by the orbital wobbles. Without the amplification from carbon dioxide, global temperatures would have hardly moved.

Shakun et al.'s work helped solve one mystery about the glacial–interglacial cycles: why the small orbital nudges from the Milankovitch cycles could produce such large effects on climate. But their research sheds

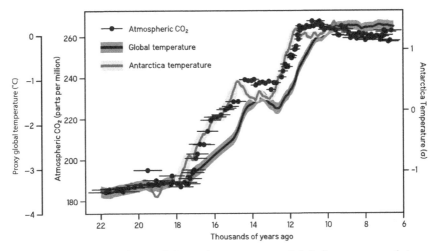

Figure 2.6 Atmospheric CO_2 and temperature (global average and Antarctica) over the past 22,000 years.

Source: Shakun et al. (2012).

light on another important question, too. The orbital wobbles influence the seasons, and the seasons are reversed between the Northern and Southern Hemispheres. Milankovitch's orbital nudges should have opposite effects in the two hemispheres, but the entire planet undergoes glacial and interglacial conditions at pretty much the same time, in tune with the Northern Hemisphere's seasons. Why?

Scientists have recognized for some time that the answer must lie at least partly with the oceans. Oceans cover over 70% of Earth's surface and have a huge capacity for storing and releasing heat (just think of question 7, where we looked at climate features such as El Niño and the Atlantic Multidecadal Oscillation). They're also good at moving heat from one place to another: warm ocean currents taking heat from the equator toward the North Pole are a major reason why western Europe and Scandinavia are as warm as they are, for example. In fact, scientists sometimes refer to the worldwide circulation of the oceans as the *conveyor belt*, for their ability to move heat around the world from the equator to the poles, and from one hemisphere to the other. Changes in how the oceans circulate can therefore have a big effect on climate: slow down or stop the conveyor belt, and heat piles up at one end, causing warming, while the interrupted supply of heat causes temperatures to plummet at the other end.

When the last glacial period drew to a close, here's what seems to have happened. The orbital wobbles nudged the Northern Hemisphere—but not the Southern Hemisphere—toward warmer conditions. The giant glacial-period ice sheets of the Northern Hemisphere started to melt in response. The melting ice became freshwater flowing into the North Atlantic Ocean, changing how salty it was. This upset the balance of temperature and salinity that's a major driving force behind ocean circulation, and the conveyor belt ground to a halt. Heat that would have been transported from the South Atlantic to the North Atlantic got backed up, warming the Southern Hemisphere, but slowing down, or stopping, the warming in the Northern Hemisphere that was brought on by the orbital wobbles. Finally, like an upset stomach, the disturbed ocean circulation released gas—specifically, carbon dioxide. Because the gas easily spreads throughout the entire atmosphere, this slug of carbon dioxide warmed the entire planet, ultimately overwhelming the temporary cooling of the Northern Hemisphere brought on by the clogged conveyor belt and bringing the planet out of its freezing glacial period and into today's interglacial.

That's a complicated sequence of events, but it ties together a lot of research over the past 30 years or so, and Shakun et al.'s collection of proxies provides strong evidence that this is how the last glacial–interglacial transition probably happened. In fact, the gray line in Figure 2.6 shows that temperatures in Antarctica, unlike most of the rest of the world, warmed up slightly ahead of the rise in carbon dioxide. This would make sense if the complex sequence of events described earlier is correct: the interrupted conveyor belt would have warmed the South Atlantic, which in turn would have released carbon dioxide. For Antarctica (and elsewhere in the Southern Hemisphere), the warming preceded the release of carbon dioxide. For the planet as a whole, though, the release of carbon dioxide came first, causing the warming.

Unfortunately, some books and websites, and even a television documentary, present only a small part of this story. They emphasize the point that initial temperature changes happen before changes in carbon dioxide, but leave it at that. They fail to mention that the initial warming from the orbital wobbles is very small and that most of the planet warmed *after* the change in carbon dioxide. In a 2011 blog post, Dr. Tim Ball wrote, "Temperature change before CO_2 change is the case in every record for any period or duration. . . . It is logical to assume that if CO_2 change follows temperature change in every record then CO_2 cannot be a greenhouse gas." However, we know from the detailed research conducted by the U.S. Air Force, among others, that carbon dioxide most assuredly *is* a greenhouse gas. Ball ends his story too soon.

Making a similar point, here's Steve Goreham (2013), in *The Mad, Mad, Mad World of Climatism*: "Since carbon dioxide rose centuries *after* temperature, *it could not be the cause* of the temperature change resulting in the ice ages" (p. 80; emphasis in original). However, this statement refers only to ice cores from Antarctica and neglects the rest of the planet. As we've seen, there are good reasons why Antarctic temperatures rose before carbon dioxide, and they do not negate the basic physics of the greenhouse effect. Carbon dioxide traps heat, no matter when it's released. As with Tim Ball's blog post, Steve Goreham's statement leaves out most of the story: in one part of the world, the change in carbon dioxide does indeed follow the initial change in temperature toward a glacial or inter-glacial period, because the initial temperature change is triggered by an external forcing, Milankovitch's orbital wobbles. The rest of the story, as discussed earlier, is that the carbon dioxide change then amplifies the ini-tial temperature change and spreads the warming to the rest of the planet. The orbital wobbles alone are too weak to produce the full magnitude of the glacial and interglacial periods.

Goreham and Ball are cherry-picking the data by neglecting most of the planet, where warming happens after the change in carbon dioxide. By ignoring the amplifying effect of carbon dioxide, Goreham and Ball are also presenting a false dichotomy. They are arguing that either carbon dioxide changes cause temperature changes, or it's the other way around. In truth, both occur—the causal relationship between carbon dioxide and temperature goes both ways. This false dichotomy is like observing a chicken hatch out of an egg and arguing that this proves that eggs don't come out of chickens!

Some of the sources of this particular misconception use the peer-reviewed scientific literature to make their point. Unfortunately, they tend to quote selectively, again telling only part of the story. Both Fred Singer and Dennis Avery's (2008) book, *Unstoppable Global Warming: Every 1500 Years*, and the 2007 television documentary *The Great Global Warming Swindle* by Martin Durkin (still available on YouTube, see Fur-ther Reading) refer to an important study by a team led by Nicholas Caillon (Caillon et al., 2003). Caillon and his team examined a switch from glacial to interglacial conditions around 240,000 years ago in a long ice core from Russia's Vostok station in Antarctica, finding a roughly 800-year lag between temperature increase and the following carbon dioxide increase. "This confirms that CO_2 is not the forcing that ini-tially drives the climatic system during a deglaciation" (p. 1730), they concluded. This sentence is quoted by both Singer and Avery (2008) and Durkin (2007) as evidence that "CO_2 hasn't controlled Earth's past temperatures" (Singer and Avery, 2008, p. 107; the quote from Caillon et al., 2003, appears on page 109).

A more accurate picture of Caillon et al.'s research would have been provided if their next sentence had also been quoted. They go on to say, "Rather, deglaciation is probably initiated by some insolation [sunlight] forcing, which influences first the temperature change in Antarctica (and possibly in part of the southern hemisphere) and then the CO_2. *This sequence of events is still in full agreement with the idea that CO_2 plays, through its greenhouse effect, a key role in amplifying the initial forcing*" (p. 1730, emphasis added). Their final sentence is even more telling: "The radiative forcing due to CO_2 may serve as an amplifier of initial orbital forcing, which is then further amplified by fast feedbacks that are also at work for the present day and future climate" (p. 1731).

Singer and Avery (2008) and Durkin (2007) quote the scientific literature selectively. This selective quoting does a disservice to the scientists whose work is being misrepresented. More recent mentions of this myth neglect to mention Shakun et al.'s (2012) research finding that most of the planet warmed *after* the change in CO_2.

FURTHER READING

Alley, R. B. (2011). *Earth: The Operators' Manual*. W.W. Norton & Company.

Ball, T. (2011). Whether it is warming or climate change, it cannot be the CO_2. Posted to DrTimBall.com blog, November 9, 2011, available at http://drtimball.com/2011/whether-it-is-warming-or-climate-change-it-cannot-be-the-co2/. Accessed May 12, 2015.

Caillon, N., Severinghaus, J. P., Jouzel, J., Barnola, J. M., Kang, J., and Lipenkov, V. Y. (2003). Timing of atmospheric CO_2 and Antarctic temperature changes across Termination III. *Science*, 299(5613), 1728–1731.

Durkin, M. (2007). The Great Global Warming Swindle. WAG TV Production for Channel 4, 2007. Available at https://www.youtube.com/watch?v=52Mx0_8YEtg. Accessed August 21, 2015.

Goreham, S. (2013). *The Mad, Mad, Mad World of Climatism: Mankind and Climate Change Mania*. New Lenox Books.

Shakun, J. D., Clark, P. U., He, F., Marcott, S. A., Mix, A. C., Liu, Z., . . ., and Bard, E. (2012). Global warming preceded by increasing carbon dioxide concentrations during the last deglaciation. *Nature*, 484(7392), 49–54.

Q18. WHICH PRODUCES MORE CARBON DIOXIDE: VOLCANOES, OR BURNING FOSSIL FUELS?

Answer: Multiple independent lines of evidence find that human burning of fossil fuels adds almost 140 times more carbon dioxide than volcanoes do. Human use of fossil fuels is, in effect, a constantly burning megavolcano.

The Facts: In the 1990s, a scientist named Ralph Keeling, working with various colleagues, found a telling change in the chemistry of the atmosphere. His measurements showed that, year after year, the amount of oxygen was very gradually, but clearly, going down. Ongoing measurements show that this pattern continues to the present day. Nobody needs to worry about running out of oxygen, as the annual rate of change is tiny, about 19 per meg, meaning that each year, out of every million oxygen molecules, 19 are lost (Scripps Institution of Oceanography, 2015; see Figure 2.7). The finding is nevertheless important because of what it reveals about the cause of another significant change in the atmosphere: the buildup of carbon dioxide.

Keeling was no newcomer to the carbon dioxide issue. His father was Charles David Keeling, the first person to measure reliably the levels of carbon dioxide in the atmosphere, and the instigator of the continuous measurement program at Mauna Loa Observatory that began in 1958 (a readable history is provided by Justin Gillis in *The New York Times*, 2010). In fact, the graph of increasing carbon dioxide over time from Mauna Loa (see Figure 2.4) is often referred to as the Keeling Curve. Keeling Senior's work showed clearly that carbon dioxide was building up year after year. Ralph Keeling's work has made a significant contribution to proving that the carbon dioxide must be coming from burning fossil fuels and cannot be coming from natural sources such as volcanoes.

How does a steady decline in oxygen in the air point the finger at fossil fuels? Keep in mind that a sure way to put out a fire is to cut off its air supply. Fire needs oxygen to burn. Burning coal, oil, or natural gas is no different. The energy stored in these fossil fuels is released when burning oxidizes them, reacting oxygen with the carbon that they're largely made up of. The result is heat, which boils water into steam for turning turbines and generating electricity—and carbon dioxide. The slight but steady decline in oxygen correlates very well with the increase in carbon dioxide. This is strong evidence that the carbon dioxide is forming when carbon combines with oxygen in burning.

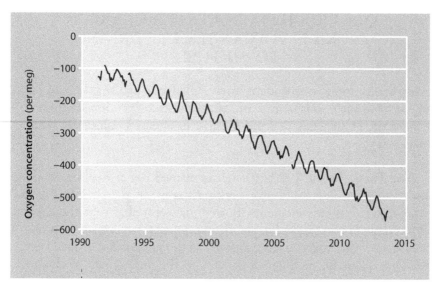

Figure 2.7 Declining oxygen concentration in the atmosphere, measured at Mauna Loa Observatory, Hawaii. Graph shows monthly average oxygen concentration. Mauna Loa is one of nine locations worldwide where similar measurements are taken. All show similar declines in oxygen.

Source: Data from Scripps Institution of Oceanography (2015), available at http://scrippso2.ucsd.edu/sites/default/files/data/o2_data/o2_monthly/mloo.txt. Accessed May 14, 2015.

Other evidence supports Keeling's oxygen findings that humans are contributing to the rise in atmospheric carbon dioxide. All naturally occurring chemical elements come in a variety of flavors, known as isotopes. Isotopes are distinguished from each other by having different numbers of neutrons in the atomic nucleus. Neutrons are neutral in terms of electrical charge, neither positive nor negative, so they don't affect how the different isotopes of a chemical element react with other elements. Hydrogen and oxygen will combine to form water regardless of the isotopes involved. But although neutrons don't have a charge, they do have mass, so the more neutrons there are, the heavier an atom becomes, though only very, very slightly. Because different isotopes are lighter or heavier, they behave in different ways physically, even though they behave in the same ways chemically.

For example, the most common isotope of carbon is called carbon-12. Add a neutron and you get the slightly heavier carbon-13; add another and you get carbon-14, which is heavier still. Together, these make up the three isotopes of carbon known to exist. Because carbon-12 is the lightest of the three, it's easier for plants to manipulate when they build sugars out of carbon dioxide and water through photosynthesis. Plants therefore tend to absorb more carbon dioxide molecules made out of carbon-12, and carbon-12 becomes more concentrated in plant tissues than the air it's being absorbed from. Burning a plant releases the carbon-12 back into the atmosphere.

Coal is fossilized plant matter, many millions of years old, formed under a very specific set of circumstances. Natural gas and oil are similarly derived from fossilized plants. Consequently, when fossil fuels are burned, not only does the burning use oxygen, as Ralph Keeling discovered, but also the carbon released into the atmosphere is rich in carbon-12. As shown in Figure 2.8, the ratio of carbon-12 compared with carbon-13 in the atmosphere has been changing markedly since the beginning of the Industrial Revolution, as carbon-12 pours into the air, swamping the carbon-13. It's a bit like adding milk to a cup of coffee. The more milk you add, the fuller your cup gets—just as the total amount of carbon dioxide in the atmosphere is going up—but the more dilute your caffeine fix becomes, as the

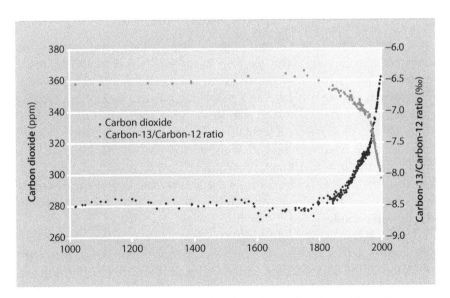

Figure 2.8 The changing ratio of carbon-12 and carbon-13 in the atmosphere, and increase in total carbon dioxide, over the past 1,000 years as measured in air bubbles trapped in ice in Antarctica's Law Dome.
Source: Rubino et al. (2013).

coffee is swamped with milk. The ratio of milk to coffee changes, just as the ratio of carbon-12 to carbon-13 is changing in the atmosphere.

But where does carbon-14 come in? Carbon-14 is radioactive and forms high in the atmosphere when carbon atoms interact with high-energy cosmic rays. All living things—plants, animals, and humans—are made of carbon (among other elements), so we all contain some of this radioactive element, a tiny amount and not remotely enough to be dangerous. While carbon-14 may not be dangerous, it can be useful, for example, in radio-carbon dating. All radioactive elements decay at a known rate (called the half-life), so the amount of a radioactive element can indicate how old something is. When a person or a plant dies, it stops taking in carbon-14, and the radioactive clock starts. This helps archeologists, for example, to determine how old ancient human settlements are.

Different radioactive elements have different half-lives, and carbon-14's is relatively short, a little over 5,700 years. This means that carbon dat-ing cannot be used on very old things, because all the carbon-14 will have decayed (into a stable isotope of nitrogen). Fossil fuels, being many millions of years old, therefore have no carbon-14 at all, unlike living plants. And again, measurements of the atmosphere show a dramatic change. The proportion of carbon-14 in the atmosphere, like the propor-tion of carbon-13, is going down as more carbon-12 floods in, diluting the radioactive carbon (Figure 2.9).

The behaviors of the different isotopes, and the measurements showing an increase in carbon-12, but declines in carbon-13 and carbon-14, make it possible to tell where the carbon in the atmosphere is coming from. The increase in carbon-12 points to plants, but the lack of a matching increase in carbon-14 points to plants that have been dead for a very long time. That's a description of fossil fuels. Add to the isotope data the slight, steady decline in oxygen and we see the extra carbon dioxide must be a result of burning something. Again, this points to fossil fuels. So taken together, the changing chemistry of the atmosphere tells us that burning fossil fuels, not natural sources such as volcanoes, must be the source of the carbon dioxide.

The U.S. Department of Energy's Carbon Dioxide Information Anal-ysis Center backs up the atmospheric chemistry measurements with estimates of the total amount of carbon dioxide emitted by burning fos-sil fuels. They compile statistics on consumption of fossil fuels by coun-tries from all over the world and estimate the amount of carbon dioxide emitted as a result. The latest estimate, for 2013, shows that burning fos-sil fuels, together with making cement, pumped over 36 billion metric tons, or gigatons (Gt), of carbon dioxide into the atmosphere (Le Quéré

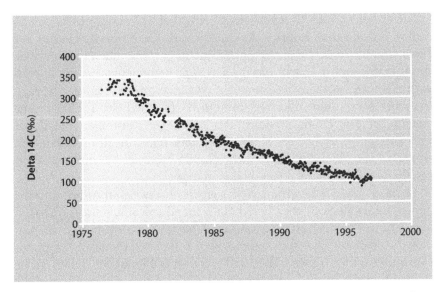

Figure 2.9 The changing proportion of radioactive carbon-14 in carbon dioxide in the atmosphere, as measured from 1977 to 1997 at Schauinsland, Germany. The vertical axis is a measure of the proportion of carbon-14 called delta 14C. Schauinsland is one of several sites where this has been measured, and they all show the same trend (see data from the Carbon Dioxide Information Analysis Center, http://cdiac.ornl.gov/carbonisotopes.html). The proportion of radioactive carbon is declining as the atmosphere is flooded with non-radioactive, fossil carbon.

Source: Data from Levin and Kromer (1997).

et al., 2015). Although some gets absorbed by plants or dissolves in the oceans—causing its own problems, as we'll see in question 23—more than half stays in the atmosphere, causing the steady buildup, year after year, that we've looked at in previous questions. The prodigious quantity of carbon dioxide that human civilization emits calls to mind a giant volcano: a constantly burning, artificial megavolcano.

Even this description falls short of reality, though. U.S. Geological Survey (USGS) expert Terry Gerlach has pointed out that estimates of global volcanic emissions of carbon dioxide are at most only about 0.26 Gt per year, which makes emissions from burning fossil fuels nearly 140 times the amount that comes from volcanoes (see USGS's website on volcanic gases and climate change [USGS, 2015]; a short, but more technical, peer-reviewed paper is Gerlach, 2011). Next to humanity's artificial megavolcano, real volcanoes are little more than firecrackers.

Nevertheless, there is a persistent myth that volcanoes produce more carbon dioxide than humans do. Ian Plimer's (2009) book, *Heaven and Earth*, and his subsequent writings online have done much to popularize this misconception. Plimer has made several statements that are at odds with the available data, for example: "Volcanoes produce more CO_2 than the world's cars and industries combined" (p. 413). In a 2009 online column for The Drum, a companion site to the Australian Broadcasting Corporation's television show of the same name, he dismissed human emissions of carbon dioxide over the past 250 years as insignificant, writing: "One volcanic cough can do this in a day."

Numbers provided by the USGS suggest otherwise. In addition to the annual total emissions of carbon dioxide for all volcanic sources (0.26 Gt, as mentioned earlier), estimates are available for the contributions of individual volcanoes. Take, for example, two of the largest volcanic eruptions over the past few decades. The 1980 eruption of Mount St. Helens in the United States produced an estimated 0.01 Gt of carbon dioxide, and the 1991 eruption of Mount Pinatubo in the Philippines produced around 0.05 Gt of carbon dioxide. Recall that burning fossil fuels released an estimated 36 Gt in 2013. There's no doubt that standing near an erupting volcano is a truly awe-inspiring experience and that individual eruptions can, for people living nearby, result in tragedy. But compared to human civilization's capacity to pump out carbon dioxide, they really are just firecrackers. Ian Plimer's claims that volcanoes produce more carbon dioxide than humans are not supported by the facts. (Terry Gerlach, the USGS volcano expert, wrote a comprehensive review of Ian Plimer's book at *Earth* magazine in 2010, see Further Reading.)

Ian Plimer, however, is by no means the only source of this misconception. Other sources exist online (e.g., Wylie, 2013; Felix, 2014), including some that appear to be quite rigorously argued (e.g., Casey, 2014). A common issue raised is that existing estimates for volcanic carbon dioxide—such as the USGS's figure of 0.26 Gt mentioned earlier—are far too low. What if there are hidden sources that we haven't accounted for?

On the face of it, this seems reasonable: we should always be aware of the limits to our knowledge. However, for this argument to be correct, the sheer scale of the underestimate is staggering. Gerlach (2011) points out, for example, that there would need to be the equivalent of 3,500 Mount St. Helens-scale eruptions every year to generate the same amount of carbon dioxide as burning fossil fuels does. It's hard to imagine that so much volcanic activity is escaping notice.

Even if we are missing some enormous hidden volcanic source of carbon dioxide, however, it's hard to explain the atmospheric chemistry measurements in terms of volcanic emissions. If volcanoes really were the source of the carbon dioxide, not only would they have to have stayed hidden, but they would also have had to change their carbon isotopes suddenly and dramatically at exactly the same time as the Industrial Revolution began. And even if they had somehow accomplished this feat, it still wouldn't explain the decline in oxygen that results from burning. The only source of carbon dioxide that explains all the data adequately is burning fossil fuels. This point was made earlier, but it's worth repeating: compared with the firecrackers of individual volcanoes, human civilization is a constantly burning megavolcano.

FURTHER READING

Casey, T. (2014). Volcanic carbon dioxide. Posted to Principia Scientific International website, June 15, 2014, available at http://www.principia-scientific.org/volcanic-carbon-dioxide.html. Accessed May 14, 2015.

Felix, R. (2014). Three million underwater volcanoes can't be wrong. Posted to IceAgeNow website, July 17, 2014, available at http://ice agenow.info/2014/07/million-underwater-volcanoes-wrong/. Accessed May 14, 2015.

Gerlach, T. (2010). Comment: volcanic versus anthropogenic carbon dioxide: the missing science. *Earth* 55(7), 87, available at http://www.earthmagazine.org/article/comment-volcanic-versus-anthropo genic-carbon-dioxide-missing-science. Accessed May 14, 2014.

Gerlach, T. (2011). Volcanic versus anthropogenic carbon dioxide. *Eos, Transactions American Geophysical Union*, 92(24), 201–202.

Gillis, J. (2010). A scientist, his work and a climate reckoning. *The New York Times*, December 2010, available at http://www.nytimes .com/2010/12/22/science/earth/22carbon.html?scp=1&sq=a%20scie ntist%20his%20work%20and%20a%20climate%20reckoning& st=cse. Accessed May 9, 2015.

Le Quéré, C., Moriarty, R., Andrew, R. M., Peters, G. P., Ciais, P., Fried lingstein, P., . . ., and Steinhoff, T. (2015). Global carbon budget 2014. *Earth System Science Data*, 7, 47–85. Data set available from the Carbon Dioxide Information Analysis Center, Oak Ridge National Laboratory, U.S. Department of Energy, Oak Ridge, Tennessee, available at http://cdiac.ornl.gov/GCP/. Accessed August 28, 2015.

Levin, I., and Kromer, B. (1997). Atmospheric $^{14}CO_2$ measurements from Schauinsland, Germany. Data set available from the U.S. Department of Energy Carbon Dioxide Information and Analysis Center, available at http://cdiac.ornl.gov/ftp/trends/co2/schauinsland.c14. Accessed May 15, 2015.

Plimer. I. (2009). *Heaven and Earth*. Taylor Trade.

Plimer, I. (2010). Legislative time bomb. Posted to The Drum online, August 13, 2009, updated September 28, 2010, available at http://www .abc.net.au/news/2009-08-13/29320. Accessed May 14, 2015.

Rubino, M., Etheridge, D. M., Trudinger, C. M., Allison, C. E., Battle, M. O., Langenfelds, R. L., . . ., and Francey, R. J. (2013). A revised 1000 year atmospheric δ13C-CO$_2$ record from Law Dome and South Pole, Antarctica. *Journal of Geophysical Research: Atmospheres, 118*(15), 8482–8499.

Scripps Institution of Oceanography. (2015). Scripps O$_2$ Program-Atmospheric Oxygen Research. Available at http://scrippso2.ucsd .edu/. Accessed May 14, 2015.

USGS. (2015). Volcanic Gases and Climate Change Overview. Available at http://volcanoes.usgs.gov/hazards/gas/climate.php. Accessed May 14, 2015.

Wylie, R. (2013). Long invisible, research shows volcanic CO$_2$ levels are staggering (op-ed). Posted to LiveScience.com website, October 15, 2013, available at http://www.livescience.com/40451-volcanic-co2-levels-are-staggering.html. Accessed May 14, 2015.

3

The Likely Impacts of Climate Change

Q19. HOW WELL DO COMPUTER MODELS REPRODUCE EARTH'S CLIMATE?

Answer: Climate models successfully reproduce many (though not all) aspects of Earth's climate, including the observed warming over the course of the 20th and early 21st centuries.

The Facts: Computer simulations of Earth's climate—commonly known as climate models—provide an important thread in the cable of evidence supporting the case that global warming is real, caused by humans, and very likely to be a serious problem. However, there are perhaps more misconceptions and myth variants about climate models than about any other aspect of climate science. It's therefore important to be clear on exactly what climate models are and are not, and what they can and cannot do.

First, the basics: a computer climate model is a simulation of the climate based on known physical laws, relationships, and behaviors. It's basically a very complex computer program that instructs the computer to solve a series of equations for lots of different locations, horizontally across the Earth and vertically upward into the atmosphere (and sometimes down into the oceans as well). The solutions to the equations indicate climate variables, such as temperature, humidity, or rainfall.

A more familiar example of the same basic idea might be a car-racing computer game. The computer code that the game is built from must include the physics of how cars accelerate and decelerate, how they handle corners, and so on. This produces a simulation of how a high-performance car behaves. Climate models take the physics of the atmosphere to produce a simulation of the climate. But unlike a simple car-racing game, climate models are trying to solve a vastly larger and more complex set of equations, and are striving for a much closer match between the simulation and reality. All of this explains why today's climate models require the processing power of the world's most powerful supercomputers in order to run.

The same powerful supercomputers, and somewhat similar models, are used to make weather forecasts. But the similarities between weather forecasting and climate simulation more or less end there. The inherent short-term variability of weather, which happens because of the butterfly effect that we described in question 6, means it becomes increasingly difficult to make accurate weather forecasts the further into the future you try to look. Most people rightly have a lot more confidence in a weather forecast for later today or tomorrow than they do in a forecast for next week—and it's probably impossible to predict anything at all about the weather more than about 10–14 days ahead.

Climate models, though, have a lot more wiggle room than weather forecasts, because they're trying to simulate something different. Instead of trying to determine exactly what the temperature or rainfall will be on any given day in the future—that is, the weather—they're trying to determine the *average* conditions—that is, the climate. We can see the difference clearly when we think about planning an important event, like a wedding. For an outdoor event, you need good weather—but you have to set the date, and send out the invitations, at least a few months in advance so your guests can make plans to attend. Weather forecasts are simply not capable of telling you what the weather will be like that far off in the future. To figure out the date that will give you the best chance of good weather, you might instead look at the *typical* weather—in other words, the climate—for several different possible dates for the wedding. The statistics can give you a sense of which days hold the best chance of clear skies and not-too-hot temperatures, but they can't guarantee that the weather on the day will do what you want. Weather and climate are different things. Looking at climate statistics can give you a sense of your odds but can never guarantee the outcome. Climate models are trying to simulate what's typical, which is why they're different from weather forecasts.

Despite this fundamental difference, weather forecasting and climate modeling face some common challenges. For example, both struggle to simulate clouds accurately, partly because the physics is still not fully understood and partly because clouds form at scales much smaller than models can represent. The chicken-and-egg feedback relationships we've seen in questions 6 and 17 are another challenge. Because many feedbacks serve to amplify changes, small errors in estimating the strength of the feedback can produce large errors in the end result. For reasons such as these, climate modelers are usually pretty careful to say what their simulations can and can't do. The IPCC's most recent (2013) report states, for example, "There remains *low confidence* in the representation and quantification of [cloud and air pollution] processes" (IPCC, 2013, p. 16). NASA climate scientist James Hansen, while presenting climate model results to Congress in 1988, pointed out that "there are major uncertainties in the model" (Hansen, 1988, p. 38).

How seriously do these problems affect the computer models' ability to re-create climate? There are several different major climate models around the world, and each modeling team tries to address the challenges in its own way. Consequently, no two models are exactly alike, and each one produces unique results. Some models probably do a better job of simulating the effects of sea ice, for example; others might be a bit closer to reality when it comes to cloud processes. Each model has its own strengths and weaknesses. Because of this, models are used in groups, called *ensembles*. While individual models can give results that are pretty different from the observed reality, the ensemble average fits the observations quite well. So, while the difficulties with clouds and feedbacks and other aspects of the climate system are real, and do affect model performance, the ensemble approach helps to minimize the errors that result.

This is one indication that, despite the shortcomings, the fundamental physics underlying the models is reasonably sound. Another indication is that several predictions about the pattern of climate change made using models all the way back in the 1980s have turned out to be correct. These include more warming in the Arctic, more warming over land than over the oceans, and warming of the troposphere combined with cooling of the stratosphere (see Hansen, 1988, p. 40).

Models certainly don't get everything right. They have an especially hard time replicating precipitation patterns, and their match with reality becomes increasingly tenuous as you zoom into smaller and smaller areas—they do well at the global scale, quite well at the scale of continents, adequately at the scale of regions within continents, such as the southwestern United States, and not at all well at scales finer-grained than that. So long as model results are used at appropriate scales, and in ensembles instead of on their own, they recreate the existing climate (especially temperature) reasonably well.

What about future climate? The success of ensemble model simulations of temperature suggests that model ensembles may be able to give us a sense of what the future holds, if we know how the climate forcings will change in the future. This presents modelers with the biggest uncertainty of all, one that makes clouds and feedbacks well understood by comparison: how human society will change in the future. Nevertheless, this issue is vital to include in climate model estimates of what the future holds, because as we've seen throughout this book, human activity now constitutes a forcing on the climate system, mainly through the release of carbon dioxide into the atmosphere when fossil fuels are burned.

How this forcing will change into the future is an impossible question to answer. There are so many possibilities: will we decide to use fossil fuels as much and as fast as we can, partying like there's no tomorrow, burning twice as bright for half as long? Will we decide to limit ourselves? Will the plummeting cost of solar power mean we don't have to?

Climate scientists are aware of this difficulty, and as a result, don't try to predict a single future for society. Instead, simulations of future climate are based on several possible "what-if" scenarios. These scenarios give policymakers and the rest of us an idea of *what* we might expect *if* we go down one path of energy use versus another. The different scenarios therefore define best-case and worst-case scenarios, although modelers are careful to emphasize that there is no way to know if one is more likely to happen than another. The climates associated with these different scenarios are therefore not *predictions*, but *projections*—a subtle, but important, distinction. The ensemble average for the best-case scenario is a global average warming of around 1°C (1.8°F) by 2100 compared with today's temperatures; and for the worst case, it's around 4°C (over 7°F). World leaders are currently trying to keep the warming to less than 2°C.

These are the realities of climate models. They're valuable, but imperfect, tools for assessing how climate might change in the future (see NASA climate modeler Gavin Schmidt's TED talk for a video summary, listed in Further Reading). Unfortunately, the complexities of the models and how they're used have led to a number of misconceptions about them. One overarching error is to suggest that the entire scientific case for human-induced global warming is based on these imperfect climate models. This is the background to several books, including Fred Singer and Dennis Avery's 2008 *Unstoppable Global Warming: Every 1500 Years* and Nigel Lawson's 2009 *An Appeal to Reason*. Implicit is the idea that if the models are imperfect, then there is no basis for taking action on climate change. This is not the case, as we know from basic physics that carbon dioxide is a heat-trapping greenhouse gas (question 14), and we know from studies of Earth's history that carbon dioxide has played an important role in driving climate change in the past. Models give us a more detailed look at the possible effects of amping up the greenhouse effect, but they don't provide the basic physics. Carbon dioxide traps heat whether you simulate its effects in a model or not.

Another common mistake is to equate climate projections with weather forecasts. Here's Michael Crichton, speaking through one of his characters in his 2004 novel, *State of Fear*: "Nobody tries to predict weather more than ten days in advance. Whereas computer modelers are predicting what the temperature will be one hundred years in advance. Sometimes a thousand years, three thousand years" (p. 248). While it's true that models are *projecting* (not, as Crichton states, predicting) the temperature at the end of the century or beyond, what they are projecting is future climate, an estimate of the typical conditions. This is not a weather forecast, as our earlier discussion of planning a wedding tried to show. (See also Adams, 2013, for a recent online version of this myth.)

A related error ties in with the purported "pause" in global warming we looked at in question 7. Many discussions of this issue state that none of the climate models anticipated it (Nigel Lawson's book is a good example); indeed, this is supposedly evidence that "global climate models are unable to make accurate projections of climate even 10 years ahead, let alone the 100-year period that has been adopted by policy planners" (Idso et al., 2014, p. viii). This is both inaccurate and misleading. As discussed in question 7, warming or cooling over timescales of a few decades or less constitute climate *variability*, and are extremely hard to simulate in models—but they constitute fluctuations up and down, superimposed on the larger trend of climate *change*. Models are really only intended to capture this larger trend. Features of climate variability, such as El Niños, are included in models, but because they're so hard to predict, they're programmed to appear automatically every few years, with the chances of any given year experiencing an El Niño being based on the observed odds. In effect, the computer rolls a pair of dice, and if the score is 10 or more, the model brings in an El Niño. Thus, while the ensemble average did not anticipate the so-called pause, some individual models most certainly did. (See Nuccitelli, 2014, for an easy-to-read discussion; and Rahmstorf, 2013, for a slightly more technical discussion.) Regardless, this issue is fundamentally a red herring, because the models are not intended to capture such short-term variability in any detail.

Other myth variants include the idea that climate models exaggerate the possible warming from increased carbon dioxide. This is a common refrain from several posts at the Climate Conservative Consumer website, many of which use James Hansen's 1988 model to demonstrate these exaggerations (e.g., C3 Headlines, 2015). Models, and the computers they run on, have advanced a great deal in the intervening years, so it's perhaps a little unfair to focus on output from a very early climate model. Even so, as we've seen, there's plenty that individual models simulate imperfectly, and each individual result should be taken with a pinch of salt. However, while models might overestimate some responses of the climate system to increased carbon dioxide, they also clearly *underestimate* other responses. For example, melting of Arctic sea ice is currently running ahead of where model projections expected it to be (see, e.g., Jeffries et al., 2013), and today's rate of sea level rise is at the very highest end of where climate models, run back in 1990, projected it to be (Rahmstorf et al., 2007). There is uncertainty in climate model projections of the future—but that uncertainty will not necessarily work in our favor. Some aspects of future climate may not be as bad as models suggest—but other aspects may be worse.

It's clear, then, that models are far from perfect, but they can be useful. Like any tool, however, they need to be used for the appropriate job, and with an understanding of their limitations.

FURTHER READING

Adams, M. (2013). Global warming computer models collapse; Arctic ice sheets rapidly expand as planet plunges into global cooling. Posted to NaturalNews.com, September 10, 2013, available at http://www .naturalnews.com/041981_global_warming_computer_models_cooling .html#. Accessed May 17, 2015.

Bindoff, N. L., Stott, P. A., Achuta Rao, K. M., Allen, M. R., Gillett, N., Gutzler, D., Hansingo, K., Hegerl, G., Hu, Y., Jain, S., Mokhov, I. I., Overland, J., Perlwitz, J., Sebbari, R., and Zhang, X. (2013). Detection and Attribution of Climate Change: From Global to Regional. In *Climate Change 2013: The Physical Science Basis. Contribution of Working Group I to the Fifth Assessment Report of the Intergovernmental Panel on Climate Change*, T. F. Stocker, D. Qin, G.-K. Plattner, M. Tignor, S. K. Allen, J. Boschung, A. Nauels, Y. Xia, V. Bex, and P. M. Midgley (eds.). Cambridge University Press, Cambridge, United Kingdom, and New York, NY, pp. 867–952, doi:10.1017/CBO9781107415324.022, available at http://www.climatechange2013.org/report/. Accessed April 21, 2015.

C3 Headlines. (2015). 2014: NASA/Hansen climate model output vs. climate reality—failure is always ugly. Posted to C3Headlines.com, February 7, 2015, available at http://www.c3headlines.com/2015/02/2014-nasa-hansen-climate-model-output-vs-climate-reality-failure-its-still-ugly.html. Accessed May 17, 2015.

Crichton, M. (2004). *State of Fear*. HarperCollins, New York, New York.

Hansen, J. E. (1988). The Greenhouse Effect: Impacts on Current Global Temperature and Regional Heat Waves. Testimony presented at Hearing on the Greenhouse Effect and Global Climate Change, Committee on Energy and Natural Resources, US Senate, One Hundredth Congress. Reprinted in Abrahamson, D. E. (Ed.). (1989). *The Challenge of Global Warming*. Island Press. Chapter 2, pp. 35–43.

Idso, C. D, Idso, S. B., Carter, R. M., and Singer, S. F. (Eds.). (2014). *Climate Change Reconsidered II: Biological Impacts*. The Heartland Institute, Chicago, IL, available at https://www.heartland.org/media-library/pdfs/CCR-IIb/Full-Report.pdf. Accessed May 19, 2015.

IPCC (2013). Summary for Policymakers. In *Climate Change 2013: The Physical Science Basis. Contribution of Working Group I to the Fifth Assessment Report of the Intergovernmental Panel on Climate Change*, T. F. Stocker, D. Qin, G.-K. Plattner, M. Tignor, S. K. Allen, J. Boschung, A. Nauels, Y. Xia, V. Bex, and P. M. Midgley (eds.). Cambridge University Press, Cambridge, United Kingdom, and New York, NY.

Jeffries, M. O., Overland, J. E., and Perovich, D. K. (2013). The Arctic shifts to a new normal. *Physics Today*, 66(10), 35–40.

Lawson, N. (2009). *An Appeal to Reason: A Cool Look at Global Warming*. Duckworth Overlook, London and New York.

Nuccitelli, D. (2014). Climate models accurately predicted global warming when reflecting natural ocean cycles. Posted to *The Guardian* online, July 21, 2014, available at http://www.theguardian.com/environment/climate-consensus-97-per-cent/2014/jul/21/realistic-climate-models-accurately-predicted-global-warming. Accessed May 17, 2015.

Rahmstorf, S. (2013). The global temperature jigsaw. Posted to RealClimate.org, December 17, 2013, available at http://www.realclimate.org/index.php/archives/2013/12/the-global-temperature-jigsaw/. Accessed May 17, 2015.

Rahmstorf, S., Cazenave, A., Church, J. A., Hansen, J. E., Keeling, R. F., Parker, D. E., and Somerville, R. C. (2007). Recent climate observations compared to projections. *Science, 316*(5825), 709–709.

Schmidt, G. (2014). The emergent patterns of climate change. TED Talk filmed, March 10, 2014, available at http://www.ted.com/talks/

gavin_schmidt_the_emergent_patterns_of_climate_change?language=en.
    Accessed August 28, 2015.
Singer, S. F., and Avery, D. T. (2008). *Unstoppable Global Warming: Every
    1500 Years*. Updated and expanded edition. Rowman & Littlefield.

Q20. CAN AN INCREASE IN ATMOSPHERIC CARBON DIOXIDE CAUSE A SIGNIFICANT WARMING OF GLOBAL TEMPERATURES?

Answer: A wide range of evidence supports the view that doubling carbon dioxide will lead to a significant global average warming (between 1.5°C and 4.5°C, with 3.0°C being the most likely outcome). The direct warming caused by a doubling of carbon dioxide is around 1°C, but this initial warming is roughly tripled by reinforcing climate feedbacks.

The Facts: Many different pieces of the climate system are connected: the atmosphere and the oceans, for example (question 7), or the jet stream and changes in the Arctic (question 6). Some of these connections, as discussed in question 15, can take the form of feedbacks, those chicken-and-egg relationships where one thing affects another, which affects the first thing again, in an endless loop. Some of these feedbacks amplify, while others diminish, any initial changes. Exactly how climate will respond to any given external forcing therefore depends on the overall effect of these different feedbacks: will the amplifiers or the diminishers win out?

A sizeable body of evidence suggests that, at the timescales relevant to human-caused climate change, the feedbacks overall work to amplify initial changes. For example, questions 9 and 17 discussed how the forcing from Milankovitch's orbital wobbles are too small to explain the large changes in climate that resulted. The effect of the wobbles must have been amplified, most likely by carbon dioxide—but other feedbacks are also at work. As warming melts ice, for example, it exposes darker surfaces underneath, which absorb more sunlight than the ice did, increasing the warming and accelerating the melting. There are other feedbacks, too, but the key idea is that external forcings trigger a set of feedbacks. Some amplify and some diminish the initial change, but the amplifiers win out: the end result is a much larger climate change than the original forcing would suggest.

As discussed in question 9, the increased level of carbon dioxide in the atmosphere from fossil fuel burning itself constitutes a climate forcing. If the glacial–interglacial cycles are anything to go by, the forcing from carbon dioxide should be amplified by feedbacks. Is there any evidence that this might be happening now?

Scientists have documented evidence of several feedbacks currently in progress. The Arctic is undergoing a dramatic loss of reflective sea ice, helping to amplify the local warming to at least twice the global average rate and possibly affecting conditions elsewhere (question 6). But another, possibly more important, feedback seems to be at work in the atmosphere. As temperatures are rising, observations are recording an increase in our most abundant greenhouse gas: water vapor.

Theory suggests that an initial warming, from whatever source, should lead to more evaporation from the oceans (warmer water evaporates more easily), and less condensation once the water vapor is in the atmosphere (warmer air can hold more water vapor). Water vapor is a greenhouse gas, so more of it should induce more warming—and, once again, we have an amplifying feedback loop. Observations show that as the Earth has been getting warmer, the atmosphere has indeed been taking on more water vapor. The NOAA State of the Climate global overview of humidity for 2013 (the most recent available at the time of writing) states, "Overall, water vapor in the surface atmosphere has increased over land and ocean relative to the 1970s" (NOAA, 2014), a statement based on measurements of humidity taken from weather stations on the ground. Satellites and weather balloons confirm that this change is not limited to the surface but instead seems to be happening throughout the lower atmosphere, the troposphere, according to the IPCC's latest report summarizing numerous studies of the issue (Hartmann et al., 2013). There are variations from place to place and over time, as with many other features of the climate system that we've examined so far, but the overall global average trend is for more water vapor in the atmosphere.

These observations confirm the theoretical idea that warming should add more water vapor to the atmosphere, generating more warming. Yet more support comes from studies of the effects of the eruption of Mount Pinatubo, a large volcano in the Philippines, in 1991. As discussed in question 9, volcanic eruptions cause a short-lived cooling effect by injecting tiny, reflective particles (sulfates) into the stratosphere—and Pinatubo did indeed cause a global average cooling of about 0.5°C for the year after the eruption. If the ideas behind the water vapor feedback are correct, the cooling from Mount Pinatubo should have cut the levels of water vapor, amplifying the direct effect of the volcano itself. Measurements show that water vapor did, in fact, decline abruptly in 1992, and computer simulations of Pinatubo's cooling effects are unable to match what actually happened, unless the models include the water vapor feedback (Soden et al., 2002).

It's pretty clear, then, from both theory and observations, that water vapor feedback is real. Combined with other feedbacks, the overall effect is to amplify warming, regardless of the initial source. In the case of glacial–interglacial cycles, the warming first comes from orbital wobbles; in the case of human-caused climate change, the warming comes from the increase of carbon dioxide due to burning fossil fuels. In this latter case, the feedbacks mean that the overall warming is greater than would result from the heat-trapping effects of carbon dioxide alone. This gives rise to the concept of *climate sensitivity*. Climate sensitivity is actually quite a subtle and complex idea (NASA's Gavin Schmidt has a nice discussion of the issues in a 2013 post at the climate science blog RealClimate.org), but put simply, it's the amount of global warming that results from a doubling of carbon dioxide. Current estimates from the Intergovernmental Panel on Climate Change place this at between 1.5°C and 4.5°C, with 3.0°C being the most likely (Stocker et al., 2013, p. 83). This is based not only on observations of feedbacks like the water vapor feedback but also on studies of climate changes from Earth's past, such as the glacial and interglacial periods.

A widespread misconception about climate sensitivity, however, is that the estimate noted earlier is too high and that global average temperature responds little, if at all, to increases in carbon dioxide. This is typically argued by focusing on water vapor feedback. Fred Singer and Dennis Avery (2008), for example, in a section titled "The failures of the greenhouse theory," list water vapor feedback as failure number 8. "Eighth, the greenhouse theory requires that the warming effect of additional CO_2 to be amplified by increased water vapour in the atmosphere. But there is no evidence that the upper atmosphere is retaining more water vapour" (p. 107), a claim echoed by Steve Goreham's (2013) *The Mad, Mad, Mad World of Climatism* on page 87. As we've seen, this is not supported by the facts. Multiple sources of evidence indicate that water vapor levels in the atmosphere have risen since the 1970s.

A more intriguing argument made by these authors, though, is that the water vapor feedback as a whole does not work as advertised. Instead of water vapor strongly amplifying any initial warming, they suggest that water vapor feedback might only be very weak, or might actually work to *diminish* an initial warming. The reasoning here is that, although warming in the tropics should cause more evaporation, it might also cause a change in the cloud patterns. High-altitude cirrus clouds trap heat, so if the area covered by these clouds were to contract, more heat could escape to space, counteracting the warming from carbon dioxide. This is sometimes referred to as the heat vent, or "iris" hypothesis. This idea has been researched and championed mainly by Massachusetts Institute of Technology meteorologist Richard Lindzen, an accomplished climate scientist, and his work on this issue has mostly been published in well-respected peer-reviewed journals (Lindzen et al., 2001; Lindzen and Choi, 2009, 2011). This by itself, however, doesn't mean it's right—and a host of follow-up studies, by several different research teams, have found Lindzen's work to contain many fundamental errors. (A relatively easy-to-read discussion was posted to RealClimate.org by climate scientist Andrew Dessler in 2015.)

This is how science progresses, of course: research gets published; then other scientists try to poke holes in it. Sometimes they're unable to; but sometimes, as with this issue, they find serious problems; the flawed ideas are discarded and everybody moves on. Unfortunately, however, in this case, writers such as Fred Singer and Dennis Avery, Steve Goreham, and Nigel Lawson (2009) continue to refer to this obsolete work, which is a good example of what's sometimes called "zombie science": ideas that have been disproved several times over but keep being resurrected in popular outlets. As with the focus on a small body of work finding flaws with the "hockey stick" from question 11, as opposed to the large body of work that has independently confirmed it, this is a form of cherry-picking. In this case, the cherries are the particular studies that find the desired result, with other research being sidelined. This is an innate human tendency, as suggested in question 13, and it's why the processes of science are so valuable. But in order for them to work effectively, and help us separate what's real from what we would merely like to be real, we need to look at the whole body of research, not just the parts we like.

FURTHER READING

Dessler, A. (2015). The return of the iris effect? Posted to RealClimate.org, April 24, 2015, available at http://www.realclimate.org/index.php/archives/2015/04/the-return-of-the-iris-effect/. Accessed May 18, 2015.

Goreham, S. (2013). *The Mad, Mad, Mad World of Climatism: Mankind and Climate Change Mania.* New Lenox Books.

Hartmann, D. L., Klein Tank, A. M. G., Rusticucci, M., Alexander, L. V., Brönnimann, S., Charabi, Y., Dentener, F. J., Dlugokencky, E. J., Easterling, D. R., Kaplan, A., Soden, B. J., Thorne, P. W., Wild, M., and Zhai, P. M. (2013). Observations: Atmosphere and Surface. In

Climate Change 2013: The Physical Science Basis. Contribution of Working Group I to the Fifth Assessment Report of the Intergovernmental Panel on Climate Change, T. F. Stocker, D. Qin, G.-K. Plattner, M. Tignor, S. K. Allen, J. Boschung, A. Nauels, Y. Xia, V. Bex, and P. M. Midgley (eds.). Cambridge University Press, Cambridge, United Kingdom, and New York, NY.

Lawson, N. (2009). *An Appeal to Reason: A Cool Look at Global Warming.* Duckworth Overlook, London and New York.

Lindzen, R. S., and Choi, Y. S. (2009). On the determination of climate feedbacks from ERBE data. *Geophysical Research Letters, 36*(16), DOI: 10.1029/2009GL039628.

Lindzen, R. S., and Choi, Y. S. (2011). On the observational determination of climate sensitivity and its implications. *Asia-Pacific Journal of Atmospheric Sciences, 47*(4), 377–390.

Lindzen, R. S., Chou, M. D., and Hou, A. (2001). Does the earth have an adaptive infrared iris? *Bulletin of the American Meteorological Society, 82*(3), 417–432.

NOAA. (2014). State of the Climate 2013: Humidity. Available at http://www.climate.gov/news-features/understanding-climate/2013-state-climate-humidity. Accessed May 18, 2015.

Schmidt, G. (2013). On sensitivity—part I. Posted to RealClimate.org, January 3, 2013, available at http://www.realclimate.org/index.php/archives/2013/01/on-sensitivity-part-i/. Accessed May 18, 2015.

Singer, S. F., and Avery, D. T. (2008). *Unstoppable Global Warming: Every 1500 Years.* Updated and expanded edition. Rowman & Littlefield.

Soden, B. J., Wetherald, R. T., Stenchikov, G. L., and Robock, A. (2002). Global cooling after the eruption of Mount Pinatubo: a test of climate feedback by water vapor. *Science, 296*(5568), 727–730.

Stocker, T. F., Qin, D., Plattner, G.-K., Alexander, L. V., Allen, S. K., Bindoff, N. L., Bréon, F.-M., Church, J. A., Cubasch, U., Emori, S., Forster, P., Friedlingstein, P., Gillett, N., Gregory, J. M., Hartmann, D. L., Jansen, E., Kirtman, B., Knutti, R., Krishna Kumar, K., Lemke, P., Marotzke, J., Masson-Delmotte, V., Meehl, G. A., Mokhov, I. I., Piao, S., Ramaswamy, V., Randall, D., Rhein, M., Rojas, M., Sabine, C., Shindell, D., Talley, L. D., Vaughan, D. G., and Xie, S.-P. (2013). Technical Summary. In *Climate Change 2013: The Physical Science Basis. Contribution of Working Group I to the Fifth Assessment Report of the Intergovernmental Panel on Climate Change,* T. F. Stocker, D. Qin, G.-K. Plattner, M. Tignor, S. K. Allen, J. Boschung, A. Nauels, Y. Xia, V. Bex, and P. M. Midgley (eds.). Cambridge University Press, Cambridge, United Kingdom, and New York, NY.

Q21. HOW WILL CLIMATE CHANGE
IMPACT SOCIETY?

Answer: Climate scientists and economists believe that the negative consequences of climate change will far outweigh any local and regional benefits. Problems include lower crop yields in many places, more floods and droughts, and more people dying in heat waves, though in some places this may be slightly offset by fewer people dying from cold.

The Facts: Climate scientists emphasize that the severity of global warming in coming decades depends heavily on the choices that policy-makers make now. Will nations reduce their dependence on fossil fuels or burn them like there's no tomorrow? Will the world muddle along without really doing much to reduce carbon dioxide emissions? It's very difficult to predict, so climate scientists have posited a range of possibilities, with global average warming by 2100 probably running somewhere between 1°C and 4°C (just under 2°F to just over 7°F).

But this is quite an abstract set of numbers. People live in specific places, not the world as a whole, so how will the climate change where you live? And how do those climate changes translate into impacts on people's daily lives? Although climate model results get more unreliable at finer scales, they're reasonably accurate down to the scale of regions, such as places the size of the eastern, Midwestern, or western United States. At these scales, there's quite a lot of variation from region to region (see IPCC, 2013a, for an atlas of regional-scale climate change; another great resource, describing regional variation across the United States, is the 2014 U.S. National Climate Assessment, by Jerry Melillo and co-authors).

However, a few generalizations can be made. Overall, more heatwaves and fewer cold snaps are expected, and there will probably be more floods and more droughts. As glaciers and ice sheets on land melt (question 2), the water flows into the sea; and as the oceans get warmer, they expand. These two effects combined are expected to cause global average sea level to rise by between about 0.4 and 0.6 m (roughly 1 to 2 feet) by 2100, causing coastal flooding. Partly because richer countries are better placed to throw money at the problem and adapt to these changes, for example with more air conditioning or by building stronger bridges that are less likely to get swept away by floods, the impacts are expected to be a lot more serious in poor countries that lack this capacity; poor people in rich countries are also typically more vulnerable (see IPCC, 2013b, p. 7, 2014, p. 6).

However, this is not to say that rich countries will be unaffected. The United States makes an interesting case study. Here, in 2014, a report was released by a group called the Risky Business Project (Gordon, 2014). This group is co-chaired by Michael Bloomberg, the billionaire former mayor of New York City; Hank Paulson, former U.S. secretary of the Treasury; and Thomas Steyer, retired founder of a global investment company called Farallon Capital Management. The committee includes George Shultz, U.S. secretary of state for President Ronald Reagan. The Risky Business report is specifically aimed at identifying, and assessing the costs of, the risks presented to the United States by climate change. Among other things, it finds that rising sea levels, combined with the increased threat of severe storms, will likely increase the cost of coastal flooding damage along the eastern seaboard and the Gulf of Mexico by an average of $7.3 billion every year. This is not a cost that will hit sometime by the end of the century: this is expected within the next 15 years. By 2050, the report estimates that "between $66 billion and $106 billion worth of existing coastal property will likely be below sea level nationwide, with $238 billion to $507 billion worth of property below sea level by 2100" (Gordon, 2014, p. 4).

The costs to the United States do not stop with the effects of rising sea levels. Increased temperatures, and the greater chance of extreme heat from heat waves, should make it harder to work outside, affecting construction workers, farmers, and utility maintenance crews. The Risky Business report estimates that productivity in these areas could be cut by up to 3% by 2100 (Gordon, 2014, p. 4), which looks like a small number but is actually huge in this context. The increased temperatures will probably mean a lot of new air conditioning, which will mean a lot of new electricity in order to run the cooling systems. The expected cost of the new power plants is $12 billion a year for residential and commercial ratepayers—again, not in the distant future, but within 25 years (Gordon, 2014, p. 3).

These are significant costs, to be paid by ordinary people. While those inclined to be dismissive of climate change as a serious issue tend to unfairly deride the work of the IPCC or government scientists as doom and gloom, or, as Steve Goreham (2013) puts it, "The usual Climatist mantra of submerging coastal cities, famine from droughts and floods, and more intense tropical storms" (p. 133), it's perhaps difficult to describe the Risky Business Project, a group of hard-headed business people, in quite the same terms—yet they're raising the alarm about climate change just as much as the scientists are.

And it's not just the business community joining with scientists to raise the alarm about climate change. Moving beyond purely economic costs, the U.S. Department of Defense (DoD) sees climate change as imposing a cost to national security. In its most recent Quadrennial Defense Review, a four-yearly overview of strategy and future security challenges, the DoD stated: "Climate change may exacerbate water scarcity and lead to sharp increases in food costs. The pressures caused by climate change will influence resource competition while placing additional burdens on economies, societies, and governance institutions around the world. These effects are threat multipliers that will aggravate stressors abroad such as poverty, environmental degradation, political instability, and social tensions—conditions that can enable terrorist activity and other forms of violence" (Hagel, 2014, p. 8). Indeed, one recent paper found that drought increases in many parts of the world are likely to be severe even under optimistic projections of future emissions of carbon dioxide (Zhao and Dai, 2015); another found that drought, probably enhanced by global warming, was a likely contributing factor in the destabilizing of Syria (Kelley et al., 2015).

The overall impacts of climate change will vary a lot from place to place, both because the climate change itself will vary and because the capabilities of countries to respond and adapt will vary. Even so, the Risky Business report suggests that there will be substantial economic costs associated with climate change, even for a wealthy country like the United States, and globally, the impacts of climate change are likely to make the world less safe for American servicemen and women. However, there is no shortage of sources claiming that climate change impacts won't be that bad, or might even be beneficial. In light of the concerns raised by these highly credible sources, how are these claims possible?

The central point in this line of reasoning is the balance between the *costs* of climate change and any possible *benefits*. It would be inaccurate to claim that all impacts of climate change will be negative. Depending on the baseline climate, for example, warmer winters in some places could mean less snow, with reduced costs for keeping roads cleared and airports open. Lower yields for some crops, because of temperatures that are too high, might occur simultaneously with higher yields for other crops, because it's no longer so cold. In determining whether climate change is overall good or bad, the critical question is how the negatives and positives stack up against each other.

The answer from economists leans strongly toward the negatives far outweighing any positives, certainly at the global scale. One recent thorough study found that economic productivity for all countries tends to peak at an annual average temperature of 13°C (about 55°F) and drops off sharply as it gets warmer (Burke et al., 2015). This study went on to explain that, if carbon emissions continue as they have been doing, unchecked, the resulting warming could cut global incomes by about 23% relative to a situation without warming. The impacts would be different depending on how warm the countries are to begin with: warmer countries are much harder hit, cooler countries, such as Russia or Canada, might actually benefit. However, the overall balance of costs and benefits comes down strongly on the costs side. Furthermore, because the hardest hit, warmer-to-begin-with countries are typically poorer, while the cooler countries are typically richer, the gap between the richest and poorest countries could grow substantially as a result of global warming, exacerbating existing challenges such as migration from poor countries to rich ones. And in a globally interconnected world, the cooler places that might benefit economically from some warming are unlikely to be isolated from the problems affecting other places. The breakdown of Syria, for example, has spurred an ongoing refugee crisis in Europe, as of summer 2015. Whether or not Syria's collapse was helped along by climate change, a possibility suggested earlier, the fallout has not been restricted to Syria alone.

Efforts to argue that global warming will not cause serious problems, or could be overall beneficial, rely on overstating the benefits and understating the costs. There are many variants, each addressing a specific aspect of climate change, but all ultimately misrepresent the cost–benefit balance. Two examples give a sense of how this is typically done: first, the argument that carbon dioxide is plant food, and second, the idea that, in a warmer world, fewer people will die from cold, more than making up for the deaths from heat.

The claim that carbon dioxide is plant food is an especially popular one in books, blogs, and websites. It's based on the concept that carbon dioxide is an essential ingredient in photosynthesis: plants make sugars from it. So, the reasoning goes, crops will grow better as atmospheric carbon dioxide levels continue to climb. This argument is made by Steve Goreham (2013, pp. 131–132), Fred Singer and Dennis Avery (2008, pp. 192–193), and Craig Idso and the co-authors of the Heartland Institute's 2014 report, *Climate Change Reconsidered II: Biological Impacts* (e.g., p. ix, pp. 483–596). Television advertisements aired in 2006 (and still available on YouTube), commissioned by the Competitive Enterprise Institute and largely paid for by the fossil fuel industry, used the slogan, "Carbon dioxide: They call it pollution. We call it life." (See Competitive Enterprise Institute, 2006a, 2006b; meteorologist Jeff Masters posted an interesting discussion of the adverts on his Weather Underground blog when they came out.)

Like many of the misconceptions we've already looked at, this one has a grain of truth. Carbon dioxide *is* essential for photosynthesis, and experiments conducted in greenhouses show that higher levels of carbon dioxide do stimulate more growth—for some plants. This is known as the CO_2 *fertilization effect*. It's real. But there are at least three challenges to the idea that the world will be better off because of it. First, not all plants respond equally to increases in CO_2. Several crops that are staples of tropical countries, like sorghum, maize, and millet, show little if any increase in growth. Second, the experiments were conducted under highly controlled conditions. When exposed to the more realistic conditions of the world outside a greenhouse, the effect is diminished. And finally, there are many other influences on plant growth besides carbon dioxide, notably heat stress and water availability, both of which are expected to cause problems for agriculture. The Risky Business report indicates that in the United States, without adaptation, "some states in the Southeast, lower Great Plains, and Midwest risk up to a 50% to 70% loss in average annual crop yields (corn, soy, cotton, and wheat)" (Gordon, 2014, p. 5). Importantly, the report finds that gains in currently cooler, more northern states will be more than offset by these losses, making the United States as a whole somewhat worse off economically due to climate change. Although some people in some places might benefit, most people in most places will not. The see-saw of costs and benefits comes down hard on the costs side.

The argument that climate change will be beneficial because of the CO_2 fertilization effect can really only be made on the erroneous assumption that other aspects of the climate, such as temperature, won't change much—and as we've seen in earlier questions, this assumption is not supportable by current science. While some research supports the basic idea of the fertilization effect, it is a serious oversimplification to claim that the world will be better off because of it. Indeed, there is considerable evidence, documented by science historian Naomi Oreskes (2010), that this particular misconception has formed the core of a marketing campaign by the fossil fuels industry since the 1990s, intended to change people's views about global warming. Unfortunately, persuasive though it may be, the facts do not support it.

So much for the idea that carbon dioxide is plant food. The other claim mentioned earlier is the idea that, while warming will probably increase the number of people dying from the heat, it will *decrease* the number of people dying from the cold. Again, this sounds reasonable and does have some support from current research. However, evidence suggests that the two will not balance out: the increase in heat-related deaths is expected to be much greater than the decrease in cold-related deaths. The most obvious reason for this is that the majority of the world's population lives in the relatively warm tropics, where cold-related deaths are a minor issue (IPCC, 2014, pp. 19–20). But even in cooler countries, extreme heat is often more of a problem than extreme cold. In the United States since 1986, according to the National Weather Service, extreme heat has killed over five times the number of people who have died from extreme cold; even factoring in all winter deaths, from blizzards and ice, extreme heat has still killed more than twice as many people as winter and cold combined (National Weather Service, 2014; see also Melillo et al.'s, 2014, National Climate Assessment). Climate change in these cooler countries will help solve a minor problem, while making a major problem a lot worse.

What's the basis for claims to the contrary? Many people make such claims, including Danish author Bjorn Lomborg, in his 2007 book, *Cool It*, and some of the authors mentioned in previous questions: Steve Goreham (2013) and Craig Idso and co-authors (2014), among others. The arguments they make tend to be based on examining the effects of the relatively small changes in base climate that we can expect from global warming: an increase in average temperature of a few degrees (either Celsius or Fahrenheit).

However, this ignores the fact that a warmer climate is also likely to have more variability—hence the concept of *global weirding* mentioned at the very beginning of this book. This means the odds of experiencing a severe heat wave go up. The small increases in average temperature are less of a problem than the increased chances of extreme heat, and the effects of heat waves are rarely mentioned in arguments that global warming will lead to fewer people dying from cold. Currently, record heat waves are five times more likely than they would have been in a world with no global warming. As Figure 3.1 shows, if we continue burning fossil fuels in a business-as-usual future, the risk from heat waves will be 12 times greater by 2040.

Even if we were to ignore the errors in the claim about fewer cold deaths, it really makes sense only for countries where large numbers of people die from cold. As we've seen, in the United States, significantly fewer people die from cold than from heat, and in tropical countries, this is even more the case. This brings us back to an important issue, one that we raised at the beginning of this question: the impacts of climate change are likely to be much greater in poor countries, and for poor people in rich countries. The research cited earlier, which found an optimum temperature for economic productivity of 13°C, also found that "average income in the poorest 40% of countries declines by 75% by 2100 relative to a world without climate change, while the richest 20% experience slight gains" (Burke et al., 2015, p. 238). Ironically, the countries that have

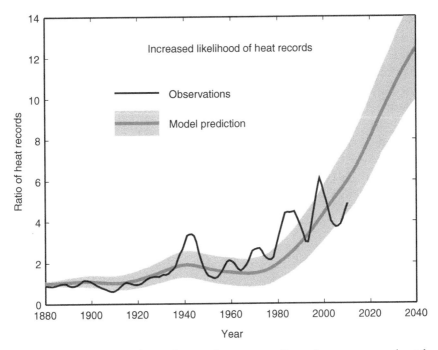

Figure 3.1 The number of records compared to those expected with no global warming has increased 5-fold over the last century. In a business-as-usual future, heat records are expected to increase 12-fold by 2040.
Source: Coumou et al. (2013).

done the least to cause the problem of climate change are the ones that are currently expected to bear the greatest burden. This is a challenge to many people's sense of fairness.

FURTHER READING

Burke, M., Hsiang, S. M., and Miguel, E. (2015). Global non-linear effect of temperature on economic production. *Nature* 527, 235–239.

Competitive Enterprise Institute. (2006a). Energy. Posted to YouTube, May 18, 2006, available at https://www.youtube.com/watch?v=7sGKv DNdJNA. Accessed May 19, 2015.

Competitive Enterprise Institute. (2006b). Glaciers. Posted to YouTube, May 18, 2006, available at https://www.youtube.com/watch?v=Wq_Bj-av3g0. Accessed May 19, 2015.

Coumou, D., Robinson, A., and Rahmstorf, S. (2013). Global increase in record-breaking monthly-mean temperatures. *Climatic Change*, 118, 771–782.

Gordon, K. (2014). Risky Business: The Economic Risks of Climate Change in the United States. Risky Business Project. Available at http://risky business.org/uploads/files/RiskyBusiness_Report_WEB_09_08_14.pdf. Accessed May 20, 2015.

Goreham, S. (2013). *The Mad, Mad, Mad World of Climatism: Mankind and Climate Change Mania*. New Lenox Books.

Hagel, C. T. (2014). *Quadrennial Defense Review*. Department of Defense, Washington, DC, March 4, 2014, available at http://archive.defense.gov/pubs/2014_Quadrennial_Defense_Review.pdf. Accessed November 24, 2015.

Idso, C. D., Idso, S. B., Carter, R. M., and Singer, S. F. (Eds.). 2014. *Climate Change Reconsidered II: Biological Impacts*. The Heartland Institute, Chicago, IL, available at https://www.heartland.org/media-library/pdfs/CCR-IIb/Full-Report.pdf. Accessed May 23, 2015.

IPCC. (2013a). Annex I: Atlas of Global and Regional Climate Projections [G. J. van Oldenborgh, M. Collins, J. Arblaster, J. H. Christensen, J. Marotzke, S. B. Power, M. Rummukainen, and T. Zhou (eds.)]. In *Climate Change 2013: The Physical Science Basis. Contribution of Working Group I to the Fifth Assessment Report of the Intergovernmental Panel on Climate Change*, T. F. Stocker, D. Qin, G.-K. Plattner, M. Tignor, S. K. Allen, J. Boschung, A. Nauels, Y. Xia, V. Bex, and P. M. Midgley (eds.). Cambridge University Press, Cambridge, United Kingdom, and New York, NY. Available at http://www.climatechange2013.org/images/report/WG1AR5_AnnexI_FINAL.pdf. Accessed May 20, 2015.

IPCC. (2013b). Summary for Policymakers. In *Climate Change 2013: The Physical Science Basis. Contribution of Working Group I to the Fifth Assessment Report of the Intergovernmental Panel on Climate Change*, T. F. Stocker, D. Qin, G.-K. Plattner, M. Tignor, S. K. Allen, J. Boschung, A. Nauels, Y. Xia, V. Bex, and P. M. Midgley (eds.). Cambridge University Press, Cambridge, United Kingdom, and New York, NY. Available at http://www.climatechange2013.org/images/report/WG1AR5_SPM_FINAL.pdf. Accessed May 20, 2015.

IPCC (2014). Summary for Policymakers. In *Climate Change 2014: Impacts, Adaptation, and Vulnerability. Part A: Global and Sectoral Aspects. Contribution of Working Group II to the Fifth Assessment Report of the Intergovernmental Panel on Climate Change*, C. B. Field, V. R. Barros, D. J. Dokken, K. J. Mach, M. D. Mastrandrea, T. E. Bilir, M. Chatterjee, K. L. Ebi, Y. O. Estrada, R. C. Genova, B. Girma, E. S. Kissel, A. N. Levy, S. MacCracken, P. R. Mastrandrea, and L. L. White (eds.).

Cambridge University Press, Cambridge, United Kingdom, and New York, NY, pp. 1–32. Available at http://ipcc-wg2.gov/AR5/images/uploads/WGIIAR5-SPM_FINAL.pdf. Accessed May 20, 2015.

Kelley, C. P., Mohtadi, S., Cane, M. A., Seager, R., and Kushnir, Y. (2015). Climate change in the fertile crescent and implications of the recent Syrian drought. *Proceedings of the National Academy of Sciences, 112*(11), 3241–3246.

Lomborg, B. (2007). *Cool It: The Skeptical Environmentalist's Guide to Global Warming.* Vintage Books.

Masters, J. (2006). Is carbon dioxide a pollutant? Posted to Weather Underground blog, May 24, 2006, available at http://www.wunderground.com/resources/climate/cei.asp. Accessed May 20, 2015.

Melillo, Jerry M., Terese (T. C.) Richmond, and Gary W. Yohe (Eds.). (2014). *Climate Change Impacts in the United States: The Third National Climate Assessment.* U.S. Global Change Research Program, 841 pp. doi:10.7930/J0Z31WJ2, available at http://nca2014.globalchange.gov/. Accessed May 20, 2015.

National Weather Service. (2014). 74-Year List of Severe Weather Fatalities. Available at http://www.nws.noaa.gov/os/hazstats/resources/weather_fatalities.pdf. Accessed May 20, 2015.

Oreskes, N. (2010). My Facts Are Better Than Your Facts: Spreading Good News about Global Warming. In *How Do Facts Travel?* M. S. Morgan and P. Howlett (eds.). Cambridge University Press, pp. 135–166.

Singer, S. F., and Avery, D. T. (2008). *Unstoppable Global Warming: Every 1500 Years.* Updated and expanded edition. Rowman & Littlefield.

Zhao, T., and Dai, A. (2015). The magnitude and causes of global drought changes in the 21st century under a low-moderate emissions scenario. *Journal of Climate, 28*(11), 4490–4512.

Q22. HAVE THE DANGERS OF CLIMATE CHANGE BEEN UNDERSTATED OR OVERSTATED BY SCIENTISTS AND THE NEWS MEDIA?

Answer: Many of the observed changes in the climate system are happening faster and more dramatically than scientists predicted, including melting of Arctic sea ice, rising sea level, and emissions of carbon dioxide. Scientific assessments of climate change and its consequences have therefore tended to understate their seriousness. News reports, meanwhile, have tended to understate the level of scientific agreement about climate change and its likely impact.

The Facts: The popular perception of scientists tends to be that they are cool, calm, rational, and unflappable. Like many stereotypes, there may be some truth to it. Randy Olson, a scientist turned film maker, has observed: "I have heard scientist friends of mine over the years rave about how much they enjoy field and laboratory research. . . . it's all so rational, so logical, so objective" (Olson, 2009, p. 31). To be sure, as discussed in question 8, scientists are only human, too—even Mr. Spock from *Star Trek* cracks and lets his emotions show sometimes—but there's a common view that scientists are no-drama people. It's possible that scientists even believe this about themselves, that this is how they're *supposed* to be, and try to act accordingly, to a fault. This is what's called a *cultural norm*, and this particular cultural norm for scientists has been labelled Erring on the Side of Least Drama (Brysse et al., 2013). This is not necessarily a good thing. While shouting "Fire!" in a crowded theater is dangerous, so is waffling when a real fire presents a real threat.

A good example of the tendency for scientists to err toward caution is the work of the Intergovernmental Panel on Climate Change (IPCC). Hundreds of scientists from around the world serve as unpaid volunteers, combing through the scientific literature to produce three giant reports roughly every five years. There's a report for each of the IPCC's three working groups, one on physical science, one on impacts, and one on what we can do about the problem. These reports are intensively peer reviewed and represent the best-available picture of the state of scientific knowledge on climate change.

But they're not immune to erring on the side of least drama. There are several examples of projections in the earlier IPCC reports that later events have shown to be underestimates of the speed and significance of climate change. These include the rate of melting of Arctic sea ice and the rate of warming of the oceans, all of which have happened more quickly than the IPCC reports indicated (see Brysse et al., 2013, for details; many of these are also documented in an assessment of climate change science by several of the world's leading climate scientists, *The Copenhagen Diagnosis* [Allison et al., 2009]). The rate of carbon dioxide emissions has tended to follow the IPCC's worst-case scenario (and, as of this writing, global carbon dioxide emissions are actually slightly higher than the IPCC's current worst-case scenario). Perhaps the clearest example of the IPCC's tendency to err on the side of least drama, though, is a consistent underestimating of the rate of sea level rise.

In the IPCC's 2007 report, the highest that sea level was projected to rise by the end of the century, under the worst-case outcome for the worst-case scenario, was 59 cm, a hair less than 2 feet. But, according to oceanographer

Stefan Rahmstorf, this figure was actually artificially low, for several reasons (Rahmstorf discusses his reasoning in a 2010 post to the climate science blog RealClimate.org). First, it was calculated using a smaller maximum warming than the IPCC itself projected, limiting the expansion that seawater undergoes as it warms up; second, it was calculated out to the year 2095, not 2100, so the sea level had a few years less to rise; and finally, the big ice sheets of Greenland and Antarctica had recently been found to be melting at ever faster rates—but the science was so new that any potential implications for sea level of this accelerating melt were simply left out of the calculation. Rahmstorf wrote: "IPCC would never have published an implausibly high upper limit [on sea level rise] like this, but it did not hesitate with the implausibly low 59 cm. That is because within the IPCC culture, being 'alarmist' is *bad* and being 'conservative' (i.e. underestimating the potential severity of things) is *good*" (emphasis in original).

Looking at specific examples is instructive, but even more striking is a broader look at the overall predictions of the IPCC. One analysis looked at news reports of scientific findings published after IPCC predictions. As Figure 3.2 shows, the IPCC turns out to have been more than 20 times more likely to underestimate climate impacts than overestimate

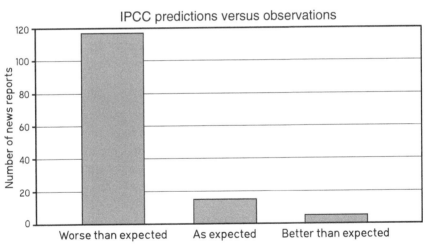

Figure 3.2 Number of news reports for the period 1998–2002, and 2008, showing whether new scientific findings were worse than, better than, or about the same as expected by the IPCC. The diagram shows that, as reported in the prestige news media, new scientific findings that were worse than expected outnumber those that were better than expected by more than 20 to 1.

Source: Freudenburg and Muselli (2010).

(Freudenburg and Muselli, 2010). This track record presents a compelling case that scientists err toward caution rather than alarm.

As we've noted before, science is a human undertaking prone to human failings. The previous examples show the IPCC is no exception. There has been, to our knowledge, one genuine instance of an exaggerated claim appearing in an IPCC report, the unrealistically early melting of all Himalayan glaciers by 2035 that we mentioned in question 3. In comparison, however, the tendency to err on the side of least drama has produced low estimates of at least four elements of the climate system: sea level, Arctic ice melt, warming of the ocean, and emissions of carbon dioxide (Allison et al., 2009).

Furthermore, the most-publicized, and probably the most widely read, section of each of the IPCC's reports is the short distillation that is the Summary for Policymakers (SPM). Unlike the rest of the report, the SPM is subject to line-by-line approval by delegations sent by national governments, and all the delegations have to agree. If even one country objects to a word or a sentence in the SPM, the text must be changed. In effect, the IPCC's rules mean that every country has a veto—so countries whose economies depend heavily on the export of fossil fuels, such as Saudi Arabia, have the power to remove sections that sound too alarming. There are several accounts from the drafting of the 2014 Working Group 3 SPM, in the news media and from people involved in the drafting process, showing that these rules led to a watered-down document (for news articles, see Clark, 2014, and *The Economist*, 2014; for first-hand accounts, see Broome, 2014, and Stavins, 2014).

Adding to these inherent tendencies of the IPCC reports to downplay the worst outcomes is the way climate change is often reported in the news. A well-established practice in journalism is to present both sides of the story. But what if there aren't really two sides? Scientists have compiled strong evidence that climate change is real and happening because of human emissions of carbon dioxide, with potentially serious consequences. This evidence has led 90–100% of climate scientists to agree on these basic points. However, news reports on climate change have often tended to follow the "he said-she said" format of two people providing opposing viewpoints, as if there were some kind of debate about the basic facts. For example, television science presenter Bill Nye has engaged in several televised one-on-one debates in recent years, including a debate on CNN with Marc Morano in 2012. This can give a very misleading picture of the views of the scientific community as a whole, suggesting a 50–50 split and that scientists are not able to agree about climate change. A detailed study of reports in *The New York Times, Los Angeles Times, The*

Washington Post, and *Wall Street Journal* found that, from 1988 to 2002, over half of the stories on climate change suffered from this problem of false balance (Boykoff and Boykoff, 2004). Although these "prestige" newspapers have improved significantly in recent years, false balance persists in the tabloid press (Boykoff, 2011). Surveys of public opinion consistently find that people overestimate the level of disagreement between scientists.

Given the two-fold tendency for reports about climate change to be understated due to cultural norms among both scientists and journalists, claims that the IPCC and news media exaggerate the seriousness of the situation deserve close examination. One widely repeated myth is that the IPCC is biased toward exaggeration, referencing only those scientific publications that support an alarmist view and altering reports to make the threat of climate change appear much worse than it is.

Exhibit A is the events surrounding the 1995 IPCC Working Group 1 report on the physical science of climate change. In short, it's claimed that one of the lead authors of a critical chapter of the report, Ben Santer, removed key sections that emphasized uncertainty and our inability to pin climate change on carbon dioxide, and inserted a statement that the evidence "now points to a discernible human influence on global climate" (IPCC, 1996, p. 439). These alterations, it is claimed, significantly shifted the tone of the report away from the agreed version, which allegedly included much less certainty about the human influence on climate. This claim was originally made by the late Fred Seitz, a distinguished retired physicist and former president of the National Academy of Sciences, at the time working for the Science and Environmental Policy Project, a think-tank funded by the fossil fuels industry. His article appeared as a 1996 *Wall Street Journal* op-ed but has been repeated many times in books (e.g., Crichton, 2004; Singer and Avery, 2008; Goreham, 2013) and online (e.g., World Climate Report, 1996; Dawson, 2012).

However, Ben Santer was merely implementing changes that the peer review process required. Dr. Seitz's allegations were based on confusion about whether the report had been finalized or not. It hadn't been, and the changes being made were entirely in accordance with IPCC procedures. The IPCC's chairman, and 40 of the scientists involved, wrote a letter to the *Wall Street Journal* in response, but it was unfortunately heavily edited. The original version is available in the archives of the University Corporation for Atmospheric Research, the organization that is in overall charge of the U.S. National Center for Atmospheric Research (Avery et al., 1996). A thorough discussion of the relevant events is given in Naomi Oreskes and Erik Conway's remarkable, and highly readable, 2010 book, *Merchants of Doubt*. Both sources make it clear that Dr. Seitz's widely repeated allegation of wrongdoing is a misrepresentation of what actually happened.

If the IPCC doesn't exaggerate, perhaps the news media are at fault? That's the view presented by many of the same publications we've looked at previously (Singer and Avery, 2008; Goreham, 2013) as well as numerous additional ones online (e.g., the Competitive Enterprise Institute, 2006; Adams, 2013). This myth comes in two variants: first, the news media are ignoring claims that contradict the conventional wisdom on climate change, and second, they're emphasizing the worst-case studies. Although it's impossible to check every single case, the first variant is often based on misrepresentation—the studies that supposedly run counter to mainstream thinking on climate change actually don't. We saw an example of this in question 17, where research on ice cores was presented as contradicting the idea that carbon dioxide contributed to global warming in the past. It happened again with a 2006 Competitive Enterprise Institute video advert, which selectively cited parts of two studies on the big ice sheets of Greenland and Antarctica. The studies' findings are actually rather different from the way they're portrayed in the video (see Jeff Masters's thorough discussion from 2006 at his Weather Underground blog)—so much so that the lead author of one of the studies issued a press release denouncing the use of his work in the advert.

The second version of this myth is that the news media exaggerate the effects of climate change by focusing on worst-case scenarios. Earlier, we came across one cultural norm for journalists, the norm of balance, and another seems to be that there's a strong preference for novel, unusual, and therefore attention-grabbing studies. These tend to be newsworthy, even if, or perhaps precisely because, they lie outside the mainstream of climate science. So it's reasonable to suggest that the media have a tendency to emphasize these outlier studies, and opinion polls show that the general public thinks the news media exaggerate the issue (Dugan, 2014). An example of media exaggeration often pointed to on websites is news coverage of a 2007 study, suggesting the Arctic could be ice free in summer by 2013. Thus, Mike Adams (2013) used a BBC News report on this study as evidence that the news media exaggerate. Reading beyond the dramatic headlines, the full BBC report contained many caveats from other scientists, making it clear that the new research did not represent the mainstream scientific view—but still, the headline is what caught most people's attention. Hollywood portrayals of climate change can be even worse: the 2004 movie *The Day After Tomorrow* portrayed an ice age descending on the Northern Hemisphere in a matter of hours, violating numerous laws of physics.

It's therefore understandable that people think that the media tend to exaggerate on the issue of climate change. Indeed, we'll see another example of this tendency in question 29. But the news media tend to exaggerate lots of things, not just the consequences of climate change. As we saw earlier, they also tend to exaggerate the level of disagreement between scientists, because of the "get both sides" cultural norm of the newsroom. So media exaggeration can cut in several different directions, and the "false balance" approach that the media often take when covering climate change actually works to lower public concern about climate change. And as we saw earlier, the evidence indicates that any IPCC bias works to minimize concern rather than stoke it up.

FURTHER READING

Adams, M. (2013). Global warming computer models collapse; Arctic ice sheets rapidly expand as planet plunges into global cooling. Posted to NaturalNews.com, September 10, 2013, available at http://www.natural news.com/041981_global_warming_computer_models_cooling.html#. Accessed May 23, 2015.

Allison, I., Bindoff, N. L., Bindschadler, R. A., Cox, P. M., De Noblet, N., England, M. H., . . ., and Weaver, A. J. (2009). *The Copenhagen Diagnosis*. The University of New South Wales Climate Change Research Centre, Sidney, Australia, 60. Available at http://www.copenhagen diagnosis.com/. Accessed May 22, 2015.

Avery, S. K., Try, P. D., Anthes, R. A., and Hallgren, R. E. (1996). Special insert—an open letter to Ben Santer. *UCAR Communications Quarterly*, Summer 1996, available at http://www.ucar.edu/communications/quarterly/summer96/insert.html. Accessed May 22, 2015.

Boykoff, M. T. (2011). *Who Speaks for the Climate?: Making Sense of Media Reporting on Climate Change*. Cambridge University Press.

Boykoff, M. T., and Boykoff, J. M. (2004). Balance as bias: global warming and the US prestige press. *Global Environmental Change, 14*(2), 125–136.

Broome, J. (2014). At the IPCC. Posted to the London Review of Books blog, May 8, 2014, available at http://www.lrb.co.uk/blog/2014/05/08/john-broome/at-the-ipcc/. Accessed May 21, 2015.

Brysse, K., Oreskes, N., O'Reilly, J., and Oppenheimer, M. (2013). Climate change prediction: erring on the side of least drama? *Global Environmental Change, 23*(1), 327–337.

Clark, P. (2014). Climate change report was watered down says senior economist. *Financial Times*, April 26.

CNN. (2012). Battleground America: Global Warming. Available at https://www.youtube.com/watch?v=gWT-EWKIR3M. Accessed May 22, 2015.

Competitive Enterprise Institute. (2006). Glaciers. Posted to YouTube, May 18, 2006, available at https://www.youtube.com/watch?v=Wq_Bj-av3g0. Accessed May 19, 2015.

Cook, J., Oreskes, N., Doran, P. T., Anderegg, W. R., Verheggen, B., Maibach, E. W., Carlton, S.J., Lewandowsky, S., Skuce, A.G., Green, S.A., Nuccitelli, D., Jacobs, P., Richardson, M., Winkler, B., Painting, R., and Rice, K. (2016). Consensus on consensus: a synthesis of consensus estimates on human-caused global warming. Environmental Research Letters, 11(4), 048002.

Crichton, M. (2004). *State of Fear*. HarperCollins, New York, New York.

Dawson, C. (2012). 16 years since the SAR where the "consensus" of the "anointed one" was created. The same 16 years during which there has been no global warming. Posted to the website of the Lord Monckton Foundation, December 20, 2012, available at http://www.lordmoncktonfoundation.com/blog/view/315/16_years_since_the_sar_where_the__consensus__of_the__anointed_one__was_created__the_same_16_years_during_which_there_has_been_no_global_warming__. Accessed May 22, 2015.

Dugan, A. (2014). Americans most likely to say global warming is exaggerated. Posted to the Gallup website, March 17, 2104, available at http://www.gallup.com/poll/167960/americans-likely-say-global-warming-exaggerated.aspx. Accessed May 24, 2015.

The Economist. (2014). Climate Change: Inside the Sausage Factory. May 10, 2014. Available at http://www.economist.com/news/science-and-technology/21601813-scientists-versus-diplomats-intergovernmental-panel-climate. Accessed May 21, 2015.

Freudenburg, W. R., and Muselli, V. (2010). Global warming estimates, media expectations, and the asymmetry of scientific challenge. *Global Environmental Change*, doi:10.1016/j.gloenvcha.2010.04.003.

Goreham, S. (2013). *The Mad, Mad, Mad World of Climatism: Mankind and Climate Change Mania*. New Lenox Books.

IPCC. (1996). Climate change 1995: the science of climate change—contribution of working group I to the second assessment report of the intergovernmental panel on climate change. Houghton, J.T., Meira Filho, L.G., Callander, B.A., Harris, N., Kattenberg, A., Maskell, K. (eds). Cambridge University Press, Cambridge, UK.

IPCC. (2007). Summary for Policymakers. In *Climate Change 2007: The Physical Science Basis. Contribution of Working Group I to the Fourth Assessment*

Report of the Intergovernmental Panel on Climate Change, S. Solomon, D. Qin, M. Manning, Z. Chen, M. Marquis, K. B. Averyt, M. Tignor, and H. L. Miller (eds.). Cambridge University Press, Cambridge, United Kingdom, and New York, NY, available at http://ipcc.ch/publications_and_data/ar4/wg1/en/spmsspm-projections-of.html. Accessed May 22, 2015.

Masters, J. (2006). Is carbon dioxide a pollutant? Posted to Weather Underground blog, May 24, 2006, available at http://www.wunderground.com/resources/climate/cei.asp. Accessed May 20, 2015.

Olson, R. (2009). *Don't Be Such a Scientist*. Island Press.

Oreskes, N., and Conway, E. M. (2010). *Merchants of Doubt: How a Handful of Scientists Obscured the Truth on Issues from Tobacco Smoke to Global Warming*. Bloomsbury Publishing USA.

Santer, B. D., Wigley, T. M. L., Barnett, T. P., and Anyamba, E. (1996). Detection of climate change and attribution of causes. Chapter 8 in Houghton, J. T., Meira Filho, L. G., Callendar, B. A., Harris, N., Kattenberg, A., and Maskell, K. (Eds.). (1996). *Climate Change 1995: The Science of Climate Change: Contribution of Working Group 1 to the Second Assessment Report of the Intergovernmental Panel on Climate Change*. Cambridge University Press, pp. 407–443.

Seitz, F. (1996). A major deception on global warming. *The Wall Street Journal*, June 12, available at http://stephenschneider.stanford.edu/Publications/PDF_Papers/WSJ_June12.pdf. Accessed May 22, 2015.

Singer, S. F., and Avery, D. T. (2008). *Unstoppable Global Warming: Every 1500 Years*. Updated and expanded edition. Rowman & Littlefield.

Stavins, R. (2014). Is the IPCC Government Approval Process Broken? Posted to blog An Economic View of the Environment, April 25, 2014, available at http://www.robertstavinsblog.org/2014/04/25/is-the-ipcc-government-approval-process-broken-2/. Accessed May 21, 2015.

World Climate Report. (1996). Bait and switch? IPCC pares down the consensus. *World Climate Report*, 1(19), available at http://www.worldclimatereport.com/archive/previous_issues/vol1/v1n19/feature.htm. Accessed May 22, 2015.

Q23. ARE CARBON DIOXIDE EMISSIONS ACIDIFYING THE OCEAN?

Answer: Observations show that the oceans are becoming more acidic, as carbon dioxide from the atmosphere dissolves in seawater. This is impacting ocean organisms which are particularly sensitive to ocean chemistry, such as shellfish and corals.

The Facts: In standard Western music, the scale has eight notes, A, B, C, D, E, F, and G. As you move up the scale, hitting progressively higher notes, eventually you reach G, the end. But keep going and you reach A again, the same note you started from, only eight notes (an octave) higher. On the piano keyboard, the center point of this system of notes is called middle C. Music can go up and down relative to this middle note, or relative to other notes on the scale. One note might be described as being lower than another, for example, as opposed to being less high than another. It's an intuitive way to talk about music.

In chemistry, the equivalent idea to the musical scale is the pH scale, which puts a number on exactly how acidic something is. It's an *inverse logarithmic* scale, which simply means that smaller numbers mean more acidity, and each whole-number change in pH is a 10-fold change in acidity (measured by the number of hydrogen ions). Lemon juice has a pH of about 2, while battery acid has a pH of 0, making it 100 times more acidic than lemon juice. A milder substance, like black coffee, has a pH of about 5, making it 1,000 times less acidic than lemon juice.

At the other end of the scale, high pH numbers show very alkaline (also called basic) substances. Milk of magnesia has a pH around 10, and drain cleaner has a pH around 14. Neutral substances, neither acidic nor alkaline, have a pH of 7, the pH scale's middle C. The salts dissolved in seawater make it slightly alkaline, weighing in with typical values for the surface ocean of around 8.1 or 8.2, although there are large variations from one part of the ocean to another.

However, measurements of ocean surface pH carried out since the late 1980s and early 1990s show that the numbers are dropping (IPCC, 2013, p. 12). Measurements from the Atlantic and Pacific Oceans find that pH has dropped from around 8.12 to a little over 8.06 in the past 25 years. The IPCC concluded in 2013, with high confidence, that global average surface ocean pH has dropped by 0.1 since the beginning of the Industrial Revolution (IPCC, 2013, p. 12). While 0.1 might not sound like a lot, remember that pH is a logarithmic scale. A pH drop of 0.1 is equivalent to a 30% increase in acidity. The oceans are becoming more acidic, less alkaline.

This phenomenon was anticipated at least as far back as the early 1980s by applying some fundamental principles of chemistry. When carbon dioxide dissolves in water, it forms carbonic acid. The large-scale buildup of carbon dioxide in the atmosphere should theoretically lead to at least some of the extra gas dissolving in the oceans.

Estimates of carbon dioxide emissions based on how much fossil fuel the world burns (see question 18), compared with how much is measured to be accumulating in the atmosphere (see question 14), show that we're adding significantly more carbon dioxide into the atmosphere than is actually staying there. So what's happening to the rest of it? While some is probably being used by plants as a result of the carbon dioxide fertilization effect (see question 21), some should be dissolving in seawater. The measurements of changing ocean pH show that this is exactly what's happening.

Scientists use the term "ocean acidification" to describe this phenomenon, because the surface ocean is becoming more acidic. It would be equally accurate, but a lot more cumbersome, to describe this as ocean de-alkalinization, much as people tend to describe one musical note as being lower than another, rather than less high. Despite the increasing acidity, the pH of seawater is currently still slightly alkaline. Nobody going for a swim in the ocean is going to dissolve. However, some organisms are acutely sensitive to changes in pH, particularly shellfish and corals. As pH drops, it becomes increasingly difficult for these *calcifying organisms* to pull calcium carbonate out of solution and into solid form. There is widespread scientific concern about the potential impacts of ocean acidification on coral reefs, shellfish, and shellfish fisheries. Costs may run into the billions of dollars per year. (For a short, readable account, see Winner, 2013.) Small changes in pH can, therefore, have potentially devastating consequences.

It's a focus on the pH changes being small that seems to be behind the claim that the term "ocean acidification" is misleading, an alarmist phrase meant to scare people. This argument is raised to varying degrees by Roy Spencer (2008) and Steve Goreham (2013), and in chapter 6 of the Heartland Institute's *Climate Change Reconsidered II: Biological Impacts*, by Craig Idso and co-authors (2014). These sources (among others) point to the small change in pH, along with the fact that ocean surface water, while acidifying, remains on the alkaline side of neutral. As we've seen, though, it's no more misleading to say the oceans are becoming more acidic than it is to say one musical note is lower than another, rather than less high. The objection to the term "acidification" is a misrepresentation of the situation that distracts from the serious impacts that changing pH is having on coral reefs.

"Ocean acidification" is therefore an accurate term. But is it alarmist, or unduly frightening? To bolster their case that it is, Idso et al.'s, 2014, report for the Heartland Institute points to a 2009 paper by Pieter Tans, a highly respected geochemist working for NOAA's Earth System Research Laboratory. Tans, they claim, demonstrates that atmospheric carbon dioxide will peak "well before 2100 and at only 500 ppm as compared to the 800 ppm predicted in one of IPCC's scenarios" (Idso et al., 2014, p. 822). Thus, the case is presented that the IPCC is exaggerating (see also question 22), based on Tan's work. These levels of atmospheric carbon dioxide translate into a drop in surface ocean pH of 0.2, compared with an almost 0.5 drop for the IPCC scenario referenced. This claim, including the same reference to Pieter Tans's 2009 paper, appears on the website CO2Science.org.

These documents seriously misrepresent Tans's work. In the original paper, Tans calculated two scenarios for fossil fuel use, atmospheric carbon dioxide levels and surface ocean pH. As discussed in question 19, it's a nearly impossible task to predict how humanity will or will not keep using fossil fuels in the future, so it's a good idea to consider a range of possible scenarios, bracketing best-case and worst-case scenarios, or answering more general "what-if" questions. Idso et al.'s Heartland Institute report and the CO2Science website mention only one scenario from Tans's paper, thereby making the difference with the IPCC reports look much larger than it really is. The second scenario in Tans's 2009 paper gives atmospheric carbon dioxide levels peaking at around 600 ppm, and ocean surface pH dropping by almost 0.3, well in line with IPCC projections (see Figure 3.3 for a comparison of graphs in Tans's original paper with the revised version from Idso et al.'s report). In an e-mail, Tans described the misrepresentation of his work thus: "In science this kind of deliberate misrepresentation is called fraud. These people only pretend to engage in a scientific discussion. Perhaps it is acceptable behavior in a court of law, where one can be totally one-sided and even knowingly wrong, but in the court of science this behavior merits contempt" (quoted with permission).

Misrepresentation of good science like this is an unfortunate way to make an argument. The reality is that "ocean acidification" is an accurate term, and if it's alarming then that's because the phenomenon it's describing is alarming. A board of scientists is currently in the process of deciding whether to officially designate the time since the Industrial Revolution as a new geological epoch. The reasoning is that human activity is so drastically changing the nature of the planet that the geologic record will retain the evidence for millions of years. We have markers of several major events in Earth's history, including the extinction of the dinosaurs. It's likely that the changes being wrought by humans are similar in scale. If so, a major contributor will be the effects of human activity on ocean chemistry, and the consequent impacts on marine life. The proposed name for this new epoch is the Anthropocene. (For more on the Anthropocene, see the Subcommission on Quaternary Stratigraphy's Working Group on the Anthropocene website; for a readable discussion, see Stromberg, 2013.)

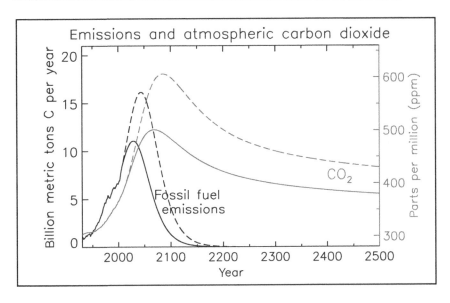

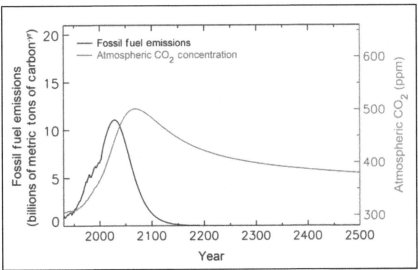

Figure 3.3 Comparison of diagrams from Pieter Tans's (2009, p. 32) original work (top) and as represented in the Heartland Institute's *Climate Change Reconsidered II* (Idso et al., 2014, p. 822) (bottom).

FURTHER READING

Goreham, S. (2013). *The Mad, Mad, Mad World of Climatism: Mankind and Climate Change Mania.* New Lenox Books.

Idso, C. D, Idso, S. B., Carter, R. M., and Singer, S. F. (Eds.). (2014). *Climate Change Reconsidered II: Biological Impacts*. The Heartland Institute, Chicago, IL, available at https://www.heartland.org/media-library/pdfs/CCR-IIb/Full-Report.pdf. Accessed May 23, 2015.

IPCC. (2013). Summary for Policymakers. In *Climate Change 2013: The Physical Science Basis. Contribution of Working Group I to the Fifth Assessment Report of the Intergovernmental Panel on Climate Change*, T. F. Stocker, D. Qin, G.-K. Plattner, M. Tignor, S. K. Allen, J. Boschung, A. Nauels, Y. Xia, V. Bex, and P. M. Midgley (eds.). Cambridge University Press, Cambridge, United Kingdom, and New York, NY.

Spencer, R. (2008). More carbon dioxide, please. Posted to the website of *National Review*, May 1, 2008, available at http://www.national review.com/article/224319/more-carbon-dioxide-please-roy-spencer. Accessed May 23, 2015.

Stromberg, J. (2013). What is the Anthropocene, and are we in it? *Smithsonian Magazine*, January 2013, available at http://www.smith sonianmag.com/science-nature/what-is-the-anthropocene-and-are-we-in-it-164801414/?no-ist. Accessed May 23, 2015.

Subcommission on Quaternary Stratigraphy. (2015). Working Group on the Anthropocene. Available at http://quaternary.stratigraphy.org/workinggroups/anthropocene/. Accessed May 22, 2015.

Tans, P. P. (2009). An accounting of the observed increase in oceanic and atmospheric CO_2 and an outlook for the future. *Oceanography*, *22*(4) 26–35.

Winner, C. (2013). The socioeconomic costs of ocean acidification. *Oceanus Magazine*, *50*(2), 74–76, available at http://www.whoi.edu/oceanus/flipbook/oceanus50n2/index.html. Accessed May 23, 2015.

Q24. HOW ARE PLANTS AND ANIMALS AFFECTED BY RAPID CLIMATE CHANGE?

Answer: Climate change will increase the risk of extinction for many species. Already, the rate of species extinction is 100 to 1,000 times higher than if humans weren't around. Some species, such as polar bears, are already showing signs of stress due to climate change.

The Facts: Climate change is posing a challenging new environment for many species. Some of the new environmental conditions can be adapted to, but eventually conditions cross a line: either the rate of change is too fast, or the new conditions defy adaptation. This is true not only for people but for plants and animals as well. Climate change and its associated effects, such as sea level rise and ocean acidification, are seen by scientists as posing serious threats to the natural world. As the 2014 IPCC report puts it, "A large fraction of both terrestrial and freshwater species faces increased extinction risk under projected climate change during and beyond the 21st century. . . . Extinction risk is increased under all [emissions] scenarios with risk increasing with both magnitude and rate of climate change" (IPCC, 2014, pp. 14–15).

While this is the bottom line, there are nuances to this basic story. As we've seen in previous questions, it's important to understand these nuances, not only for a proper understanding of the science but also to see how those voices that are dismissive of climate change use them to construct their arguments. A first important nuance is that extinction is a natural process that is now being helped along by humans at an accelerating rate. A similar idea is that the greenhouse effect is a natural phenomenon, but human additions of greenhouse gases to the atmosphere are giving it an unnatural boost. With extinctions, species that are unable to adapt to changing conditions die out. Changing conditions can include loss of habitat, the arrival of upstart new competitors, or changing climate. These kinds of events are constantly going on, giving rise to a natural "background rate" of extinctions, but every so often changes occur extraordinarily quickly, and many species go extinct. The fossil record shows when these *mass extinctions* happened, and how severe they were. The mass extinction at the end of geology's Cretaceous period, 65 million years ago, wiped out not only the dinosaurs but an estimated 75% of all species on the planet. While there's ongoing debate about what killed the dinosaurs—growing evidence now points to a series of massive volcanic eruptions, rather than the impact of an asteroid—it's widely accepted that we are now undergoing a new mass extinction event, the sixth in Earth's history, with extinction rates 100 to 1,000 times higher than the background rate (see, e.g., the Millennium Ecosystem Assessment, 2005; Barnosky et al., 2011; de Vos et al., 2015). There's also widespread agreement about the cause: humans. (For a readable account, see Elizabeth Kolbert's 2014 book, *The Sixth Extinction*.)

Many aspects of human behavior contribute to this sixth mass extinction. Some are things we've been doing for thousands of years, such as the development of agriculture; others are more recent, such as tropical deforestation, or global travel allowing aggressive invasive species and infectious diseases to hitch a free ride. However, the scale of human impacts on the natural world has grown with our technological capacity, especially since the Industrial Revolution allowed us to harness the energy stored in fossil fuels. And as we've seen in earlier chapters, the megavolcano that is human burning of those fossil fuels is causing a massive increase in concentrations of atmospheric carbon dioxide. This causes two effects with potentially very large consequences for plants and animals: ocean acidification and climate change. These are only a part of the story of human impact on the natural world, but they have the potential to be a large part.

We looked at ocean acidification in question 23, but how might climate change contribute to species extinction? Because different species have different tolerances and preferences for warm or cold, wet or dry conditions, climate change is likely to prompt migrations as the planet warms, and different places become wetter or drier. This has happened before in response to climate changes in Earth's past—in fact, fossils of particular plant and animal species are used as indicators of how climate has changed over time in specific locations, for example, tropical plant fossils being found in the Arctic. Clearly, plants and animals have moved in response to climate change in the past. Why shouldn't they do so again?

There are at least two reasons why it might be more difficult this time. First, the pace of climate change could be significantly faster than species have experienced in the past, potentially outstripping their ability to relocate. Just how fast the climate will change isn't known for sure, because it depends on how fast we burn fossil fuels, and on exactly how sensitive the climate is to increasing carbon dioxide. But the faster the climate changes, the smaller the number of species able to migrate quickly enough in response.

Second, previous migrations happened without the other effects of humans on the natural world. Today, a remarkable network of roads, fences, cities, and farms chops up the landscape into many pieces. Crossing these artificial barriers may prove difficult or impossible for some species.

Other species, however, could benefit from climate change. For example, there's evidence that the pine bark beetle has been thriving in the forests of the western United States. As higher temperatures and drought stress the trees, their defenses weaken, making them more vulnerable to beetle infestations, killing huge numbers of trees and increasing the fuel available for wildfires. Climate change has been good for the pine bark beetle, but not so good for the pines—or for wildfire fighters, or anyone who owns property near the affected forests.

There's considerable nuance, then, to the picture of climate change impacts on plants and animals, but there is widespread agreement among scientists that climate change poses a serious threat. If we're lucky, things might not turn out as badly as the IPCC anticipates—but recall from question 22 that the IPCC has a tendency to underestimate climate impacts. It's the nuances, though, that allow some authors to claim that plants and animals can adapt to climate change. Those nuances allow the construction of arguments that are persuasive on the surface, but with a little probing are exposed as being misleading. To see how the nuances can be used in this way, it's instructive to look in detail at a case study of one particular species: polar bears.

Polar bears have featured prominently in the conversation about climate change, appearing in Al Gore's 2007 movie *An Inconvenient Truth*, and in what sometimes seems like every news report on global warming. Images of polar bears on melting sea ice have become iconic, easy ways to communicate the threat of climate change. They've received so much attention for three reasons: they're beautiful animals, the climate change impacts are obvious, and they were listed as a threatened species in 2008 by the U.S. Fish and Wildlife Service, thus bringing a policy dimension into play.

Polar bears were listed as threatened because of their dependence on Arctic sea ice, which they use as a platform from which to hunt their main prey, ringed seals. The high fat content of seals is an essential part of the polar bear diet, which requires huge numbers of calories to sustain these large animals, correctly described as the largest land carnivores. As we saw in question 1, the sea ice is in dramatic decline. Logically, therefore, one might expect significant impacts on numbers of polar bear.

However, it's surprisingly difficult to say with certainty that polar bear populations as a whole are in decline. The International Union for the Conservation of Nature's (IUCN) Polar Bear Specialist Group identifies 19 different subpopulations of polar bears across the Arctic, of which 9 were identified as "data deficient" as of 2014—meaning that for almost half of the subpopulations, we simply don't have enough data to say whether they're growing, shrinking, or remaining stable (IUCN, 2015). Of the other 10 subpopulations, 3 are declining, 1 is increasing, and 6 are stable. So the data are scarce for many parts of the Arctic, and for the places we do know about, there's a mixed picture.

Where populations are declining, however, scientists are certain of the cause: melting sea ice. Summarizing several recent studies, the IPCC's 2014 assessment stated: "Of the two subpopulations where data are adequate for assessing abundance effects, it is *very likely* that the recorded population declines are caused by reductions in sea ice extent" (Larsen et al., 2014, p. 1570, emphasis in original). Note that the IPCC lists only two declining populations against the IUCN's three, because the IUCN report is more recent. Furthermore, studies are also show-ing impacts on overall polar bear population health: bears are getting thinner and weaker, and having fewer cubs. The total numbers of bears may not yet be showing reductions outside of two or three subpopula-tions, but the signs do not bode well for the future. The 2014 IPCC report again: "Declining ice is causing lower body condition, reduced individual growth rates, lower fasting endurance, lower reproductive rates, and lower survival (*high confidence*). . . . Condition is a precursor to demographic change (*very high confidence*)" (Larsen et al., 2014, p. 1576, emphasis in original).

It's commonly argued by those dismissive of climate change, however, that because polar bear populations have not yet shown steep decline, pro-jected future declines in sea ice will have no effect. This seems to be the reasoning behind Craig Idso and co-authors' 2014 report for the Heart-land Institute, *Climate Change Reconsidered II: Biological Impacts*. This is a little like jumping out of a 10th-floor window and, halfway down, saying "So far, so good!" The available evidence indicates that declines in sea ice are moving polar bear populations into conditions of ever-greater stress. So far, that stress is appearing as declining overall health of the bears, but eventually, it will manifest as declining numbers.

Other sources suggest that polar bear numbers might actually be increasing. Bjorn Lomborg, in his book *Cool It*, does this by relying on population estimates from the 1960s; Steve Goreham (2013, p. 137) does it by pointing to a 2007 finding of population increase since 1970 in one subpopulation, in the Northern Beaufort Sea region of the Arctic. Both of these claims are problematic, however. First, rigorous polar bear measure-ment techniques were not introduced until the 1970s and were not widely implemented until the 1980s, so any statements about polar bear popu-lations changing with reference to the 1960s, like Lomborg's, should be treated with appropriate skepticism. Second, extrapolating from a single growing subpopulation to the entire polar bear population, as Goreham does, is misguided. As the IUCN report mentioned earlier makes clear, the data are patchy and currently show three declining subpopulations, and only one increasing. Looking at one subpopulation is not necessarily informative about the others. Furthermore, it's worth pointing out that Goreham's source is a report by the eminent polar bear biologist Ian Stir-ling and co-authors. It ends with a discussion of future trends, emphasiz-ing concerns over declining sea ice (Stirling et al., 2007, p. 14). As with arguments we've examined in previous questions, the case that polar bear populations are increasing is sometimes based on incomplete references to careful, rigorous scientific studies.

Other variants of myths relating to polar bears include the idea that they have adapted to warm conditions in the past, so they can adapt this time (see, e.g., Goreham, 2013, p. 137). A key line of reasoning here is that polar bears have survived through glacial and interglacial cycles, demonstrating their resilience to climate change (this is argued, for example, by Idso et al., 2014). However, as we saw in question 9, current levels of atmospheric carbon dioxide are substantially higher than the natural glacial–interglacial cycles have seen. Warming in the 21st century may well take the Arctic beyond any warming that polar bears have experienced before. This is why the IPCC's 2014 report states: "According to model projections, within 50 to 70 years, loss of hunting habitats may lead to elimination of polar bears from seasonally ice-covered areas, where two-thirds of their world population currently live" (Larsen et al., 2014, p. 1596). And again, crucially, the rate of change over the next century is expected to be faster than climate change experienced over past glacial–interglacial cycles.

As polar bears are forced onto land to forage for whatever food they can find, people are sighting them more often. This has led to the misperception that there are more bears (U.S. Fish and Wildlife Service, 2006). It has also led to claims that polar bears will be able to adapt to the loss of sea ice by eating off the land, like the much smaller brown bears do. This is the argument proposed by Burnett (2006), but several recent studies have shown that the food resources available on land lack the calories to sustain polar bears, even if they were well adapted to eating them (they aren't), and didn't face competition from animals already using these resources (they do). (A 2015 paper by Karyn Rode and co-authors gives a useful overview; a user-friendly account is provided by Mathiesen, 2015.) Thus, glib claims that polar bears can simply move onto land are not well supported by the latest science.

The picture of climate change impacts on polar bears is highly nuanced, and the nuances are easily utilized for the purposes of building a persuasive, if misleading, argument. The same is true for climate change impacts on plants and animals as a whole. A valuable take-home message is that it's always worth checking the details of any source being cited in discussions about climate change.

FURTHER READING

Barnosky, A. D., Matzke, N., Tomiya, S., Wogan, G. O., Swartz, B., Quental, T. B., Marshall, C., McGuire, J. L., Lindsey, E. L., Maguire, K. C., Mersey, B., and Ferrer, E. A. (2011). Has the Earth/'s sixth mass extinction already arrived? *Nature, 471*(7336), 51–57.

Burnett, H. S. (2006). Polar bears on thin ice, not really! National Center for Policy Analysis Brief Analysis No. 551, available at https://www.heartland.org/sites/all/modules/custom/heartland_migration/files/pdfs/19960.pdf. Accessed May 25, 2015.

De Vos, J. M., Joppa, L. N., Gittleman, J. L., Stephens, P. R., and Pimm, S. L. (2015). Estimating the normal background rate of species extinction. *Conservation Biology*, 29, 452–462. doi:10.1111/cobi.12380.

Goreham, S. (2013). *The Mad, Mad, Mad World of Climatism: Mankind and Climate Change Mania*. New Lenox Books.

Idso, C. D, Idso, S. B., Carter, R. M., and Singer, S. F. (Eds.). (2014). *Climate Change Reconsidered II: Biological Impacts*. The Heartland Institute, Chicago, IL, available at https://www.heartland.org/media-library/pdfs/CCR-IIb/Full-Report.pdf. Accessed May 23, 2015.

IPCC. (2014). Summary for Policymakers. In *Climate Change 2014: Impacts, Adaptation, and Vulnerability. Part A: Global and Sectoral Aspects. Contribution of Working Group II to the Fifth Assessment Report of the Intergovernmental Panel on Climate Change*, C. B. Field, V. R. Barros, D. J. Dokken, K. J. Mach, M. D. Mastrandrea, T. E. Bilir, M. Chatterjee, K. L. Ebi, Y. O. Estrada, R. C. Genova, B. Girma, E. S. Kissel, A. N. Levy, S. MacCracken, P. R. Mastrandrea, and L. L. White (eds.). Cambridge University Press, Cambridge, United Kingdom, and New York, NY, pp. 1–32, available at http://ipcc-wg2.gov/AR5/images/uploads/WGIIAR5-SPM_FINAL.pdf. Accessed May 25, 2015.

IUCN. (2015). Summary of polar bear population status per 2014. Posted to the IUCN Polar Bear Specialist Group website, January 24, 2015, available at http://pbsg.npolar.no/en/status/status-table.html. Accessed May 25, 2015.

Kolbert, E. (2014). *The Sixth Extinction: An Unnatural History*. A&C Black.

Larsen, J. N., Anisimov, O. A., Constable, A., Hollowed, A. B., Maynard, N., Prestrud, P., Prowse, T. D., and Stone, J. M. R. (2014). Polar Regions. In *Climate Change 2014: Impacts, Adaptation, and Vulnerability. Part B: Regional Aspects. Contribution of Working Group II to the Fifth Assessment Report of the Intergovernmental Panel on Climate Change*, V. R. Barros, C. B. Field, D. J. Dokken, M. D. Mastrandrea, K. J. Mach, T. E. Bilir, M. Chatterjee, K. L. Ebi, Y. O. Estrada, R. C. Genova, B. Girma, E. S. Kissel, A. N. Levy, S. MacCracken, P. R. Mastrandrea, and L. L. White (eds.). Cambridge University Press, Cambridge, United Kingdom, and New York, NY, pp. 1567–1612, available at http://ipcc-wg2.gov/AR5/images/uploads/WGIIAR5-Chap28_FINAL.pdf. Accessed May 25, 2015.

Lomborg, B. (2007). *Cool It: The Skeptical Environmentalist's Guide to Global Warming*. Vintage Books.

Mathiesen, K. (2015). Polar bears face starvation as unlikely to adapt to a land-based diet, says report. Posted to *The Guardian* website, April 1, 2015, available at http://www.theguardian.com/environment/2015/apr/01/polar-bears-face-starvation-unlikely-adapt-to-land-based-diet. Accessed May 25, 2015.

Millennium Ecosystem Assessment. (2005). *Ecosystems and Human Well-Being: Biodiversity Synthesis*. World Resources Institute, Washington, DC, available at http://www.millenniumassessment.org/documents/document.354.aspx.pdf. Accessed November 22, 2015.

Rode, K. D., Robbins, C. T., Nelson, L., and Amstrup, S. C. (2015). Can polar bears use terrestrial foods to offset lost ice-based hunting opportunities? *Frontiers in Ecology and the Environment, 13*(3): 138–145.

Stirling, I., McDonald, T. L., Richardson, E. S., and Regehr, E. V. (2007). *Polar Bear Population Status in the Northern Beaufort Sea*. U.S. Department of the Interior, U.S. Geological Survey, available at http://www.usgs.gov/newsroom/special/polar_bears/docs/USGS_PolarBear_Stirling_NBeaufortSea.pdf. Accessed May 25, 2015.

U.S. Fish and Wildlife Service. (2006). Frequently asked questions: U.S. Fish and Wildlife Service proposal to list polar bears as threatened species. Posted to U.S. Fish and Wildlife Service website, December 27, 2006, available at http://www.doi.gov/news/archive/06_News_Releases/061227faq.html. Accessed May 25, 2015.

Q25. HOW IS CLIMATE CHANGE INFLUENCING EXTREME WEATHER?

Answer: Climate change is making the atmosphere generally warmer and more humid. Because all weather occurs in this context, climate change is contributing to all extreme weather events to some degree; heat waves and intense downpours are among the extreme weather events that have shown an increase in recent decades.

The Facts: "Extreme weather" is a catch-all term that includes tornadoes, intense rainfall, heat waves, and hurricanes. Some of these show a clear change over time, plausibly showing the handiwork of climate change, but for others, trends are harder to detect.

Whenever there's an extreme weather event, reporters often ask climate scientists if it was caused by climate change. But Kevin Trenberth, a distinguished senior scientist at the National Center for Atmospheric Research, says that's the wrong question (see Trenberth, 2012, for a technical, but readable, discussion). As noted in question 7, the ever-thickening blanket of greenhouse gases in the Earth's atmosphere is adding over four atomic bombs' worth of heat to the climate system every second. This is making the atmosphere in general warmer (questions 4 and 5) and more humid (question 20). Because weather is happening in warmer, more humid conditions, Trenberth points out, all extreme weather events are being affected to some degree. The question is therefore not "Was any given extreme event caused or not caused by climate change?" Instead, it's "How much did climate change contribute?"

This brings the issue back to the differences between weather and climate, climate variability and climate change that were examined in questions 6 and 7. Recall that weather and climate can be compared to a game of pinball. Weather is the pinball, bouncing around unpredictably from place to place, while climate is the pinball machine within which the bouncing occurs. Climate change is the equivalent of tilting the machine so that the pinball bounces more toward one end—but it's random enough that it still bounces to the other end from time to time. When the random bounces coincide with the direction the machine is being tilted, the ball can hit the end of the machine hard. In the same way, when the natural variability of the climate system lines up with the warming effects of climate change, records get broken, giving us new extremes of weather, and making the old extremes more commonplace.

One of the more challenging issues surrounding extreme weather events is the fact that they are, by definition, rare, so it can take a long time to gather conclusive evidence that they're increasing. As a result, statistics on extreme weather events can easily be constructed in such a way as to show that they're not increasing. From this, it's easy to conclude that global warming has no effect on them, but that would be a mistake. It's like watching the pinball game for just a few moments, noticing the ball bouncing around at the opposite end from which the machine was being tilted, and concluding that gravity doesn't cause the ball to be pulled in the direction of the tilt. That's a mistake because the game simply wasn't watched for a sufficient amount of time. Watching for a longer period would reveal that the ball actually does bounce more toward one end when the machine is tilted. Similarly, with extreme weather events, it can take time for a pattern to emerge, because extremes don't happen all that often. As a result, for some kinds of extreme weather, there's no clear evidence of an increase—yet. (Stefan Rahmstorf posted a readable explanation of this idea to the climate science blog RealClimate.org in 2014, and the National Center for Atmospheric Research maintains a web page with several excellent resources on extreme weather and climate change.)

However, some extreme weather events are better observed than others. For example, because tornadoes are short lived and affect only a relatively small swath of countryside, they're notoriously difficult to observe. By contrast, information on how temperature and rainfall have changed is much more extensive and easy to track, with the exception of a few data-scarce blind spots in certain parts of the world such as Africa. For the well-observed weather extremes, scientists have already compiled extensive evidence that they're increasing. Worldwide, according to the IPCC's 2013 report, the number of warm days and nights seems to be going up, and there's good evidence that heat waves are becoming more common in Europe, Asia, and Australia. Intense rain events seem to be happening more often everywhere, though there's better evidence in North America and Europe than for the rest of the world. The less well-observed extreme weather events haven't shown the same kinds of patterns: there is no evidence of an increase in tornado intensity, for example. But as Kevin Trenberth suggested, this doesn't mean that climate change isn't having an effect. It's just that we can't see it yet.

Perhaps the best illustration of this idea is what's happening with tropical cyclones, the severe storms known as hurricanes in the Atlantic Ocean, and typhoons in the Pacific. One important contributor to the strength of tropical cyclones is warm ocean water. As the warm water evaporates from the ocean and condenses in the atmosphere, huge amounts of latent heat are released, fueling the storm (and, incidentally, the evaporation cools the ocean, so energy has been transferred from the ocean to the atmosphere). As global warming continues, adding heat to the oceans and raising their temperature, most scientists expect that tropical cyclones will become more intense but less frequent (see, e.g., Knutson et al., 2010).

However, warm water is by no means the only thing that affects the intensity of tropical cyclones, just as the tilt of the pinball machine is not the only thing that affects where the ball ends up. Furthermore, it's difficult to measure in detail the characteristics of the storms without flying a plane through them, and this is done rarely for the Atlantic, and incredibly rarely everywhere else. Overall, the available data are simply not detailed enough, covering a period long enough, to say much with certainty. The only ocean basin that so far shows a clear and unequivocal increase in storm strength is the North Atlantic. For other ocean basins, increases in storm strength are not obviously different from natural variability, so despite the clear signal from the North Atlantic, the global average picture remains murky. While recent years have seen what may have been the most powerful storm on record hit the Philippines, 2013's Typhoon Haiyan, it's not clear that this exceptionally strong storm marks part of a trend.

But many scientists emphasize that the absence of clear trends probably says more about the holes in our measurements than it does about the intensity of tropical cyclones. Scientific understanding of the underpinnings of tropical cyclones indicates that they should get stronger eventually. Because the buildup of greenhouse gases is unquestionably adding heat to the climate system, that extra energy has to show up somewhere, and more powerful tropical storms are one likely outlet. It's a little bit like switching on an electric kettle. The water may not have boiled yet, but it will. The questions being debated by scientists about tropical cyclones focus not so much on whether storms will get stronger, but on when, and by how much.

Some of the work that dismisses the seriousness of climate change tends to miss these nuances. There's often a focus on the extreme weather events where increases are not as easily documented, such as tornadoes or tropical cyclones, while ignoring those that have increased, such as heat waves or intense rain events. Fred Singer and Dennis Avery (2008), for example, dismiss these events when they write: "By itself . . . moderate rainfall increase poses little danger" (p. 208). In reality, however, the northeastern United States has experienced a 71% rise in the frequency of the top 1% of rain events since 1958, while in the Midwest these events occur 37% more often, according to the U.S. National Climate Assessment (Melillo et al., 2014). The Great Plains have seen a 16% increase, and as of this writing, torrential rains in Texas and Oklahoma had just caused the deaths of at least 5 people in floods, with 12 more missing, according to *The New York Times* (Gaskill and Wines, 2015).

Other sources use inappropriate measurements of extreme weather to argue that there has been no increase in extreme weather in specific locations, typically the United States. For example, Michael Crichton's 2004 novel *State of Fear* includes a graph showing the number of hurricanes hitting the United States from 1900 to 2004. Because there is no clear trend, the author uses these data to claim that there has been no increase in extreme weather. However, it's not the number of hurricanes *in total* that matters but the number of *intense* hurricanes: one estimate suggests that the most intense 24% of hurricanes making landfall in the United States have historically accounted for 85% of the damage (Pielke et al., 2008). And, as noted earlier, while tropical cyclones at the global average level have not (yet) clearly increased in intensity, in the North Atlantic, they most definitely have. When this is taken into account, it becomes evident that there has, in fact, been an increase in the amount of energy unleashed on the U.S. coastline by hurricanes, according to the U.S. National Climate Assessment (Melillo et al., 2014). Crichton's observation that the number of hurricanes hitting the United States has not gone up over time is accurate but irrelevant.

While most of the sources dismissive of climate change focus on what hasn't happened, instead of what has, this continues to miss the point. All storms are taking place in the context of an atmosphere made warmer and more humid by anthropogenic climate change. We're already seeing the effects for some extreme weather events, like intense rain. For others, like tropical cyclones, scientists agree that it's not a case of if, but when.

FURTHER READING

Crichton, M. (2004). *State of Fear*. HarperCollins, New York, New York.

Gaskill, M., and Wines, M. (2015). At least 5 are killed and 12 are missing as storms ravage Texas and Oklahoma. *The New York Times*, May 25, 2015, available at http://www.nytimes.com/2015/05/26/us/texas-and-oklahoma-ravaged-by-severe-weather-and-flooding.html?_r=0. Accessed May 26, 2015.

IPCC. (2013). Summary for Policymakers. In *Climate Change 2013: The Physical Science Basis. Contribution of Working Group I to the Fifth Assessment Report of the Intergovernmental Panel on Climate Change*, T. F. Stocker, D. Qin, G.-K. Plattner, M. Tignor, S. K. Allen, J. Boschung, A. Nauels, Y. Xia, V. Bex, and P. M. Midgley (eds.). Cambridge University Press, Cambridge, United Kingdom, and New York, NY, available at http://www.climatechange2013.org/images/report/WG1AR5_SPM_FINAL.pdf. Accessed May 20, 2015.

Knutson, T.R., McBride, J.L., Chan, J., Emanuel, K., Holland, G., Landsea, C., . . ., and Sugi, M. (2010). Tropical cyclones and climate change. *Nature Geoscience*, 3(3), 157–163.

Melillo, Jerry M., Terese (T. C.) Richmond, and Gary W. Yohe (Eds.). (2014). *Climate Change Impacts in the United States: The Third National Climate Assessment*. U.S. Global Change Research Program, 841 pp. doi:10.7930/J0Z31WJ2. Available at http://nca2014.globalchange.gov/. Accessed May 20, 2015.

National Center for Atmospheric Research. (2015). In Depth: Weather on Steroids. Available at https://www2.ucar.edu/atmosnews/attribution. Accessed May 26, 2015.

Pielke, Jr., R. A., Gratz, J., Landsea, C. W., Collins, D., Saunders, M., and Musulin, R. (2008). Normalized hurricane damages in the United States: 1900–2005. *Natural Hazards Review, 9,* 29–42.

Rahmstorf, S. (2014). The most common fallacy in discussing extreme weather events. Posted to RealClimate.org, March 25, 2014, available at http://www.realclimate.org/index.php/archives/2014/03/the-most-common-fallacy-in-discussing-extreme-weather-events/. Accessed May 26, 2015.

Seneviratne, S. I., Nicholls, N., Easterling, D., Goodess, C. M., Kanae, S., Kossin, J., Luo, Y., Marengo, J., McInnes, K., Rahimi, M., Reichstein, M., Sorteberg, A., Vera, C., and Zhang, X. (2012). Changes in Climate Extremes and Their Impacts on the Natural Physical Environment. In *Managing the Risks of Extreme Events and Disasters to Advance Climate Change Adaptation,* C. B. Field, V. Barros, T. F. Stocker, D. Qin, D. J. Dokken, K. L. Ebi, M. D. Mastrandrea, K. J. Mach, G.-K. Plattner, S. K. Allen, M. Tignor, and P. M. Midgley (eds.). *A Special Report of Working Groups I and II of the Intergovernmental Panel on Climate Change* (IPCC). Cambridge University Press, Cambridge, United Kingdom, and New York, NY, pp. 109–230, available at http://www.ipcc-wg2.gov/SREX/images/uploads/SREX-All_FINAL.pdf. Accessed May 26, 2015.

Singer, S. F., and Avery, D. T. (2008). *Unstoppable Global Warming: Every 1500 Years.* Updated and expanded edition. Rowman & Littlefield.

Trenberth, K. E. (2012). Framing the way to relate climate extremes to climate change. *Climatic Change, 115,* 283–290.

4

Scientific Consensus on
Climate Change

Q26. WHAT PERCENTAGE OF CLIMATE
SCIENTISTS AGREE THAT HUMANS ARE
CAUSING GLOBAL WARMING?

Answer: Multiple assessments of the views of the expert climate science community, using different methods, find around 97% agreement that the world is warming because of human emissions of greenhouse gases.

The Facts: Imagine this: you're driving your car one day, when you hear a strange sound coming from the engine. Concerned, you take it to a mechanic. She looks it over and tells you there's a serious problem, but if you fix it now it shouldn't cost too much, and the car will run better. You're not convinced that the work is necessary, so you take the car to a different shop. The mechanic gives you the same diagnosis. Try another place. Same story. Running out of options, you see a motorboat repair place and try there—after all, an engine is an engine, isn't it? The mechanic there isn't familiar with your make of car but doesn't see anything seriously wrong. Reassured, you drive home and decide to take one last look at the engine yourself. A passerby sees you at work and offers to help, telling you he's a surgeon. "The human body is a lot like an engine," he says, and, after a quick look, tells you the car is fine. Who do you think is most likely to be right: the three auto mechanics, or the boat engine guy and the surgeon?

This scenario helps shed light on the concept of a *scientific consensus*. We've mentioned this idea before, in questions 8 and 11, but in this question and the next one, we'll examine it more thoroughly. A scientific consensus forms when people with relevant expertise independently assess the available evidence and draw the same conclusions. In the car-repair example, the scientific consensus is that your car needs work. That's the conclusion of the experts, each looking at the evidence (your car) independently. The assessments of people with expertise in other areas don't change that fact. In the case of climate change, the situation is similar, but you'd need to take your car to 100 specialist mechanics and have 97 of them independently tell you the same thing.

A point worth emphasizing about a scientific consensus is that it's not the same as people simply agreeing. Instead, it's about independent assessments of the evidence showing the same thing. The car mechanics aren't getting together and agreeing about your engine; they're each looking at it independently of the others and using their training, skill, and experience to diagnose the problem and come up with a solution. The processes of science allow the same thing to happen with issues like climate change. In fact, scientists don't much like agreeing with each other, and by training, culture, and temperament tend to be highly critical. They (we) love to pick apart other people's findings and often think they can do something that little bit better than everyone else, as the example of Richard Muller's Berkeley Earth project, from question 4, shows.

This picking apart is formalized in peer review, the process that ruthlessly weeds out mistakes over time (questions 8 and 11). Peer review is conducted by experts in the field and happens before research is published, preventing flawed research from being published, like a bouncer at a nightclub keeping out the obvious troublemakers. Crucially, though, peer review also happens *after* research is published. Reviewers are only human, and incorrect papers do get published. But other scientists then look at the published work and try to challenge it. As a result, the peer-reviewed literature can contain examples of research coming to opposing conclusions, as one paper is disputed by another. What matters to the formation of a scientific consensus is how this plays out over time. How many new studies, bringing new evidence and analysis to the debate, confirm one side versus the other of a scientific question? There's no hard-and-fast rule, but once the weight of studies supporting a particular view becomes overwhelming, most scientists would agree that it's probably right. That's a scientific consensus. Once overwhelming agreement on a scientific question is reached, the scientific community moves on and attacks a different problem. (Science historian Naomi Oreskes has an excellent 2007 essay on scientific consensus, see Further Reading.)

This is very much what has happened with regard to anthropogenic climate change. Multiple lines of evidence tell us the world is warming: melting Arctic sea ice, melting glaciers and ice sheets, and the surface and satellite temperature records. Multiple lines of evidence tell us this is happening because of human burning of fossil fuels: the physics of greenhouse gases, the changes in carbon isotopes, the patterns of warming consistent with greenhouse warming, and the inability of models to simulate what has happened without including human effects. The recent slight dimming of the Sun allows us to rule it out as an alternative cause, as do observed patterns opposite to those expected if the Sun was the culprit. The dust has settled on the basic points of anthropogenic climate change: the world is warming because of human emissions of greenhouse gases, and will continue to do so, with potentially serious consequences, as long as the energy imbalance caused by the extra greenhouse gases remains. Scientists are no longer debating these issues but have moved on to others: not whether global warming will strengthen tropical cyclones, for example, but by how much (question 25). There's no shortage of scientific debate, but not on the basic points.

How do we know this? One way to judge is to attend scientific conferences like the American Geophysical Union's meeting each December in San Francisco. This is the largest gathering of climate scientists in the world, and it's clear from the conference program, from attending the presentations, and simply from talking to other scientists, that there's nothing of interest left to be said about whether the world is warming up, or whether it's happening because of human emissions of greenhouse gases. These questions have been answered. Others are being asked.

This is no more than anecdotal evidence, though. A more rigorous approach is to survey scientists on what they think. Not just any scientists, though. Just as the surgeon's and the motorboat mechanic's views on car repair are a lot less relevant than those of the automobile engine specialists, so the views of climate scientists are more relevant than those of, say, geneticists or aerospace engineers. So the most interesting surveys of the scientific community are those that specifically identified the level of agreement among scientists who are researching and publishing research on climate change. One survey found that actively publishing climate scientists overwhelmingly agree that the world is warming due to human emissions of greenhouse gases: of 77 surveyed, 97% agreed (Doran and Zimmerman, 2009). An analysis of scientists who have signed public statements about climate change found that among the 200 most published scientists on the topic of global warming, 97.5% agreed with the consensus position on human-caused global warming (Anderegg et al., 2010). Another survey, of American Meteorological Society members, found that 93% of 124 actively publishing climate scientists were convinced that the world was warming primarily because of human activity (Stenhouse et al., 2014).

These are the opinions of scientists with relevant expertise. Another way to look at scientific consensus is to see what's in the peer-reviewed literature. A groundbreaking study by science historian Naomi Oreskes (2004, 2007) looked at 928 peer-reviewed articles on global climate change and found that none of them contradicted the fundamental tenets. Other studies, using different methods, have confirmed this general conclusion: the scientific consensus on the basic points of anthropogenic climate change is overwhelming. For example, a multiauthor team led by John Cook (this book's co-author) found that 97% of over 4,000 scientific papers that took a position on anthropogenic climate change agreed with the basic consensus (Cook et al., 2013).

While studies of the scientific view on climate change find a strong consensus, public opinion is much more confused. According to survey results from the polling company Gallup, large minorities of Americans say scientists are unsure whether global warming is even happening. Percentages answering in this way have hovered around the high 20s to low 30s since 2001 (Jones and Saad, 2014). A 2015 poll by the Yale Project on Climate Change Communication found that only about 10% of those surveyed recognized that over 90% of climate scientists think global warming is happening and caused by humans (Leiserowitz et al., 2015).

This "consensus gap" between scientists and the public probably owes something to misleading articles in the popular media. One myth about the scientific consensus is that it doesn't exist. This claim is false, as we've seen, but there are at least three different arguments made to support it. First, there's the idea that thousands of scientists disagree with the consensus position. Perhaps the best-known example is called the Global Warming Petition Project, commonly known as the Oregon Petition, organized by the Oregon Institute of Science and Medicine. The petition, which disputes the consensus position of warming due to greenhouse gases, has been signed by over 31,000 people, according to its website. While the petition is sometimes claimed to represent the views of scientists (see Goreham, 2013, p. 142), only about 1.6% have any education at all, college degree or more, in fields directly relevant to climate change, according to numbers on the petition's website. A similar document is presented by Marc Morano at the website ClimateDepot.com, but it, too, includes very few scientists with relevant expertise (Brigham Young University's Barry Bickmore has an interesting discussion of this list on his blog). These are the voices of the surgeon and the boat expert saying your car is fine, rather than the voices of the auto mechanics telling you it isn't.

If petitions constitute the first line of argument that there is no consensus, newspaper op-eds and similar public statements by individual scientists constitute the second. Princeton physicist William Happer is a good example. Professor Happer has had a long and distinguished career as an expert on the behavior of spin-polarized atoms and nuclei, but it's unclear how this makes him qualified to comment on climate change. He's entitled to his opinions, of course, but readers of his op-eds should be aware that his training and background are not in climate science (for an example of one of his op-eds, see Happer, 2012). Senator James Inhofe (2012, pp. 94–96) lists several other scientists who've publicly disavowed the consensus position on climate change, although again most of the scientists he names are not climate experts. These public statements by individual scientists supposedly demonstrate the absence of consensus on climate change. However, the number of dissenting scientists with actual relevant expertise is tiny compared to those on the other side of the argument, as the surveys of hundreds of qualified scientists discussed earlier demonstrate.

Ultimately, though, petitions and newspaper columns suffer from the same problem, regardless of the qualifications of the people involved: they're opinions. As the saying goes, "Everyone is entitled to their own opinion, but not to their own facts." The more important question is whether those opinions have hard data and rigorous analysis behind them. In other words, have they been published in the peer-reviewed literature, and have they withstood the scrutiny that comes afterward?

This is why surveys of the literature, such as Naomi Oreskes's and John Cook and his team's, are so valuable: they show clearly where the balance of scientific evidence lies. Not surprisingly, these studies have themselves come under attack. Many challenges have appeared, mostly in non-peer-reviewed venues, but the handful of peer-reviewed studies have themselves been subject to scrutiny and found wanting. The finding of an overwhelming scientific consensus has been found in multiple studies, adopting a range of independent methodologies.

The scientific consensus on climate change is a fact. It's not unanimous, and dissenting scientists can certainly be found—which demonstrates that such voices are not being silenced for political ends—but they're a tiny minority. It's also no guarantee of accuracy: the consensus could be wrong, an idea that we'll explore in more detail in question 27.

But science helps us to avoid fooling ourselves, and a scientific consensus as overwhelming as the one on climate change is a strong indicator that we're not making it all up.

FURTHER READING

Anderegg, W. R. L., Prall, J. W., Harold, J., and Schneider, S. H. (2010). Expert credibility in climate change. *Proceedings of the National Academy of Sciences of the United States of America, 107,* 12107–12109.

Bickmore, B. (2010). Another red herring survey. Posted to Climate Asylum, December 13, 2010, available at https://bbickmore.wordpress.com/2010/12/13/another-red-herring-survey/. Accessed May 27, 2015.

Cook, J., Nuccitelli, D., Green, S. A., Richardson, M., Winkler, B., Painting, R., . . ., and Skuce, A. (2013). Quantifying the consensus on anthropogenic global warming in the scientific literature. *Environmental Research Letters, 8*(2), 024024.

Cook, J., Nuccitelli, D., Skuce, A., Way, R., Jacobs, P., Painting, R., Lewandowsky, S., and Coulter, A. (2014). 24 Critical Errors in Tol (2014): Reaffirming the 97% Consensus on Anthropogenic Global Warming. Available at http://www.skepticalscience.com/docs/24_errors.pdf. Accessed April 20, 2016.

Doran, P. T., and Zimmerman, M. K. (2009). Examining the scientific consensus on climate change. *Eos, Transactions American Geophysical Union, 90*(3), 22–23.

Farnsworth, S. J., and Lichter, S. R. (2012). The structure of scientific opinion on climate change. *International Journal of Public Opinion Research, 24*(1), 93–103.

Goreham, S. (2013). *The Mad, Mad, Mad World of Climatism: Mankind and Climate Change Mania.* New Lenox Books.

Happer, W. (2012). Global warming models are wrong again. *The Wall Street Journal,* March 27, 2012, available at http://www.wsj.com/articles/SB10001424052702304636404577291352882984274. Accessed May 28, 2015.

Inhofe, J. M. (2012). *The Greatest Hoax: How the Global Warming Conspiracy Threatens Your Future.* WND Books, Washington, DC.

Jones, J., and Saad, L. (2014). Gallup Poll Social Series: Environment. Available at http://www.gallup.com/file/poll/167966/Most_Scientists_Views_on_Global_Warming_Exaggerated_140317.pdf. Accessed May 27, 2015.

Leiserowitz, A., Maibach, E., Roser-Renouf, C., Feinberg, G., and Rosenthal, S. (2015). *Climate Change in The American Mind: March, 2015.* Yale University and George Mason University. Yale Project on Climate Change Communication, New Haven, CT, available at http://environment.yale.edu/climate-communication/files/Global-Warming-CCAM-March-2015.pdf. Accessed May 27, 2015.

Morano, M. (2010). Special report: more than 1000 international scientists dissent over man-made global warming claims—challenge UN IPCC and Gore. Posted to ClimateDepot.com, December 8, 2010, available at http://www.climatedepot.com/2010/12/08/special-report-more-than-1000-international-scientists-dissent-over-manmade-global-warming-claims-challenge-un-ipcc-gore-2/. Accessed May 27, 2015.

Oregon Institute of Science and Medicine. (n.d.). Global Warming Petition Project. Available at http://www.petitionproject.org/index.php. Accessed May 27, 2015.

Oreskes, N. (2004). The scientific consensus on climate change. *Science*, 306(5702), 1686–1686.

Oreskes, N. (2007). The Scientific Consensus on Climate Change: How Do We Know We're Not Wrong? In *Climate Change: What It Means for Us, Our Children, and Our Grandchildren*, J. F. C. DiMento and P. Doughman (eds.). MIT Press, pp. 65–99.

Stenhouse, N., Maibach, E., Cobb, S., Ban, R., Bleistein, A., Croft, P., Bierly, E., Seitter, K., Rasmussen, G., and Leiserowitz, A. (2014). Meteorologists' views about global warming: a survey of American Meteorological Society Professional Members. *Bulletin of the American Meteorological Society*, 95, 1029–1040. doi: http://dx.doi.org/10.1175/BAMS-D-13-00091.1.

Tol, R.S. (2014). Quantifying the consensus on anthropogenic global warming in the literature: a re-analysis. *Energy Policy, 73*, 701–705.

Q27. WHAT DOES THE WORK OF LONE SCIENTIFIC MAVERICKS SHOW ABOUT THE IMPORTANCE OF THE SCIENTIFIC CONSENSUS ON CLIMATE CHANGE?

Answer: Science is a communal process. While brilliant individuals have successfully challenged the orthodoxy of their time, it's only when their work is confirmed by other scientists that we know they were right. By no means are all such challenges vindicated in this way.

The Facts: Many schools and universities use online plagiarism checkers. These websites use an enormous database of written materials to compare against student papers, to see if anything has been copied. It can be used punitively—if, after submitting your paper, it turns out to have been plagiarized, you fail the course. However, it can also be used to help students. After all, in the rush of trying to research and write several papers for different classes, all on a tight deadline, it can be easy to forget that a copied passage from a web source was meant for notes, not the final paper. Many students therefore plagiarize accidentally. Online plagiarism checkers can thus be used by students to check papers for unintentional plagiarism before the final submission deadline, helping to head off a failing grade. Although some universities have banned the use of online plagiarism-checking services, citing privacy concerns among others, submitting a paper to these websites is still a common experience for many students.

There are connections here, both with how science works and with why it matters that the scientific consensus on climate change is so overwhelmingly strong (question 26). If a paper has been unintentionally plagiarized, a student would not be aware of this until the failing grade comes in. Having someone else read the paper, or submitting it to a plagiarism-checking website, can catch the mistakes that the original author wasn't aware of.

Science works in a somewhat similar way, by providing an independent check on our understanding of the world. Humans are expert pattern seekers and are good at identifying patterns even when they're not real. When a scientist finds a new pattern, or a problem with an existing one, peer review helps to determine whether it's real or illusory. As we saw in question 26, peer review happens after a study has been published, as well as before. Follow-up research by other scientists metaphorically kicks the tires to see if the original work holds up under close scrutiny. It's the equivalent of using a plagiarism-checking service to look for unintended plagiarism.

We also saw in question 26 that there's an overwhelming scientific consensus that human activity is warming the planet. This is confirmed by over 90% of practicing climate scientists and around 97% of relevant climate research. How we know this is itself a good example of how science works: multiple different studies, using different methods, find similar results.

However, one frequently raised objection is that science isn't done by consensus. This viewpoint can be found in many places online, and many of those online authors quote from a single source: a speech given in 2003 at the California Institute of Technology (CalTech) by the late fiction author Michael Crichton. William O'Keefe, for example, in an essay available at the website of the George C. Marshall Institute, quotes the speech as follows: "Let's be clear: the work of science has nothing what-ever to do with consensus. Consensus is the business of politics. Science, on the contrary, requires only one investigator who happens to be right, which means that he or she has results that are verifiable by reference to the real world." In other words, when you're right, you're right, and it doesn't matter how many other people agree with you. Science isn't a popularity contest: just ask Galileo.

This argument is sometimes referred to as the Galileo gambit, because of its reference to one of the most famous scientists of all time, Galileo Galilei, who was forced by the Catholic Church to recant his view that the Earth went round the Sun instead of the other way round. In the context of discussions on climate change, references to Galileo's persecution were made in 2011 by then governor of Texas, Rick Perry, in the course of his unsuccessful campaign for the U.S. presidency, and more recently by Rep. Louie Gohmert (also of Texas) during a hearing on climate change held by the U.S. Congressional Committee on Natural Resources, on May 13, 2015 (see reports by Fountain, 2011, and Nuccitelli, 2015, respectively). The broader point seems to be that, throughout history, heroic scientists have stood alone against the forces of ignorance, and spoken the truth, when everyone else was telling them they were wrong. Although Galileo is often invoked, other scientists are sometimes referenced, such as Alfred Wegener, the father of continental drift, or Albert Einstein and the the-ory of relativity.

If this view of history, science, and the history of science is accurate, then a scientific consensus really wouldn't matter. When you're right, you're right, no matter what anybody (or everybody) else thinks. But a closer examination of Galileo's situation suggests this view misunder-stands history. As heroic as Galileo may have been, he wasn't standing alone against the Catholic Church. The idea that the Earth went round the Sun—heliocentrism—had been published by Copernicus in 1543, with mathematical calculations to support it. Johannes Kepler improved on the calculations, recognizing that the orbits of the planets were ellip-tical instead of circular. Galileo's contribution was the invention of the telescope, which could be used to observe the planets directly. In other words, we have a familiar story about how science progresses: incremen-tally, through a growing body of evidence contributed by a group of sci-entists. By the time of Galileo's trial in 1633, astronomers were largely convinced that Copernicus's heliocentric view was right (see Kuhn, 1957; Steven Sherwood, 2011, provides a fascinating comparison of several sci-entific discoveries and their reception by the public and political author-ities). Galileo may have been many things, but on this issue, he was not a maverick. He was certainly confronting ignorance, but not that of his fellow astronomers.

The idea that consensus doesn't matter, because when you're right, you're right, also misunderstands the nature of scientific consensus. As we saw in question 26, a scientific consensus isn't so much about the extent to which *scientists* agree on an idea, as it is about the extent to which *independent tests* of an idea agree. Galileo tends to get the credit, but really it should be shared, at least with Copernicus and Kepler. The Milankovitch theory of orbital wobbles causing glacial and interglacial periods is another example, having developed from ideas by other scientists, namely Louis Agassiz, Joseph Adhemar, and James Croll. This incremental building process was mentioned by Sir Isaac Newton, in his famous line, "If I have seen further, it is by standing on the shoulders of giants." Referencing Newton, the academic search engine Google Scholar uses the tagline "stand on the shoulders of giants."

Sometimes, though, the narrative of the lone heroic scientist is a bit more accurate. Alfred Wegener's proposition that the continents moved was decades ahead of its time, and although Wegener had evidence for continental drift, the understanding of the Earth's interior at the time was not sufficient to explain how it could happen. Wegener's ideas were largely ignored. As it turned out, the scientific orthodoxy was wrong on this issue. (Naomi Oreskes has a short, highly readable 2008 essay on this subject.)

However, we know this only with the benefit of hindsight. As time went on and research technology improved, so too did the evidence for continental drift, including, crucially, a mechanism explaining how it could happen. Over time, the accumulating weight of evidence led to the widespread acceptance of the idea that continents move, as explained by the theory of plate tectonics. Wegener, as it turns out, had been right—but we know this only because other independent studies verified his ideas. In other words, a scientific consensus developed due to the gradual accumulation of evidence. Michael Crichton's frequently quoted speech at CalTech, mentioned earlier, seems to recognize this concept, despite the author's vilification of the idea of scientific consensus: "In science consensus is irrelevant. What is relevant is reproducible results." The studies that reproduce the results, though, are, the foundation upon which scientific consensus is built.

Unusual ideas like Wegener's are an important part of how scientific knowledge progresses. But so, too, is the recognition that some ideas just don't hold up. This is the case for many of the ideas published by the tiny minority of active climate scientists that still disputes the fundamental ideas of anthropogenic climate change. Far from representing Alfred

Wegener–like scientific heroes, whose ideas later turn out to be right, follow-up research has tended to disprove their work. A good example is the tropical heat vent effect proposed by Richard Lindzen and co-authors in various peer-reviewed papers, and relied upon by Fred Singer and Dennis Avery (2008) for their (incorrect) view that water vapor does not amplify the warming from carbon dioxide (question 20). This idea suggested that, although rising temperatures might cause more evaporation, the warming climate should cause the area covered by high cirrus clouds to contract, allowing more heat to escape to space, counteracting the warming from carbon dioxide. This was an intriguing idea and certainly went against the prevailing scientific view—but unlike continental drift, follow-up studies did not support it, instead finding numerous flaws. In a 2014 paper, John Abraham and co-authors (including John Cook, this book's co-author) reviewed the sequence of scientific publications on the heat vent idea, finding that "[w]hile this concept gained much media attention, it was quickly and thoroughly rebutted within the scientific literature. Within approximately one year of publication of Lindzen et al. (2001), four refuting papers appeared" (p. 7). Five more papers identifying different errors had appeared by 2009, bringing the total to nine. It seems reasonable to say at this point that the balance of scientific evidence suggests that the heat vent idea is wrong. This is the fate of many new ideas in science, of course. When later work does not support them, they should be discarded. That's how science works.

The lone hero is a powerful image in our culture. Its recent manifestations include fictional characters like the Lone Ranger, Batman, and Iron Man. But unlike these heroes, the typical scientist's superpowers spring less from their abilities as individuals, extraordinary though they may be, and more from their engagement as part of a process and as part of a community of other scientists. The power of science to change the world is far more remarkable than any lone hero can muster.

FURTHER READING

Abraham, J. P., Cook, J., Fasullo, J. T., Jacobs, P. H., Mandia, S. A., and Nuccitelli, D. A. (2014). Review of the consensus and asymmetric quality of research on human-induced climate change. *Cosmopolis*, *2014*(1), 3–18.

Fountain, H. (2011). Divining Perry's meaning on Galileo remark. *The New York Times*, September 8, 2011, available at http://www .nytimes.com/2011/09/09/science/earth/09galileo.html?_r=0. Accessed May 28, 2015.

Kuhn, T. S. (1957). *The Copernican Revolution: Planetary Astronomy in the Development of Western Thought.* Harvard University Press.

Nuccitelli, D. (2015). Congress manufactures doubt and denial in climate change hearing. *The Guardian*, May 21, 2015, available at http://www .theguardian.com/environment/climate-consensus-97-per-cent/2015/ may/21/congress-manufactures-doubt-and-denial-in-climate-change-hearing. Accessed May 28, 2015.

O'Keefe, W. (2014). The corruption of science. Posted to the website of the George C. Marshall Institute, October 5, 2014, available at http://marshall.org/climate-change/the-corruption-of-science/. Accessed May 28, 2015.

Oreskes, N. (2008). The Scientific Consensus on Climate Change. In *Climate Change: Picturing the Science*, G. Schmidt, and J. Wolfe (eds.). W.W. Norton & Company, pp. 153–155.

Sherwood, S. (2011). Science controversies past and present. *Physics Today*, 64(10), 39.

Singer, S. F., and Avery, D. T. (2008). *Unstoppable Global Warming: Every 1500 Years.* Updated and expanded edition. Rowman & Littlefield.

Q28. WHAT MOTIVATES CLIMATE SCIENTISTS?

Answer: Climate scientists are generally motivated by a fascination with the natural world and a desire to prevent lasting damage to the planet.

The Facts: Meet Andrew Dessler. He's a professor of atmospheric sciences at Texas A&M University, where his main research focus is water vapor and clouds. In other words, he's a climate scientist.

In many respects, Dr. Dessler is unremarkable. In an e-mail, he explained why he loves doing what he's doing: "The Eureka! thrill of being the first person in the history of the world to understand some aspect of the climate system. That's a great and humbling experience that easily justifies spending my life doing science." Research on the psychology of scientists finds that this is a common explanation for why people enter and stay in science. Although there's a nuanced range of motivations, an important one is that scientists love to solve puzzles, figure out how things work (e.g., research by Lam, 2011, and Lounsbury et al., 2012). So with regard to why Dr. Dessler spends his time researching water vapor, he's a lot like thousands of other scientists studying the climate system.

In other ways, though, he's quite unusual. First, he's very good at what he does. He's published several papers in the leading climate science journals which have contributed significantly to our understanding of the water vapor feedback, for example. He's also written a well-received textbook on climate change and a book on the overlap between climate science and policy. The excellence of his science was recognized with a 2012 Ascent Award, given to outstanding mid-career researchers by the American Geophysical Union's Atmospheric Sciences section. The excellence of his writing was recognized with a 2014 Louis J. Battan Author's Award from the American Meteorological Society. Dr. Dessler can reasonably be described as exceptional in terms of the quality of his work.

But he's different from most climate scientists in another interesting way, too: he used to be an investment banker working on Wall Street. Why the radical career change? "The reason I left investment banking and went to graduate school is that I realized I was simply not motivated enough by money to take a boring job. . . .[M]y salary in grad school was about 25% of what it was at First Boston (that's the bank I worked for). But the real pay cut came down the road. One of the analysts in my FB class got a bonus of $10M a few years ago. I'm pretty sure I'm the lowest paid person from the FB analyst class of '86."

Research on the motivations of scientists tends to show that financial rewards rank low on the list of incentives. And recall from question 22 that scientists working on the IPCC reports are unpaid volunteers. People don't go into science if they want to make a lot of money—and Andrew Dessler went *away* from money to go into science. It's always possible to find exceptions, of course, but in general, scientists tend to be driven by less materialistic motivations.

It's curious, then, to see suggestions to the contrary popping up on the Internet. In a 2015 opinion piece for the *National Review*, Patrick Michaels discusses "the corruption of science that can be caused by massive amounts of money." He writes: "The United States has disbursed tens of billions of dollars to climate scientists who would not have received those funds had their research shown climate change to be beneficial or even modest in its effects. Are these scientists being tempted by money?" Alex Newman, in a 2014 post at the website New American.com, calls out climate scientists in general, and President Barack Obama's science adviser, John Holdren, in particular, writing: "Ridiculous forecasts have been made by other 'climate scientists' who, like Holdren, continue to reap huge amounts of U.S. taxpayer dollars in salaries, grants, and benefits despite being consistently wrong." An op-ed in the *Wall Street Journal* in 2012 by 16 scientists asked why there was so much passion about global warming, and suggested, "There are several reasons, but a good place to start is the old question 'cui bono?' Or the modern update, 'Follow the money'" (Allegre et al., 2012). Dr. Tim Ball has a 2014 book whose title says it all: *The Deliberate Corruption of Climate Science*.

Conspiracy theories of this sort don't typically provide any real evidence for their claims. Insinuation, yes, but hard evidence, not so much. This makes grappling with the claim of corrupt climate scientists a little tricky. Still, two main points are worth making in response to this charge. First, as mentioned earlier, studies of what motivates scientists in general suggest that money is not high on the list. For example, Lounsbury et al. (2012) examined over 2,000 personality tests from physical scientists and found that intrinsic motivations, such as the challenge of solving a problem, or the significance of the work, were important. Lam (2011) reported that 36 individual interviews and 735 online questionnaires completed by scientists at British universities showed that financial considerations were not important motivators—even for scientists seeking commercial applications for their work. As with any profession, there is variation from person to person, and no two scientists are exactly alike—but as a group, evidence points to scientists not being especially motivated by financial rewards.

Andrew Dessler's story is a good example: if money is what you want, why not stay on Wall Street and work toward that $10 million bonus? And grant money doesn't come close to matching the rewards of a lucrative career in high finance. Spending of grant money is tightly regulated, and at universities, where most of the science and engineering research in the United States is conducted (National Science Board, 2014), grants can be used only to buy equipment, support graduate students, pay for travel to conferences, and cover three months' worth of the scientist's university salary (typical contracts allow for the university paying for nine months of work). Grants are used to support research activities, not for personal enrichment: it's against the law for scientists to siphon off large amounts of grant money into their own pockets. In this light, the likelihood that climate scientists are engaged in a huge international effort to con politicians and the public so that they can keep reaping personal financial benefit is remote.

Second, the message from climate scientists has become progressively clearer and stronger as time has gone on. The scientific case that changing concentrations of atmospheric carbon dioxide could change the Earth's climate dates back to an 1896 paper by Swedish chemist Svante Arrhenius. It's been building progressively since then. Thus, not only does the fundamental science predate the availability of large government grants to support it, but the message of climate science hasn't swung with the political winds. If climate scientists want to get government money, and the way to do that is to tell political leaders what they want to hear, then surely the conclusions would have changed with the views of whoever was in office. The perspectives on global warming varied quite dramatically from 1992 to 2015, for example, as the Clinton, George W. Bush, and Obama administrations took office, and as control of Congress switched back and forth between Democrats and Republicans. Yet the message from climate scientists hasn't changed much over that time, except to become more confident that the basic science is correct. (Yale economist William Nordhaus has a point-by-point response to the *Wall Street Journal* op-ed mentioned earlier, in which he makes this very argument; see Nordhaus, 2012.)

So from a logical standpoint, the claim that scientists have been corrupted by the prospect of large government grants doesn't really hold up. It's a little like saying that Galileo supported heliocentrism only so he could sell more telescopes. It impugns the motivations of scientists, and it's unfortunate that people still make this claim, despite the lack of evidence to support it and despite its logical failings.

FURTHER READING

Allegre, C., Armstrong, J. S., Breslow, J., Cohen, R., David, E., Happer, W., Kelly, M., Kininmonth, W., Lindzen, R., McGrath, J., Nichols, R., Rutan, B., Schmitt, H., Shaviv, N., Tennekes, H., and Zichichi, A. (2012). No need to panic about global warming. *Wall Street Journal, 27*, available at http://www.wsj.com/articles/SB10001424052970204301404577171531838421366. Accessed June 1, 2015.

Ball, T. F. (2014). *The Deliberate Corruption of Climate Science.* Stairway Press.

Lam, A. (2011). What motivates academic scientists to engage in research commercialization: 'gold', 'ribbon' or 'puzzle'? *Research Policy, 40*(10), 1354–1368.

Lounsbury, J. W., Foster, N., Patel, H., Carmody, P., Gibson, L. W., and Stairs, D. R. (2012). An investigation of the personality traits of scientists versus nonscientists and their relationship with career satisfaction. *R&D Management, 42*(1), 47–59.

Michaels, P. (2015). If the pope wants to have a truly moral climate-change debate, here are a few ideas. Posted to *National Review*, April 27, 2015, available at http://www.nationalreview.com/article/417520/if-pope-wants-have-truly-moral-climate-change-debate-here-are-few-ideas-patrick-j. Accessed May 31, 2015.

National Science Board. (2014). *Science and Engineering Indicators 2014: Chapter 5, Academic Research and Development*. National Science Foundation (NSB 14-01), Arlington, VA, available at http://www.nsf.gov/statistics/seind14/index.cfm/chapter-5/c5s1.htm. Accessed November 8, 2015.

Newman, A. (2014). Embarrassing predictions haunt the global warming industry. Posted to The New American.com, August 12, 2014, available at http://www.thenewamerican.com/tech/environment/item/18888-embarrassing-predictions-haunt-the-global-warming-industry. Accessed May 31, 2015.

Nordhaus, W. D. (2012). Why the global warming skeptics are wrong. *The New York Review of Books*, 59(5), 32–34.

Schneider, S. H. (2009). *Science as a Contact Sport: Inside The Battle to Save Earth's Climate*. National Geographic Books.

Q29. IN THE 1970s, WERE MOST CLIMATE SCIENTISTS CONCERNED ABOUT GLOBAL WARMING OR GLOBAL COOLING?

Answer: Before the modern global warming trend began in the 1970s, the majority of climate scientists were anticipating global warming due to increased greenhouse gases. In fact, by the end of the 1970s, scientific papers anticipating global warming outnumbered those warning of potential global cooling by more than six to one. Scientists were vindicated when the modern global warming trend began in the late 1970s.

The Facts: The 1970s were an exciting time for climate science. New technologies had allowed scientists to identify the timing of the glacial and interglacial cycles going back over 400,000 years in the past. The new evidence showed that major cold and warm periods had occurred exactly, or very nearly, when Milankovitch's orbital wobble theory had said they should. Milankovitch's idea had been shown to be right (Hays et al., 1976). Although many questions still remained, there was a sense in the air that a major scientific mystery had been solved.

Something else was in the air in the 1970s, too: pollution. When World War II came to an end, there followed an unprecedented boom in prosperity, especially in the United States but in many other parts of the world, too. This boom was fueled by abundant, cheap energy. But burning fossil fuels at a prodigious rate released not only large amounts of carbon dioxide but also other types of pollution.

Air pollution comes in many forms, with one of them being tiny particles known to climate scientists as *aerosols*, or perhaps less confusingly, *particulate pollution*. Like a major volcanic eruption, particulate pollution exerts a cooling influence on Earth's climate by reflecting sunlight. Unlike aerosols erupted by volcanoes, though, particulate pollution doesn't get as high into the atmosphere, so it can be washed out by rain and snow within a few days. But also unlike volcanoes, particulate pollution is constantly being replenished by human activity: driving cars, burning coal to make electricity, and so on. By the 1970s, air pollution had become a serious issue. Its impacts on human health were becoming apparent. So, too, were its impacts on climate.

This prompted the other big climate science discussion of the 1970s, besides Milankovitch cycles and glacial–interglacial periods. As fossil fuels are burned, both carbon dioxide, which traps heat, and aerosols, which reflect sunlight, are released. This sets up a climate tug-of-war. Which influence is stronger, cooling from aerosols or warming from carbon dioxide? And if pollution rates were to continue as they had been, what would this mean for the future of Earth's climate?

In 2008, climate scientist Tom Peterson and co-authors published a detailed examination of the scientific research of the late 1960s and 1970s. How did the scientific process resolve these questions? Was the emphasis on warming or cooling, or was the debate never settled conclusively one way or the other?

Their study found that, by the end of the 1970s, scientists had published 44 papers identifying warming from carbon dioxide as the most likely outcome. By contrast, cooling from aerosols received support in just seven papers. The scientific consensus of the 1970s was clear, by a ratio of more than six to one (see Figure 4.1). Most climate science of the 1970s was predicting global warming.

Many contemporary news reports accurately conveyed the back-and-forth scientific discussions of the time, as well as the shift toward concerns about future warming. For example, a 1975 *New York Times* article by Walter Sullivan reported: "The world's climate is changing. Of that scientists are firmly convinced. But in what direction and why are subjects of deepening debate." As it turned out, the debate was just turning toward a resolution in 1975 (see Figure 4.1), but this is a fair characterization of the situation at the time, based on the Peterson study.

However, possibly because of the constant need for journalists to find a fresh new angle on a story (question 22), other reports emphasized the global cooling side of the discussion, largely ignoring the warming side. *Time* magazine ran a story in 1974 warning of an impending ice age; Peter

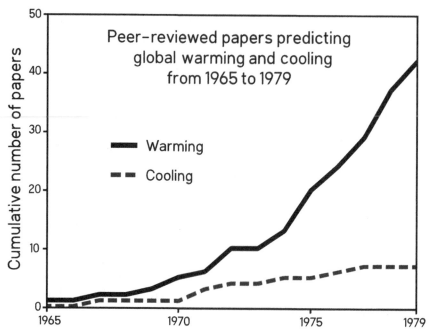

Figure 4.1 Number of scientific papers published between 1965 and 1979 predicting warming or cooling, shown as a cumulative total. By 1979, 44 papers had been published on warming and only 7 on cooling.
Source: Data from Peterson et al. (2008).

Gwynne, writing in *Newsweek* in 1975, warned of the dangers ahead for a cooling world. It's reports like these that are sometimes used to convey the misleading impression that scientists in the 1970s were largely speaking with one voice on this issue, sounding the alarm about global cooling. The reasoning is that if climate scientists got it wrong in the 1970s, then this brings today's clear and overwhelming consensus on global warming into doubt.

This argument is on display in numerous print and Internet sources. For example, both Glenn Beck's 2007 *An Inconvenient Book* and Sen. James Inhofe's 2012 *The Greatest Hoax* highlight Peter Gwynne's 1975 *Newsweek* article. Gwynne himself has expressed concern about this, writing in 2014 that it's time "to stop using an old magazine story as ammunition against the consensus of today's climate scientists." But his article is not the only one used (or misused) in this discussion. Nicholas Loris, in a 2010 briefing posted to the website of conservative think-tank the Heritage Foundation, uses other news articles. Specifically, in a section called The Shifting Consensus, he relies on Walter Sullivan's eminently balanced 1975 *New York Times* article, mentioned earlier, to claim that "not long ago, scientists thought that global *cooling* was a threat to the planet." As we've seen, some scientists did indeed think this—but they were a small minority. Claiming that global cooling was the consensus of the 1970s misrepresents the science of the time.

While many sources for this myth rely on news articles, some reference scientific reports. In a 2003 op-ed in *The Washington Post*, former U.S. energy secretary James Schlesinger quoted a 1972 report by the National Science Board, the governing body of the National Science Foundation. The quote was used in support of the usual argument on this issue, that climate scientists in the 1970s were sounding the alarm over global cooling, even an imminent new ice age. Here's the quote as used by Schlesinger: "Judging from the record of the past interglacial ages, the present time of high temperatures should be drawing to an end . . . leading into the next glacial age." However, this version misses out some important pieces. Here's the complete section, with missing pieces highlighted in italic (not in original): "Judging from the record of the past interglacial ages, the present time of high temperatures should be drawing to an end, *to be followed by a long period of considerably colder temperatures* leading to the next glacial age *some 20,000 years from now. However, it is possible, or even likely, that human interference has already altered the environment so much that the climatic pattern of the near future will follow a different path*" (National Science Board, 1972, p. 55). One of the human interferences the report lists is warming due to industrial emissions of carbon dioxide. The restored sections make it clear that the National Science Board was trying to say something very different from Schlesinger's version. Given the excitement in climate science over new discoveries relating to the glacial and interglacial cycles, it's not surprising that the National Science Board should discuss this issue. However, it's a mistake to confuse scientists' interest in these much longer-term climate changes with concern that the next ice age was just around the corner. This may have appeared in some of the popular media of the period, like the *Time* article mentioned earlier, but for the most part, it wasn't what scientists were saying. Nonetheless, Senator Inhofe repeats Schlesinger's misleading version of the quote in his 2012 book.

Previous questions have shown that there is an overwhelming scientific consensus on anthropogenic global warming, based on many independent lines of evidence. We've explained why this consensus matters. We've shown that the tiny minority of contrary research does not represent the work of heroic individuals who will be vindicated in time, but rather represents ideas that have been shown to be wrong by repeated testing. In this question, we've seen the evidence that, by the end of the 1970s, many more scientists were concerned about global warming than global cooling. This shows that the scientific consensus on climate change has not undergone rapid changes in outlook, flipping from cooling to warming. It's not like the weather, changing from day to day. Instead, like the changing climate, it's been gradually moving more and more clearly in one direction: global warming from increased greenhouse gases.

FURTHER READING

Beck, G. (2007). *An Inconvenient Book: Real Solutions to the World's Biggest Problems*. Simon and Schuster.

Gwynne, P. (1975). The cooling world. *Newsweek*, April 28, 1975, p. 22.

Gwynne, P. (2014). My 1975 "Cooling World" story doesn't make today's climate scientists wrong. Posted to Inside Science.com, May 21, 2014, available at http://www.insidescience.org/content/my-1975-cooling-world-story-doesnt-make-todays-climate-scientists-wrong/1640. Accessed January 9, 2015.

Hays, J. D., Imbrie, J., and Shackleton, N. J. (1976). Variations in the Earth's orbit: pacemaker of the ice ages. *Science*, 194(4270), 1121–1132.

Inhofe, J. M. (2012). *The Greatest Hoax: How The Global Warming Conspiracy Threatens Your Future*. WND Books, Washington, DC.

Loris, N. (2010). How the "scientific consensus" on global warming affects American business—and consumers. Backgrounder #2479 on Energy and Environment. Posted to the website of the Heritage Foundation, October 26, 2010, available at http://www.heritage.org/research/reports/2010/10/how-the-scientific-consensus-on-global-warming-affects-american-business-and-consumers. Accessed May 29, 2015.

National Science Board. (1972). *Patterns and Perspectives in Environmental Science*. National Science Foundation, 426 pp, available at http://www.nsf.gov/nsb/publications/1971/nsb0671.pdf. Accessed May 29, 2015.

Peterson, T. C., Connolley, W. M., and Fleck, J. (2008). The myth of the 1970s global cooling scientific consensus. *Bulletin of the American Meteorological Society*, 89(9), 1325–1337.

Schlesinger, J. (2003). Climate change: the science isn't settled. *Washington Post*, July 7, A17.

Sullivan, W. (1975). Scientists ask why world climate is changing; major cooling may be ahead. *The New York Times*, May 21, 1975.

Time. (1974). Another ice age? Published June 24, 1974.

5

Responding to Climate Change

Q30. IS IT POSSIBLE TO REDUCE GREENHOUSE GAS EMISSIONS WITHOUT DAMAGING THE ECONOMY?

Answer: Practical examples, as well as economic theory, show that it's possible to cut carbon emissions without impeding economic growth.

The Facts: Weber State University is a medium-sized, undergraduate-focused university in northern Utah, about 35 miles from Salt Lake City and about 30 minutes from a world-class ski resort. It's also a national leader in cutting carbon emissions through smart use of energy efficiency and renewable power.

In 2007, the university's then president signed the Association of College and University Presidents Climate Commitment. Among other things, the university had to come up with a plan for becoming *carbon neutral* by 2050, meaning it had to cut its emissions and balance whatever couldn't be cut with things that take in carbon, like planting trees (or, as a last resort, paying other people to plant trees). To do this, the university has embarked on an ambitious program of energy savings. Inefficient incandescent lightbulbs have been replaced with high-efficiency compact fluorescent and light-emitting diode (LED) bulbs. Switching out the stadium lighting in the basketball arena for LEDs won the university a national award from the Environmental Protection Agency. New buildings on campus are constructed to high levels of energy and water efficiency. Solar power is increasingly used—not only to generate electricity but also to heat the water for the swimming pool. Carbon emissions from electricity generation have fallen by 28% since 2007, even as the university has gained over 300,000 square feet of new buildings and around 3,000 more students. Weber State is now on track to be carbon neutral by 2040, 10 years ahead of schedule (Bodine, 2014).

How much has this path to carbon neutrality cost? Remarkably, far from costing money, Weber State now saves over a million dollars a year on its energy bills. Although the efficiency upgrades carry an up-front cost, the savings pay back the initial investment within anything from a few months to a few years to over 10 years, and will keep paying over the lifetime of the projects, often measurable in decades. The return on investment has been significantly better than could have been earned from putting the money into the stock market.

Weber State University is a good example of how carbon emissions can be cut while protecting, or even growing, the economic bottom line. While it's just one case, there are many others like it. Universities, towns, and businesses are finding that cutting carbon can be good financial sense (several examples are provided in Energy Quest USA, the third part of Geoff Haines-Stiles and Richard Alley's excellent video series, *Earth: The Operators' Manual*). But most are fairly small-scale examples. Can efforts to tackle climate change work at larger scales? In North America, several quite large initiatives are under way. California, currently the world's eighth-largest economy, is trying to reduce emissions; so is a group of states in the northeastern United States; so are Canada's provinces of British Columbia and Alberta. Although they're using different approaches, they have one thing in common: they're trying to put a price on carbon.

Economists generally agree that if you want less of something, you make it more expensive. At the moment, almost everywhere, emitting carbon is free. The price of a gallon of gasoline includes many things: the cost of finding, extracting, and refining it; the cost of moving it to where it's sold; a profit for the oil company; sales taxes for the government; and so on. But there's no price associated with the carbon that's released when the gasoline is burned. In effect, we all get to use the atmosphere as a place to dump waste carbon, like throwing sewage into a nearby river—and we don't have to pay for it.

From an economic perspective, this is a problem. As seen earlier in this book, all that waste carbon is building up in the atmosphere and causing global warming. In the United States, we've already seen increases in some extreme weather events, such as intense rainstorms and heat waves, and we're very likely to see these increases continue into the future. Tropical cyclones may become less frequent but more intense, and coupled with rising sea levels have great potential to cause damage. All of these climate changes come at a cost, as the Risky Business report and other studies discussed in question 21 make clear. Consequently, dumping carbon into the atmosphere is not, in fact, free of charge. Even though we don't pay for it when we fill up our cars, we pay for it in other ways, such as higher electricity bills from using more air conditioning, or expensive disaster relief and cleanup operations. These hidden costs, taken together, are known as the *social cost of carbon*.

Estimating the social cost of carbon is arguably one of the most contentious issues in the economics of climate change. It requires not only estimating the future damage from climate change, a tricky job in its own right; it also requires thinking about how we value that future damage compared with today. In other words, do we care enough about our descendants to take action now? These are extraordinarily difficult questions to answer. As a result, the IPCC's 2007 report listed a range of estimates from over $350 a ton to −$10 a ton, suggesting that burning carbon is anything from really, really bad to very slightly good, respectively (Yohe et al., 2007). A widely cited figure, though, is around $30 a ton, from the work of Yale economist William Nordhaus (see also the discussion of the economics of climate change in Richard Alley's 2011 book, *Earth: The Operators' Manual*).

This is close to the price that's been applied in British Columbia's effort to cut carbon emissions: currently Can $30, or about US $25 per ton. British Columbia's approach has been to apply a tax on carbon at this rate, which translates to about 7 cents per liter of gasoline in Canada, the equivalent of about 25 cents per gallon in the United States (detailed numbers are available in reports by Stewart Elgie and Jessica McClay, 2013, as well as *The Economist*, 2014).

The experiment began in 2008. Has it worked? Although it's still fairly early to tell, it does seem to have cut greenhouse gas emissions in British Columbia. According to Elgie and McClay's research, mentioned earlier, consumption of those fuels subject to the tax has declined by 19% compared with the rest of Canada. Significantly, the carbon tax does not seem to have impeded economic growth. British Columbia's economy has grown slightly *more* than the rest of Canada's, on average, since the tax was introduced in 2008, and unemployment was slightly below the Canadian average, as of 2011. This may be partly because the carbon tax was designed to be *revenue neutral*, meaning that any gains in income the government gets from the carbon tax must be balanced by tax cuts elsewhere.

As a result, British Columbia has the lowest personal income tax rate in Canada.

This looks like another case of win–win: cut carbon emissions and grow the economy at the same time. However, it's still a fairly small step relative to the scale of the actions needed to completely eliminate our carbon emissions. To put these in perspective, two scientists at Princeton University, Stephen Pacala and Robert Socolow, developed the concept of *stabilization wedges*. Each wedge is a set of actions that cuts carbon emissions over time, starting at zero and increasing over 50 years, ultimately keeping a total of 25 billion tons of carbon from entering the atmosphere by about 2050. Seven of these wedges would be needed to level off global carbon emissions. There are several to choose from, but a few examples give a sense of just how big a challenge this is: double the fuel efficiency of cars; halve the average distance being driven; double the amount of electricity generated by nuclear power; increase the amount of energy generated by solar power by 700 times. (Princeton's Carbon Mitigation Initiative, 2015, has materials and rules online for a game based on the concept of stabilization wedges.)

So, while low-cost actions like British Columbia's might chew around the edges of climate change, taking a real bite out of the problem could be expensive, possibly very expensive. But the costs of action have to be weighed against the costs of inaction. It's very difficult to know how much climate change will really cost, as the wide range of estimates for the social cost of carbon suggests. But the costs probably won't be nothing, and they could be very high, for example, if multi-billion-dollar damage from storms like Hurricane Katrina or Superstorm Sandy gets more common. In these kinds of situations, uncertainty is not our friend, and taking out some insurance against the worst possibilities seems like a good idea. We take out fire insurance on our houses not because we expect our homes to burn down but because the consequences would be so terrible if they did. This is a reasonable analogy to the costs of action versus inaction on climate change.

Furthermore, efforts to move away from fossil fuels bring numerous additional benefits, besides reducing carbon emissions and their associated costs from the impact of climate change. For example, cutting fossil fuel use also cuts air pollution and improves peoples' health, even in countries like the United States where fairly strong clean-air regulations are already in place. Improving peoples' health also improves the economy, because people take fewer sick days (and, in extreme cases, live longer). One detailed study estimated that moving away from fossil fuels in the United States to an energy system powered entirely by wind, water, and sunlight would save approximately 46,000 premature deaths per year in 2050, saving the U.S. economy around $600 billion per year in 2050 (in 2013 dollars) (Jacobson et al., 2015). Although the study identifies a fairly wide range of possibilities, even the lowest estimates of lives and dollars saved are large: 12,000 premature deaths per year avoided, and $85 billion per year in 2013 dollars, both for the year 2050.

These health savings are just one example of what are known as *co-benefits*: good things that happen as side effects to the main goal of reducing carbon emissions. Stanford University's Solutions Project, which produced the study mentioned earlier, estimates that if all the co-benefits are included, every one of the United States' 50 states would be economically better off with an energy system powered entirely by renewable energy. The state of New York, for example, is calculated to save close to $6,000 per person per year in energy, health, and climate costs by 2050 with a completely renewable energy system; California could save well over $7,000 per person per year; Utah could save over $10,000 per person per year; and so on for all 50 states (infographics explaining the energy mix and potential savings for each state are available at the team's website, thesolutionsproject.org, as well as in Jacobson et al.'s peer-reviewed paper mentioned earlier). Overall, the Solutions Project estimates that the savings from 100% renewable energy are so large that the investment required to build such a system could be paid back in less than three years. According to this research, far from damaging the economy, investment in cutting carbon could provide a significant economic boost.

The Solutions Project is not the only team to find that cutting carbon emissions is compatible with growing the economy. The Deep Decarbonization Pathways Project is analyzing ways that substantial reductions in carbon emissions could occur, for several countries around the world. For example, the United States is estimated to be able to bring about, by the year 2050, an 80% reduction in carbon emissions from 1990's levels, at a cost of only around 1% of gross domestic product (GDP) (Williams et al., 2014), although the authors acknowledge that the actual cost could vary substantially from this figure, depending on hard-to-predict factors such as the price of oil in the future. Still, the authors calculate that the cost of transitioning to a low-carbon energy system in the United States is unlikely to be more than about 1.8% of GDP and could even have a negative cost—that is, it would pay back, rather than costing anything. The low cost of this shift to low-carbon energy comes about in large part because fossil fuel no longer needs to be purchased when energy is generated from renewable sources such as the wind or the Sun, significantly offsetting the cost of building a new energy system.

However, all these encouraging calculations can make it easy to forget that transitioning away from coal and other fossil fuels has real consequences for the people who work in those industries. The transformation of the economy described earlier is monumental, and families and communities that are heavily dependent on fossil fuel consumption for their livelihoods will face serious challenges in adjusting. But efforts to address and mitigate this pain do exist. For example, the U.S. Department of Energy already runs a training program for retiring military personnel, preparing them for civilian life by ensuring they are discharged with the skills needed to work in the solar energy industry. The Solar Ready Vets program is one example of how highly skilled, disciplined, and motivated people can be helped to move from one way of life into another. In the event that a wholesale shift away from fossil energy actually begins, similar programs could potentially help ease the pain that workers in those industries are likely to experience by retraining them for careers in other areas such as the solar energy sector, one of the fastest-growing industries in the United States (U.S. Department of Energy, 2016).

However, not all approaches to cutting carbon are the same. Simply because the Solutions Project and the Deep Decarbonization Pathways Project show that it's possible to grow the economy while transitioning to low-carbon energy, this doesn't mean it's inevitable. There's a wide range of policy options, and the precise design of any given policy will have a large effect on whether it works as advertised or not. For example, a recent effort in Germany to support electricity generation from renewable sources had the perverse effect of increasing carbon emissions, prompting a redesign of the applicable laws (see *The Economist*, 2013). So in many respects, when it comes to reducing carbon emissions, the devil is in the details. Exactly *how* deep decarbonization is approached will matter, a lot. But the findings of both the Solutions Project and the Deep Decarbonization Pathways Project, as well as small-scale practical efforts such as Weber State University, are clear: it is possible, using existing technology, to make large cuts in carbon emissions while protecting economic growth.

However, it sometimes seems as though *any* attempt to cut carbon emissions generates opposition. The Obama administration's effort to reduce power plant emissions was described in 2013 by Marita Noon, at the Center for a Constructive Tomorrow, as a proposal that will "ruin the economy and disproportionately hurt the poor." California's project to price carbon through a system known as cap-and-trade prompted an extensive (and ongoing) opposition, notably from the California Chamber of Commerce (Justin Gillis has interesting reporting on this issue at *The New York Times*).

Marlo Lewis, writing for the Competitive Enterprise Institute's website in 2012, advised that carbon taxes are a "dangerous folly." Roy Spencer, in his 2008 book *Climate Confusion*, highlights "Dumb Assumption #1: We can reduce emissions and not hurt the economy" (p. 141).

These perspectives tend to focus on cases where cutting carbon emissions has not gone hand in hand with economic growth, while ignoring both the successful cases and the scientific research finding that these two goals can be compatible at a large scale. While there's nothing inevitable about economic growth following efforts to decarbonize, critics of such efforts tend to assume the opposite, that economic disaster is inevitable instead. Research and practical examples show that this assumption is unfounded.

FURTHER READING

Alley, R. B. (2011). *Earth: The Operators' Manual*. W.W. Norton & Company.

Bodine, J. (2014). Weber State University Climate Action Plan Progress Report for FY 2013 & 2014. Available at http://apps.weber.edu/wsuimages/sustainability/PlansReports/FY2013FY2014WSUSustainabilityReport.pdf. Accessed June 2, 2015.

The Carbon Mitigation Initiative. (2015). Stabilization Wedges Game. Available at http://cmi.princeton.edu/wedges/game.php. Accessed June 2, 2015.

The Economist. (2011). Greenery in Canada: We Have a Winner, July 21, 2011. Available at http://www.economist.com/node/18989175. Accessed June 2, 2015.

The Economist. (2013). Europe's dirty secret: the unwelcome renaissance. *The Economist*, January 5, 2013, available at http://www.economist.com/news/briefing/21569039-europes-energy-policy-delivers-worst-all-possible-worlds-unwelcome-renaissance. Accessed June 2, 2015.

The Economist. (2014). British Columbia's carbon tax: the evidence mounts. Posted to *The Economist* blogs, July 31, 2014, available at http://www.economist.com/blogs/americasview/2014/07/british-columbias-carbon-tax. Accessed June 2, 2015.

Elgie, S., and McClay, J. (2013). Policy Commentary/Commentaire: BC's carbon tax shift is working well after four years (Attention Ottawa). *Canadian Public Policy*, 39, S1–S10.

Gillis, J. (2014). A price tag on carbon as a climate rescue plan. *The New York Times*, May 30, 2014, available at http://www.nytimes.com/2014/05/30/science/a-price-tag-on-carbon-as-a-climate-rescue-plan.html?_r=0. Accessed June 2, 2015.

Haines-Stiles, G. (writer, producer, director), and Alley, R. B. (host). (2011). *Energy Quest USA*, program 3 in *Earth: The Operators' Manual* (series), PBS, 2011 and 2012, available at http://www.earththeoperators manual.com/feature-video/energy-quest-usa. Accessed June 2, 2015.

Jacobson, M. Z., DeLucchi, M., Bazouin, G., Bauer, Z. A., Heavey, C. C., Fisher, E., Morris, S. B., Piekutowski, D. J. Y., Vencill, T. A., and Yeskoo, T. W. (2015). 100% clean and renewable wind, water, and sunlight (WWS) all-sector energy roadmaps for the 50 United States. *Energy & Environmental Science*, 8(7), 2093–2117.

Lewis, M. (2012). Carbon tax: bad politics, bad policy. Posted to the website of the Competitive Enterprise Institute, July 31, 2012, available at https://cei.org/op-eds-articles/carbon-tax-bad-politics-bad-policy. Accessed June 2, 2015.

Noon, M. (2013). Senate hearing proves Obama is lying about "climate change." Posted to the website of the Center for a Constructive Tomorrow, July 22, 2013, available at http://www.cfact.org/2013/07/22/senate-hearing-proves-obama-is-lying-about-climate-change/. Accessed June 2, 2015.

Nordhaus, W. D. (2008). *A Question of Balance: Weighing the Options on Global Warming Policies*. Yale University Press.

Pacala, S., and Socolow, R. (2004). Stabilization wedges: solving the climate problem for the next 50 years with current technologies. *Science*, 305(5686), 968–972.

Spencer, R. W. (2008). *Climate Confusion: How Global Warming Hysteria Leads to Bad Science, Pandering Politicians and Misguided Policies That Hurt the Poor*. Encounter Books.

U.S. Department of Energy. (2016). Solar Ready Vets. Available at http://energy.gov/eere/sunshot/solar-ready-vets. Accessed February 4, 2016.

Williams, J. H., Haley, B., Kahrl, F., Moore, J., Jones, A. D., Torn, M. S., and McJeon, H. (2014). Pathways to Deep Decarbonization in the United States. The U.S. Report of the Deep Decarbonization Pathways Project of the Sustainable Development Solutions Network and the Institute for Sustainable Development and International Relations. Revision with technical supplement, November 16, 2015, available at http://deepdecarbonization.org/wp-content/uploads/2015/11/US_Deep_Decarbonization_Technical_Report_Exec_Summary.pdf. Accessed January 8, 2016.

Yohe, G. W., Lasco, R. D., Ahmad, Q. K., Arnell, N. W., Cohen, S. J., Hope, C., Janetos, A. C., and Perez, R. T. (2007). Perspectives on Climate Change and Sustainability. In *Climate Change 2007: Impacts, Adaptation and Vulnerability. Contribution of Working Group II to the Fourth*

Assessment Report of the Intergovernmental Panel on Climate Change, M. L. Parry, O. F. Canziani, J. P. Palutikof, P. J. van der Linden, and C. E. Hanson (eds.). Cambridge University Press, Cambridge, United Kingdom, pp. 811–841, available at https://www.ipcc.ch/publications_ and_data/ar4/wg2/en/ch20.html. Accessed June 2, 2015.

Q31. WHAT EFFECT WILL CUTTING CARBON EMISSIONS HAVE ON THE POOR?

Answer: Climate change impacts will affect poor people and countries far more than rich ones. Failing to curb carbon dioxide emissions will therefore harm poor people and countries far more than rich ones. Although unintended consequences of some climate mitigation policies have the potential to harm the poor, the risks of inaction outweigh the risks of action.

The Facts: Scientists agree that climate change is caused by carbon dioxide released by burning fossil fuels and that the impacts almost certainly won't be small. In addition, advocates for policies to curb carbon emissions insist that implementing such policies need not be economically ruinous. However, although the economy as a whole might suffer only relatively small effects from carbon cutting measures (and large gains when considering the damage avoided), this scale of analysis doesn't give the full picture. Growth for the economy as a whole, for example, might hide many important details: are some groups gaining more than others? Is the growth coming at the expense of certain groups or sectors of the economy? Even though carbon policies might not have much effect on the economy as a whole, it's reasonable to ask whether some income groups might be affected differently than others.

The answer to this question is a clear "yes." Poor people and poor countries stand to gain significantly from such efforts, depending on how the specific policies are designed. This is because the impacts of climate change are expected to hit poor people and countries much harder than rich ones.

There are several reasons for this disproportionate impact. First, adaptation to climate change will cost money, which by definition is in short supply for the poor. For example, increasing temperatures will likely mean an increased need to use air conditioning for those who have access to it. This is expensive in itself, but the increased use of air conditioning could compound the problem in a broader sense. More air conditioning means greater demand for electricity, driving the price up (Gordon, 2014). Use of air conditioning may not simply be a case of being more comfortable. During the worst conditions of extreme heat, "anyone whose job requires them to work outdoors, as well as anyone lacking access to air conditioning, will face severe health risks and potential death" (Gordon, 2014, pp. 4–5). Access to air conditioning doesn't mean only physical access; it also means being able to afford to use it.

Second, poor people tend to live in more vulnerable places. This was brought home very clearly when Hurricane Katrina hit New Orleans in 2005. The poorest parts of the city were also generally the lowest lying and therefore the most prone to flooding. And the poorest residents often didn't have access to a car, so they couldn't get out of the way of the storm when it came. (Mark Muro and co-authors detailed these issues in a 2005 report for the Brookings Institution.)

These challenges apply to poor people living in rich countries such as the United States, but they apply even more strikingly to poor people living in poor countries. In an important paper in 1976, Phil O'Keefe and co-authors pointed out that the term "natural disasters" was misleading, because the impacts of identical disasters are so much more profound in poor countries than rich ones. While poor people in rich countries are vulnerable, poor people in poor countries face the added problem of a government that might be less able to provide an effective disaster response. A person's vulnerability to "natural" disasters, they argued, is therefore not simply due to whether he or she lives on an earthquake fault line or a hurricane-prone coast, but it's also due to poverty. The IPCC's 2014 report concurs, summarizing a large body of research on natural hazards (Olsson et al., 2014).

When it comes to climate change impacts, the problems of poverty are amplified by geography. Most of the world's poorest countries are relatively close to the equator, meaning that their climates are already warm. Small increases in temperature on top of this can have large effects. For example, in hot countries, crops are already growing close to the limit of what they can tolerate, temperature-wise. A small push can take them over the edge, beyond what they can tolerate, resulting in large reductions in crop yields. The same push in a cooler country wouldn't have the same effect. Summarizing recent studies, Wheeler and von Braun (2013) suggested that crops in Africa could suffer striking declines in yields by the 2050s: –17% for wheat, –5% for maize, –15% for sorghum, and –10% for millet. Simply because of their location on the Earth's surface, some countries will be hit harder than others by climate change, and those harder-hit countries tend to be poorer (Mendelsohn et al., 2006).

For all these reasons, the poor have the most to lose from global warming and consequently the most to gain from cuts in carbon emissions. However, many sources claim that cutting carbon emissions will hurt the poor. In the United States, various proposals to reduce emissions have been criticized on the grounds that they will increase energy prices, which the poor are the least able to pay for (e.g., see Marita Noon's 2013 post at the Center for a Constructive Tomorrow website). This is superficially persuasive: electricity from renewable sources, like wind or solar, is currently more expensive than fossil fuel energy, and adding the social cost of carbon onto the price of gasoline or coal would make the prices go up. British Columbia's carbon tax has added the equivalent of about 25 U.S. cents to the price of a gallon of gasoline, for example.

However, recall from question 30 that British Columbia's carbon tax is *revenue neutral*: money taken in by the government from the carbon tax is given back in the form of cuts to other taxes, with a special emphasis on the poor. It's probably still too early to say for sure how well this aspect of the carbon tax has worked, but by design it's set up to avoid disproportionately harming the poor. In fact, if climate policies are designed well, they can actually benefit the poor financially, while simultaneously avoiding the climate impacts that will hit precisely those people the hardest.

International versions of this claim often follow similar logic: transitioning from fossil fuels raises the price of energy, causing undue suffering, this time for people in poor countries overseas rather than poor people at home. Claude Allegre and 15 other scientists, in a 2012 *Wall Street Journal* op-ed, wrote that "50 more years of economic growth unimpeded by greenhouse gas controls . . . would be especially beneficial to the less-developed parts of the world that would like to share some of the same advantages of material well-being, health and life expectancy that the fully developed parts of the world enjoy now." However, they underpin this claim with a reference to work by the eminent Yale economist William Nordhaus—which Nordhaus himself pointed out had been misapplied. According to a 2012 response he wrote in the *New York Review of Books*, the authors of the op-ed had used the wrong measure by which to judge the costs and benefits of action on climate change: "My research shows that there are indeed substantial net benefits from acting now rather than waiting fifty years" (Nordhaus, 2012). This is not the first time research has been misapplied in order to support an argument—recall Pieter Tans's response to the misuse of his work on ocean acidification from question 23—but it is a particularly clear-cut example.

To be fair, there could be significant unintended consequences for poor countries of efforts to cut greenhouse gas emissions, and the IPCC's 2014 report is very clear about this possibility (Olsson et al., 2014, p. 813). Increased demand for biofuels, for example, might lead to greater plantations of fuel crops in poorer countries, displacing food crops and making hunger worse. International agreements on cutting carbon emissions are extraordinarily difficult and complicated, and a detailed discussion of the issues is far beyond the scope of this book. Nevertheless, our general point is that there is no inherent reason why cutting carbon emissions inevitably makes poor countries worse off—and economic analysis of the damage avoided suggests that it could make them a lot better off than doing nothing.

An alternative version of the myth that cutting carbon emissions hurts poor countries takes a more subtle approach. Instead of focusing on higher energy prices, it focuses on other ways to spend the money that would be needed for cutting carbon emissions. Poor countries face a huge number of serious problems: lack of access to clean water and basic sanitation, inadequate hospitals and clinics, hunger and malnutrition, poor roads, and so on. Wouldn't it be better, the argument goes, to spend money on fixing these real and urgent problems now, instead of heading off climate change in the future?

This argument has been made most prominently by Bjorn Lomborg, a Danish author. His 2007 book *Cool It* explains the ideas most fully, building on earlier versions outlined in a 2004 edited volume. The earlier book described an experiment in which a group of economists was brought together to decide how best to spend a hypothetical $50 billion over five years. Which problem should they try to solve? What would give the greatest return on investment: improving access to clean water, taking steps to prevent malaria, or cutting carbon emissions to head of climate change?

The group found that this last choice was the least effective use of the money. But as economist Jeffrey Sachs has explained, the whole exercise was set up so that short-term problems would win out over long-term ones like climate change. The amount $50 billion may sound like a lot of money, but set against any of the problems on the list, or even most rich-country foreign aid budgets, it's quite small. This biases the decisions about which problems to solve. Imagine that your house is falling down, your car needs a new transmission, and your shoes leak. If somebody gives you $50, you'll probably buy a new pair of shoes. That's the best use of the money, and it solves a real problem, but it's not the biggest problem you face. Addressing a serious health issue like malaria is not, of course, the equivalent of fixing a leaky pair of shoes. The point is that the conditions of Bjorn Lomborg's exercise made the outcome a foregone conclusion.

Social and physical science research is clear that climate change will harm poor people and poor countries far more than rich ones. Claims that cutting carbon emissions will inevitably hurt the poor typically glide over this crucial point, and neglect to say that increased energy costs can be counterbalanced with policies like income tax cuts. There is no fundamental reason why the poor would suffer more than the rich from efforts to cut carbon emissions. Quite the reverse, in fact.

FURTHER READING

Gordon, K. (2014). Risky Business: The Economic Risks of Climate Change in the United States. Risky Business Project. Available at http://risky business.org/uploads/files/RiskyBusiness_Report_WEB_09_08_14.pdf. Accessed May 20, 2015.

Lomborg, B. (Ed.). (2004). *Global Crises, Global Solutions*. Cambridge University Press.

Lomborg, B. (2008). *Cool It: The Skeptical Environmentalist's Guide to Global Warming*. Vintage Books.

Mendelsohn, R., Dinar, A., and Williams, L. (2006). The distributional impact of climate change on rich and poor countries. *Environment and Development Economics*, *11*(02), 159–178.

Muro, M., Lieu, A., Sohmer, R., Warren, D., and Park, D. (2005). *New Orleans after the Storm: Lessons from the Past, a Plan for the Future*. The Brookings Institution Metropolitan Policy Program, Washington, DC.

Noon, M. (2013). Senate hearing proves Obama is lying about "climate change." Posted to the website of the Center for a Constructive Tomorrow, July 22, 2013, available at http://www.cfact.org/2013/07/22/senate-hearing-proves-obama-is-lying-about-climate-change/. Accessed June 2, 2015.

Nordhaus, W. D. (2012). Why the global warming skeptics are wrong. *The New York Review of Books*, *59*(5), 32–34, available at http://www.nybooks.com/articles/archives/2012/mar/22/why-global-warming-skeptics-are-wrong/. Accessed June 3, 2015.

O'Keefe, P., Westgate, K., and Wisner, B. (1976). Taking the naturalness out of natural disasters. *Nature*, *260*, 566–567.

Olsson, L., Opondo, M., Tschakert, P., Agrawal, A., Eriksen, S. H., Ma, S., Perch, L. N., and Zakieldeen, S. A. (2014). Livelihoods and Poverty. In *Climate Change 2014: Impacts, Adaptation, and Vulnerability. Part A: Global and Sectoral Aspects. Contribution of Working Group II to the Fifth Assessment Report of the Intergovernmental Panel on Climate Change*, C. B. Field, V. R. Barros, D. J. Dokken, K. J. Mach, M. D.

Mastrandrea, T. E. Bilir, M. Chatterjee, K. L. Ebi, Y. O. Estrada, R. C. Genova, B. Girma, E. S. Kissel, A. N. Levy, S. MacCracken, P. R. Mastrandrea, and L. L. White (eds.). Cambridge University Press, Cambridge, United Kingdom, and New York, NY, pp. 793–832, available at http://ipcc-wg2.gov/AR5/images/uploads/WGIIAR5-Chap13_FINAL. pdf. Accessed June 3, 2015.

Sachs, J. D. (2004). Seeking a global solution. *Nature*, 430(7001), 725–726.

Wheeler, T., and von Braun, J. (2013). Climate change impacts on global food security. *Science*, 341(6145), 508–513.

Q32. WHAT IS CHINA DOING TO ADDRESS CLIMATE CHANGE?

Answer: China is rapidly deploying large-scale renewable energy systems and starting to cut its carbon emissions from coal and other fossil fuels.

The Facts: Opponents of various strategies for reducing U.S. generation of greenhouse gases often insist that it is pointless to try to cut carbon emissions in America, because any cuts will be swamped by China's massive use of fossil fuels. However, this argument is becoming a harder one to make. The six months from November 2014 to April 2015 contained two big milestones for action on climate change. The first was an historic agreement between the United States and China to cut carbon emissions. The second was a report indicating that China might actually be making progress on the problem: not just talk, but action.

The first milestone, the November 2014 agreement between the United States and China, is important for several reasons. First, China and the United States are, respectively, the number one and number two emitters of carbon dioxide, so the agreement represents a declaration by the world's fossil fuel–using heavyweights that business cannot continue as usual. Second, this marks a significant change from China's previous position, which rejected the idea that poor countries have to take any action on global warming. Finally, both countries have signed up to noteworthy cuts in carbon dioxide emissions: the United States aims to reach emissions levels 26–28% below 2005 levels by 2025, while China has agreed that its emissions will not increase after 2030, when 20% of its energy will come from renewable sources such as wind and solar power.

There are differences of opinion about which country has agreed to do more. The United States has been cutting emissions steadily since about

2005, mainly because of a huge shift from coal to natural gas—but it will have to double its rate of reductions after 2020 in order to hit its target, so perhaps the United States has the bigger burden (*The Economist*, 2014). On the other hand, China must shift its emissions in an entirely new direction, from accelerating upward to flat and then down. Like a circus strongman bending an iron bar, bending the emissions curve downward in this way takes a lot of effort—so maybe China has the bigger challenge (Nuccitelli, 2014). Whichever country has the bigger job, though, one thing is clear: China is acting on climate change.

In fact, in some ways, the U.S.-China agreement has simply added an international component to what China was already doing. In the past few years, it has become clear that China has accepted the need to act on climate change. China's economy has been growing at an astounding speed, and a huge program of building new power plants has accompanied and contributed to the growth. This has led to massive and, until recently, accelerating consumption of coal, which is the main reason why China now leads the world in carbon dioxide emissions, as mentioned earlier. However, beginning in 2012, consumption of coal slowed dramatically and now seems to be flattening out or even dropping, according to figures from the U.S. Energy Information Administration (2014) and the Global Carbon Project (Jackson et al., 2016). The decline looks set to continue, according to some news reports (Reuters, 2015).

Experience has shown that official data from China on issues ranging from air pollution to public health is not always reliable. This was borne out again late in 2015, when the Chinese government altered its historical coal consumption figures. Having identified gaps in its official records for 2000–2013, the government quietly revised their numbers sharply upward, to the tune of up to 17% a year (Buckley, 2015). Given China's truly massive use of coal, this amounts to a lot of additional carbon emissions. However, when the revised data are carefully analyzed, the trends still show a leveling out of coal consumption and a reduction in carbon emissions, according to a peer-reviewed paper by scientists affiliated with the Global Carbon Project, an international effort to track the world's carbon budget (Jackson et al., 2016). In other words, although the amount of coal being used by China in previous years was underestimated, the overall direction of the trends remains unchanged whether the old data or the revised data are used.

At the same time as coal consumption is flattening or falling, China has been investing heavily in renewable energy. In 2013, for example, China installed more renewable power capacity than it did fossil fuel and nuclear power combined (*The Economist*, 2015; Jackson et al., 2016).

China still has a huge appetite for coal, consuming almost as much as the rest of the world put together, according to a 2014 report from the U.S. Energy Information Administration. However, it looks like this is starting to change. As the saying goes, the journey of a thousand miles begins with a single step. (Geoff Haines-Stiles and Richard Alley's superb video *Earth: The Operators' Manual* looks at China in some detail.)

Some, or all, of these actions may be motivated more by concerns about air pollution than climate change. China's dependence on coal to fuel its economic miracle has hit air quality hard. Chinese cities routinely top the list of the world's most polluted, and a United Nations report in 2006 estimated that 400,000 people were dying every year from air pollution in Beijing alone (United Nations Human Settlements Programme, 2006, p. 114). China clearly has much to gain from moving away from coal, regardless of the climate benefits.

Nevertheless, China's energy shift seems to be making a noticeable difference on that front, too. This brings up the second big milestone in that six-month period mentioned earlier. In March 2015, the International Energy Agency (IEA) announced that preliminary data for 2014 showed that the global economy had grown, but carbon dioxide emissions from fossil fuels hadn't, the first time this has happened. Carbon dioxide emissions have slowed in the past, but always because of a weak economy. This traditionally tight link has prompted arguments that carbon emissions cannot be cut without harming the economy (question 30). But the IEA's 2015 announcement indicated that perhaps that link was weakening or even beginning to break. And the main reasons it suggested were the growth of renewable energy, particularly in rich countries and China, and the increasingly widespread use of energy-efficient technologies. As the IEA put it, "Recent efforts to promote more sustainable growth—including greater energy efficiency and more renewable energy—are producing the desired effect of decoupling economic growth from greenhouse gas emissions." The effects in China are presented in Figure 5.1, which shows the change in carbon dioxide emissions relatively to 2011, for the period 2011–2015. Although 2015's figures are not yet definitive and are therefore presented as a range of possibilities, even the more pessimistic estimate suggests a reduction in carbon dioxide emissions relative to the previous year.

From a climate change standpoint, all of this is encouraging news, but there are at least two reasons for caution. First, although carbon emissions do not seem to have increased in 2014, they didn't decrease, either. The world is still pumping fossil carbon into the atmosphere, beyond the capacity of natural processes to absorb it. To stop atmospheric carbon dioxide

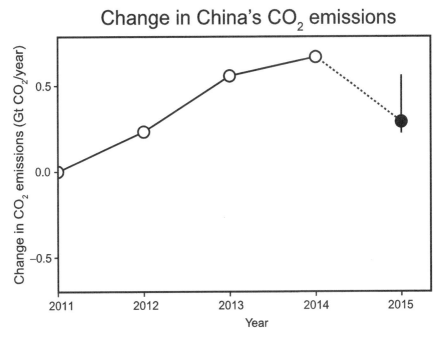

Figure 5.1 Change in China's carbon dioxide emissions, 2011–2015, relative to 2011.

Source: Jackson et al. (2016).

from increasing, emissions have to fall to zero. Until that is achieved, the amount of carbon dioxide in the atmosphere will keep going up, even if emissions have gone down. In other words, carbon would still be accumulating in the atmosphere, just not as quickly as before.

Second, the IEA announcement deals with just one year of preliminary data, so it's too soon to draw any definite conclusions. However, it does look as though renewable energy and efficiency measures are at least starting to make a difference. And most important, it seems that the economy can grow without using ever-increasing amounts of fossil energy.

China's positive new approach to energy and climate change makes obsolete a once-common argument against other countries taking action. Why should we cut our carbon emissions when China is building two major new coal-fired power plants every week, as it was between 2005 and 2011 (Larson, 2014)? Wouldn't any cuts we make just be a drop in the bucket compared to that? This argument can be found in many places, for example, on the website of the Cato Institute (Knappenberger, 2013), but it's especially strongly argued by Nigel Lawson in his 2008 book, *An*

Appeal to Reason. Describing carbon cutting measures in the European Union as "costly masochism" (p. 62) without China's involvement, he identifies the chances of an agreement with China as nonexistent: "[W]hat the United States considers an equitable sharing of the burden is worlds apart from what China and India consider equitable, and there is no prospect whatever of this chasm—it is far more than a gap—being closed" (p. 61). The events of November 2014 (and December 2015, see Postscript) suggest that times may have changed.

To be fair, claims that it was pointless to cut carbon emissions without China doing so too were, at one time, somewhat reasonable. But the argument could go in two different directions: either China's overwhelming carbon emissions mean just giving up on ever solving the problem, or they show how important it is to get China involved. Fortunately, the two milestones identified here suggest that the latter outcome may finally be coming to pass.

The case of China provides an important lesson for other seemingly insurmountable challenges. For example, India, the world's third-largest producer of greenhouse gases, is following China's lead by building coal-fired power plants hand over fist. More broadly, India's view of climate change symbolizes the divide between rich and poor countries on this issue—Nigel Lawson's chasm. With good reason, poor countries tend to see climate-changing carbon dioxide as the rich world's mess and the rich world's responsibility to clean up. It would be easy to think that India's position will never change. But this is exactly what commentators like Nigel Lawson were saying about China. However frozen the positions might seem, it's remarkable how time and a little goodwill can thaw them out. China and the United States have shown that it's possible to bridge even a gaping chasm.

FURTHER READING

Buckley, C. (2015). China burns much more coal than reported, complicating climate talks. *The New York Times*, November 3, 2015, available at http://www.nytimes.com/2015/11/04/world/asia/china-burns-much-more-coal-than-reported-complicating-climate-talks.html?_r=0. Accessed January 15, 2016.

The Economist. (2014). An uneven deal. *The Economist*, November 12, 2014, available at http://www.economist.com/news/international/2163 2412-agreement-greenhouse-gas-emissions-america-has-made-bigger-concessions-china-uneven. Accessed June 4, 2015.

The Economist. (2015). Renewables: we make our own. *The Economist*, January 17, 2015, available at http://www.economist.com/news/special-report/

21639020-renewables-are-no-longer-fad-fact-life-supercharged-advances-power. Accessed June 4, 2015.

Haines-Stiles, G. (writer, producer, director), and Alley, R. B. (host). (2011). *Earth: The Operators' Manual*, program 1 in *Earth: The Operators' Manual* (series), PBS, 2011 and 2012, available at http://earththe operatorsmanual.com/feature-video/earth-the-operators-manual. Accessed May 8, 2015.

International Energy Agency. (2015). Global energy-related emissions of carbon dioxide stalled in 2014. Posted to International Energy Agency website, March 13, 2015, available at http://www.iea.org/newsroomand events/news/2015/march/global-energy-related-emissions-of-carbon-dioxide-stalled-in-2014.html. Accessed June 4, 2015.

Jackson, R. B., Canadell, J. G., Le Quéré, C., Andrew, R. M., Korsbakken, J. I., Peters, G. P., and Nakicenovic, N. (2016). Reaching peak emissions. *Nature Climate Change*, 6, 1–4.

Knappenberger, C. (2013). US carbon dioxide emissions fall as global emissions rise. Posted to the website of the Cato Institute, June 10, 2013, available at http://www.cato.org/blog/us-carbon-dioxide-emissions-fall-global-emissions-rise. Accessed June 5, 2015.

Larson, E. (2014). China's growing coal use is world's growing problem. Posted to ClimateCentral.org, January 27, 2014, available at http://www.climatecentral.org/blogs/chinas-growing-coal-use-is-worlds-growing-problem-16999. Accessed June 4, 2015.

Lawson, N. (2008). *An Appeal to Reason: A Cool Look at Global Warming.* Penguin.

Nuccitelli, D. (2014). Fact check: China pledged bigger climate action than the USA; Republican leaders wrong. Posted to *The Guardian* website, November 14, 2014, available at http://www.theguardian.com/ environment/climate-consensus-97-per-cent/2014/nov/14/fact-check-china-pledged-bigger-climate-action-republican-leaders-wrong. Accessed June 4, 2015.

Reuters. (2015). China's coal use falling faster than expected. Posted to the website of news agency Reuters, March 26, 2015, available at http://www.reuters.com/article/2015/03/26/china-coal-idUSL3N0WL32720150326. Accessed June 4, 2015.

United Nations Human Settlements Programme (UN-HABITAT). (2006). State of the World's Cities 2006/7. Earthscan. Available at http://mirror.unhabitat.org/pmss/listItemDetails.aspx?publicationID=2101. Accessed October 10, 2015.

U.S. Energy Information Administration. (2014). China produces and consumes almost as much coal as the rest of the world combined. Posted to the U.S. Energy Information Administration website, May 14, 2014, available at http://www.eia.gov/todayinenergy/detail.cfm?id=16271#. Accessed June 4, 2015.

U.S. Energy Information Administration. (2015). International Energy Statistics. Available at http://www.eia.gov/cfapps/ipdbproject/iedindex3.cfm?tid=1&pid=1&aid=2&cid=regions&syid=1980&eyid=2012&unit=TST. Accessed June 4, 2015.

Q33. CAN CARBON DIOXIDE BE REGULATED UNDER THE CLEAN AIR ACT?

Answer: The U.S. Supreme Court ruled in 2007 and 2014 that carbon dioxide was a pollutant and should be regulated under the Clean Air Act.

The Facts: Back in 1970, responding to growing concerns about environmental degradation, the U.S. Congress and Republican president Richard Nixon passed a series of laws for dealing with pollution, among them the Clean Air Act. They also set up the Environmental Protection Agency (EPA) to put them into practice. These laws have been generally successful, helping to bring about substantial improvements in air and water quality in the decades since they were passed. However, new challenges constantly appear, and the legal system is often called upon to decide how laws passed in 1970 apply today. This is the situation regarding carbon dioxide today. Is it a pollutant under the terms of the Clean Air Act?

Yes. In 2007, the U.S. Supreme Court ended an eight-year legal battle by deciding that it is (see Supreme Court of the United States, 2007). Simply put, the Clean Air Act defines air pollution as anything in the air that might be expected to be hazardous to the public. Carbon dioxide is obviously a substance in the air, and its climate-changing properties make it hazardous. Thus, in the court's view, carbon dioxide is a pollutant. This was confirmed in a 2014 ruling (see Supreme Court of the United States, 2014).

Precision matters in legal arguments, so here are the precise wordings from the Clean Air Act. It requires the EPA to regulate "air pollution which may reasonably be anticipated to endanger public health or welfare." Air pollutants are defined broadly:

The term "air pollutant" means any air pollution agent or combination of such agents, including any physical, chemical, biological, radioactive (including source material, special nuclear material, and byproduct material) substance or matter which is emitted into or otherwise enters the ambient air.

The Clean Air Act also specifically refers to effects on welfare as including "weather, visibility, and climate, damage to and deterioration of property, and hazards to transportation, as well as effects on economic values and on personal comfort and well-being." Justice Stevens, writing the court's majority opinion, cited impacts from melting glaciers and sea level rise, among others, in support of the view that "[t]he harms associated with climate change are serious and well recognized" (Supreme Court of the United States, 2007, p. 18). The science, in this Supreme Court ruling, was deemed clear enough: carbon dioxide causes global warming; global warming is harmful; therefore, carbon dioxide is a pollutant. This ruling gave the EPA the authority to regulate it.

Actually, the ruling is even more forceful than this. The 2007 court decision dealt with a complaint raised by a group of states, local governments, and private organizations that the EPA had so far failed to regulate carbon dioxide. In effect, they claimed, the EPA was guilty of dereliction of duty. The 2007 ruling agreed—carbon dioxide is a pollutant, so the EPA had not only the *authority* to regulate it but also the *legal obligation* to do so, unless it had good reasons not to. The Supreme Court concluded that the EPA did not have good reasons for leaving carbon dioxide unregulated. Having been essentially ordered by the court to regulate carbon dioxide, the EPA took steps to comply.

Legally, then, the case is closed: carbon dioxide is a pollutant, and the EPA has the authority, even the obligation, to regulate it under the Clean Air Act. However, other definitions support the purely legal view. The Encyclopedia Britannica, for example, defines air pollution as the

> release into the atmosphere of various gases, finely divided solids, or finely dispersed liquid aerosols at rates that exceed the natural capacity of the environment to dissipate and dilute or absorb them. These substances may reach concentrations in the air that cause undesirable health, economic, or aesthetic effects. (Nathanson, 2013)

We've seen in various earlier sections of this book that this is exactly what's happening with anthropogenic carbon dioxide. It's a gas being released into the atmosphere so fast, by burning fossil fuels, that it is accumulating in the atmosphere and dissolving in the oceans, causing global warming and ocean acidification, which have undesirable health, economic, and aesthetic effects.

Merriam-Webster's dictionary provides a slightly different definition of pollution. The short version includes: "The action or process of making land, water, air, etc., dirty and not safe or suitable to use." Since carbon dioxide is colorless and odorless, it can't reasonably be said to make anything dirty, so under this definition, carbon dioxide is not a pollutant. But the dictionary provides a more complete definition, such that pollution is "the action of polluting especially by environmental contamination with man-made waste." The carbon dioxide we're concerned with clearly is man-made waste (question 18). And it's clearly an environmental contaminant, as the problem of ocean acidification shows, if not climate change (question 23). Under most ordinary definitions, as well as legal ones, carbon dioxide is a pollutant.

However, several critics continue to insist that carbon dioxide is not a pollutant. Many of these gloss over important aspects of the legal ruling we discussed earlier, in particular failing to attribute the definition of carbon dioxide as a pollutant to the Supreme Court. Tim Ball, in a 2014 guest post at the blog WattsUpWithThat.com, writes: "CO_2 continues its hold because the public believes it is a pollutant," arguing that this is because of a successful public relations campaign to mislead the public. This line of reasoning neglects to mention that it's not only the public that thinks carbon dioxide is a pollutant: the Supreme Court does, too.

Steve Goreham, in his 2013 *The Mad, Mad, Mad World of Climatism*, provides a slightly more detailed discussion of the issue: "December 7 2009 is a date that will live in infamy. Not in memory of the attack on Pearl Harbor, but on that date the Environmental Protection Agency declared carbon dioxide is a pollutant under the Clean Air Act. *That is bizarre*" (p. 128, emphasis in original). However, like Tim Ball, Goreham does not mention the 2007 Supreme Court decision. Although the EPA did place carbon dioxide on its list of substances it regulates, as Goreham says, it did so only in response to the court's ruling. The EPA was complying with the law.

Other claims about carbon dioxide not being a pollutant can be found online, at sites like CO2isgreen.org and plantsneedCO2.org. They claim that carbon dioxide is not a pollutant because it occurs naturally and plants need it. It's true, of course, that plants need carbon dioxide to photosynthesize, but this neglects the salient facts. Carbon dioxide is being emitted as a waste product from human burning of fossil fuels. It's accumulating in the atmosphere and dissolving in the oceans, disrupting our climate and causing real problems. As we noted earlier, carbon dioxide meets not only legal definitions of pollution but dictionary and encyclopedia definitions as well. Efforts to argue otherwise obscure critical details.

FURTHER READING

Ball, T. (2014). Fighting the wrong battle: public persuaded about CO_2 as pollutant—not as cause of warming. Posted to WattsUpWith-That.com, February 5, 2014, available at http://wattsupwiththat.com/2014/02/05/fighting-the-wrong-battle-public-persuaded-about-co2-as-pollutant-not-as-cause-of-warming/. Accessed June 5, 2015.

Goreham, S. (2013). *The Mad, Mad, Mad World of Climatism: Mankind and Climate Change Mania.* New Lenox Books.

Merriam-Webster's Dictionary. (2015). Pollution. Available at http://www .merriam-webster.com/dictionary/pollution. Accessed June 5, 2015.

Nathanson, J. (2013). Air pollution. *Encyclopaedia Britannica,* available at http://www.britannica.com/EBchecked/topic/10772/air-pollution. Accessed June 5, 2015.

Supreme Court of the United States. (2007). Massachusetts et al. v. Environmental Protection Agency et al. Decided on April 2, 2007. Available at http://www.supremecourt.gov/opinions/06pdf/05-1120.pdf. Accessed June 5, 2015.

Supreme Court of the United States. (2014). Utility Air Regulatory Group *v.* Environmental Protection Agency et al. Decided on June 23, 2014. Available at http://www.supremecourt.gov/opinions/13pdf/12-1146_4g18.pdf. Accessed June 5, 2015.

Q34. CAN INDIVIDUALS DO ANYTHING TO LIMIT GLOBAL WARMING?

Answer: Individual actions can add up to significant reductions in carbon dioxide emissions, being a small part of a much larger collective effort.

The Facts: In question 30, we came across British Columbia's revenue-neutral carbon tax. Four years after its implementation in 2008, consumption of fuels subject to the tax had dropped by 19% compared with the rest of Canada (Elgie and McClay, 2013). This provides an example of a sizable change in energy consumption, resulting from millions of decisions at the individual level. As people responded to the changes in the price of various fuels, they individually decided to use less, adding up to a collectively significant cut.

The success of British Columbia's carbon tax shows that individual actions do matter when it comes to reducing carbon emissions. Other studies have shown similar results. In a 2009 study, Thomas Dietz and his team examined the effects of taking simple actions by U.S. households to cut carbon dioxide emissions. Because U.S. household energy use is high relative to other countries, they found that cuts at the household level can make significant contributions to national, and even global, efforts to reduce carbon emissions. Based on 2005 data, Dietz and his team found that direct use of energy by U.S. households accounted for about 626 million metric tons of carbon. That was about 38% of total U.S. carbon dioxide emissions, or about 8% of the total for the entire world! In fact, taken together, U.S. households alone generated more carbon dioxide in 2005 than the total amount produced by any other country in the world, except China. There's a lot of room for savings, and the scale of U.S. household carbon emissions means that those savings can translate to a relatively large impact, not only at the scale of the United States but at the global scale as well.

The actions that Dietz and his team considered were all simple, affordable projects that most, if not all, households could implement today. They included weatherization projects, such as adding home insulation; changes in driving behavior, such as car pooling; and installation of energy-efficient appliances. In their study, nobody needed to install solar panels on their roof in order to make significant reductions in carbon dioxide emissions.

They also specifically factored in the reality that not everybody would engage with the activities considered. Looking at historical evidence of the most effective approaches to getting people involved, Dietz and his team calculated that anywhere from 90% to 15% of households would participate, depending on the specific action. People were more likely to participate in home weatherization, for example, but less likely to car pool. In other words, the analysis wasn't based on hypothetical ideal-world assumptions of how much carbon dioxide could be reduced if everyone in the country car pooled or bought a new energy-efficient refrigerator, but on realistic estimates grounded in what had happened in real life. Even if only 30% of U.S. households can be persuaded to tune up their air conditioning, for example, it's still enough to make a sizable dent in the country's carbon dioxide emissions.

How big a dent? Across 17 different actions, with varying degrees of participation, the study found that U.S. households could cut their emissions by about 20%. Because U.S. household energy use is so large compared with other countries, that 20% cut amounts to over 7% of the U.S. national total, which, at the time of their study, was a little more than the emissions for the entire country of France. Simple household actions therefore can make a significant contribution to cutting U.S.

carbon emissions. (The Union of Concerned Scientists' Seth Shulman and co-authors, 2013, have an excellent book on such actions.)

Arguments that individuals can't make a difference tend to focus on high-profile symbolic gestures that, by themselves, probably don't reduce carbon emissions very much. Bjorn Lomborg, for example, in his 2008 book *Cool It*, targets the global "lights out" campaign, in which cities worldwide are encouraged to switch off lights for an hour at the same time, to emphasize the need for action on climate change. Steve Goreham (2013) identifies a school in England where the heating was turned off for a day to reduce carbon emissions. It's true that these kinds of actions don't have much of an effect on carbon emissions, but they're intended as symbolic gestures rather than practical ones. Certainly, if symbolic gestures are all we engage in, then carbon emissions will be essentially unaffected.

But why restrict ourselves to symbolic gestures? We saw in question 30 that Weber State University, in Ogden, Utah, has cut its utility bills by over a million dollars a year by getting smarter about its use of energy, and carbon emissions have dropped accordingly. Similar activities, conducted at the household level and scaled up across the entire United States, can take a substantial bite out of national, and even global, carbon emissions, as Dietz's study showed. These are not symbolic gestures.

The evidence shows that smart, practical measures can add up. In much the same way that a Kickstarter campaign can get a great new business idea or art project off the ground by harnessing lots of small-scale contributions, so too can individual actions, bit by bit, affect carbon emissions. By themselves, though, they're not enough. They're a necessary part of the solution but by no means the whole thing. As Derrick Jensen pointed out, in a 2009 article for *Orion* magazine, it's important not to let household actions distract from the need for larger-scale changes as well. These are the kinds of things that can really happen only when governments set policy, so it might seem as though individuals have little or no role to play. Even when it comes to these larger-scale changes, though, individual actions can still make a contribution. One way is simply through participating in the political process. Voter turnout in the 2012 U.S. presidential election for people aged 18 to 24 was only 38%, compared with almost 70% for people aged 45 to 64, according to the U.S. Census Bureau (File, 2014). As the saying goes, the decisions are made by those who show up.

Another way to have an outsize influence on carbon emissions is by communicating with family, friends, and neighbors about climate change. A point emphasized throughout this book is that the scientific evidence showing that global warming is real, caused by humans, and associated with potentially serious consequences is very strong. However, there is also a great deal of inaccurate or misleading information circulating on the subject. It's not surprising that people might be confused about any of the aspects of climate change covered in the preceding pages. Most people in the United States, for example, are unaware that 97% of publishing climate scientists agree that humans are causing global warming. However, social science research has shown that most people shy away from information that doesn't fit their preconceptions, so communicating about climate change has become quite challenging. A solution to this problem is suggested by the fact that people are more accepting of information if it comes from a source they know and respect. Trusted messengers can be more effective in explaining the science, where strangers might fail. Individuals who know the science, not just about climate change, but about how it can be addressed, can therefore start productive conversations on this issue within their own social networks.

Finally, linking communication with action, it turns out that one of the best ways to predict whether someone will install solar panels on his or her house is if somebody else in the neighborhood has already done it. Individual action on climate change can be a bit like playing on a sports team. If one person gives up, it can damage the morale of the whole team, making failure all but inevitable. But if everyone's doing their best to win, the team becomes much more formidable. With the problem-solving ingenuity of the human race to work with, who knows what can be achieved? As climate scientist Richard Alley writes in *Earth: The Operators' Manual*: "Abraham Lincoln ran his mind and body on the same energy as a single heat-until-it-glows lightbulb. You, and Einstein, and Michelangelo, taken together, use or used less energy than a single chandelier" (p. 18).

FURTHER READING

Alley, R. B. (2011). *Earth: The Operators' Manual*. W.W. Norton & Company.

Dietz, T., Gardner, G. T., Gilligan, J., Stern, P. C., and Vandenbergh, M. P. (2009). Household actions can provide a behavioral wedge to rapidly reduce US carbon emissions. *Proceedings of the National Academy of Sciences, 106*(44), 18452–18456.

Elgie, S., and McClay, J. (2013). Policy Commentary/Commentaire: BC's carbon tax shift is working well after four years (Attention Ottawa). *Canadian Public Policy, 39*, S1–S10.

File, T. (2014). Young-Adult Voting: An Analysis of Presidential Elections, 1964–2012. Issued April 2014. Available at https://www.census.gov/prod/2014pubs/p20-573.pdf. Accessed June 9, 2015.

Goreham, S. (2013). *The Mad, Mad, Mad World of Climatism: Mankind and Climate Change Mania*. New Lenox Books.

Jensen, D. (2009). Forget shorter showers. *Orion* magazine, 15, available at https://orionmagazine.org/article/forget-shorter-showers/. Accessed June 9, 2015.

Lomborg, B. (2008). *Cool It: The Skeptical Environmentalist's Guide to Global Warming*. Vintage Books.

Shulman, S., Deyette, J., Ekwurzel, B., Friedman, D., Mellon, M., Rogers, J., and Shaw, S. (2013). *Cooler Smarter: Practical Steps for Low-Carbon Living*. Island Press.

Q35. DO SOME REPUBLICANS ACCEPT THAT ANTHROPOGENIC CLIMATE CHANGE IS OCCURRING?

Answer: Polls show that over 40% of registered Republicans accept that global warming is happening and support action to cut carbon emissions. Some of the world's most prominent climate scientists vote Republican.

The Facts: In the opening minutes of the television documentary *Earth: The Operators' Manual*, the show's presenter, climate scientist Richard Alley, lays his cards on the table: "I'm a registered Republican, play soccer on Saturdays and go to church on Sundays." Besides this, Dr. Alley is also a highly respected climate scientist. His work on ice cores retrieved from the ice sheets of Greenland and Antarctica has made significant contributions to our understanding of how and why climate has changed in the past, with important lessons for how the climate system might respond to the forcing from carbon dioxide that's being applied to it today. In common with a growing number of scientists, he's also a tireless communicator of climate research to the general public.

Another climate scientist and communicator is hurricane expert Kerry Emanuel. Dr. Emanuel's work on tropical cyclones and climate change has been widely cited; his popular books and newspaper op-eds have been widely read. He's also a self-described conservative and was a registered member of the Republican Party until about five years ago. An interesting discussion of Dr. Emanuel's political views was written for the *Los Angeles Times* in 2011 (Banerjee, 2011), and he confirmed by e-mail that he holds conservative views today.

Yet another example is Barry Bickmore. He's a geochemistry professor at Brigham Young University, a private institution owned by the Mormon

Church. He runs the spicy and provocative blog Climate Asylum (sub-title: A Republican scientist advocates sane energy policies), where he describes himself as "an active Mormon, and an active Republican" (Bickmore, n.d.).

These scientists are high-profile examples of people who occupy the right-hand end of the political spectrum and accept the science of climate change. As right-leaning voters, their views on climate change are not that unusual. Summarizing results of public opinion polls from 2012 to 2014, the Yale Project on Climate Change Communication (2015) found that 66% of U.S registered voters think global warming is happening. Republicans were somewhat less convinced, but still 44% agreed that the world is getting warmer. The poll results get more interesting as the questions get more specific: 56% of Republicans support regulation of carbon dioxide as a pollutant (question 33), and 44% even support strict carbon dioxide emissions limits on existing coal-fired power plants, a policy introduced by the Obama administration in 2015. The polling results are clear: sometimes a little less, but sometimes a little more, than half of registered Republicans see climate change as a reality and support taking action to fight it. When it comes to solutions to climate change, the results are even clearer. A different poll, conducted in August 2015 specifically to identify the views of Republican voters, found support across the political spectrum for accelerating the development and use of clean energy in the United States: 84% of voters supported this proposal, compared with 72% of Republicans and 68% of conservative Republicans. The poll was commissioned by the nonprofit group ClearPath (visit the ClearPath website at www.clearpath.org to see the complete survey).

It's easy to get the wrong impression about Republican views on climate change, though. Many of the items of misleading information concerning climate change profiled in this book find homes in conservative media outlets and think tanks. Some of the more strident voices denouncing climate change as a hoax emanate from right-wing politicians. And to be fair, opinion surveys in general do find striking differences between Republicans and Democrats on this issue. Results from the polling organization Gallup for 2001–2014 show at least a 20 percentage point difference between Republicans and Democrats when it comes to pinning the cause of global warming on humans, and the divide has grown sharply in recent years. In 2014, for example, 79% of Democrats, but only 41% of Republicans, agreed that the rise in Earth's temperature in the last century is due mainly to human activities (Saad, 2014). Results like this can easily give the impression of implacable Republican opposition to climate change science. However, they tend to focus on areas of difference rather than areas of agreement. The Yale data mentioned earlier show that attitudes are more nuanced, and there are several aspects of climate change policy that a majority of Republicans support.

Another feature of attitudes to climate change that Republicans and Democrats have in common is that neither group has a particularly strong understanding of climate science itself. A Yale survey of the general public's climate science knowledge found that 77% of those responding scored a D or an F (Leiserowitz et al., 2010); a more recent test prompted social psychologist Dan Kahan to conclude that "most people—of all cultural outlooks—don't know very much at all about 'climate science'" (Kahan, 2015, p. 26). Intriguingly, then, opinions about all aspects of climate change do not appear to be driven by knowledge of the issues. Something else must be at work.

There are several possibilities for why people might be less concerned about climate change than the facts seem to warrant. Robert Gifford calls these "dragons of inaction" (Gifford, 2011). One dragon is psychological distance—people are less concerned about a problem if it seems to happen far away or off into the future. Another dragon is pessimism bias—if the problem seems too big or too difficult to solve, people tend to deny the problem exists in the first place. However, one of the most significant dragons of inaction is an aversion to government regulation. In other words, if the science underpinning global climate change is accurate, then the policy implication is that we need to reduce CO_2 emissions, which may require regulation of the fossil fuel industry.

For many reasons, including possibly because of the prominence of former vice president Al Gore in raising awareness of the subject, climate change has come to be seen as a "Democratic issue." This can easily lead to the perception that stereotypical left-leaning solutions are inevitable: large government programs, more regulations, more bureaucracy, most, if not all, of which are not viewed kindly by those leaning to the political right. If accepting the science of climate change means accepting an expansion of government, it's not surprising that many Republicans, especially conservatives, tend to reject the science. (Naomi Oreskes and Erik Conway's 2010 book, *Merchants of Doubt*, also thoroughly documents the view among conservatives that many environmentalists are simply "watermelons": green on the outside, but red, or socialist, on the inside.)

However, solutions to climate change do not necessarily have to mean large government programs. There are market-friendly approaches to tackling climate change, such as British Columbia's revenue-neutral carbon tax. This approach has been supported by some of the United States' more conservative politicians. Bob Inglis, for example, is a former Republican Congressman from South Carolina, who now works with the Energy and Enterprise Initiative at George Mason University. The Energy and Enterprise Initiative describes itself on its website as a group of conservative "climate realists." During his time in Congress, Mr. Inglis earned a 93.5% approval rating from the American Conservative Union based on his voting record.

George Shultz, secretary of state under President Ronald Reagan, is another example. Not only is he on the committee of the Risky Business Project discussed elsewhere in this book, but he also wrote a 2015 op-ed article in *The Washington Post* advocating for a revenue-neutral carbon tax. Although this position is at odds with the views of many of today's senior Republican politicians, it is possible to find examples of both climate scientists and political figures on the right who accept the science and recognize the need to act.

In reality, there is much more certainty regarding the science of climate change than there is about the social science and politics of what to do about it. There does not seem to be any good reason why solutions to climate change can't come from the political right, any more than from the political left or middle. One way to think of the issue is that, whenever there is a gun violence tragedy, liberals and conservatives waste no time in advocating for their positions on gun ownership and gun laws: liberals typically argue for more restrictions on gun ownership, conservatives sometimes argue for wider availability of guns, to act as a deterrent. But these are arguments about *solutions*. Rarely, if ever, do people deny that the tragedy took place. With climate change, there are right-leaning climate scientists finding evidence of the problem and its many facets; there are conservative solutions, and conservative political figures advocating for them. The idea that Republicans cannot accept the science of climate change is a myth.

FURTHER READING

Althoff, E. (2015). Bob Inglis breaks from Republican Party, advocates action to fight climate change. *Washington Times*, March 24, 2015, available at http://www.washingtontimes.com/news/2015/mar/24/bob-inglis-advocates-action-to-fight-climate-chang/?page=all. Accessed June 9, 2015.

Banerjee, N. (2011). Scientist proves conservatism and belief in climate change aren't incompatible. *Los Angeles Times*, January 5, 2011, available at http://articles.latimes.com/2011/jan/05/nation/la-na-scientist-climate-20110105. Accessed June 9, 2015.

Bickmore, B. (n.d.). About the contributors. Posted to Climate Asylum blog, available at https://bbickmore.wordpress.com/about-barry-bickmore/. Accessed June 9, 2015.

ClearPath. (n.d.). Available at www.clearpath.org. Accessed November 8, 2015.

Energy and Enterprise Initiative. (2014). Who We Are. Available at http://republicen.org/about/index. Accessed April 20, 2016.

Gifford, R. (2011). The dragons of inaction: psychological barriers that limit climate change mitigation and adaptation. *American Psychologist*, 66(4), 290.

Kahan, D.M. (2015). Climate-science communication and the measurement problem. *Political Psychology*, 36(S1), 1–43.

Leiserowitz, A., Smith, N., and Marlon, J. R. (2010). *Americans' Knowledge of Climate Change*. Yale University. Yale Project on Climate Change Communication, New Haven, CT, available at http://environment. yale.edu/climate/files/ClimateChangeKnowledge2010.pdf. Accessed June 8, 2015.

Oreskes, N., and Conway, E.M. (2010). *Merchants of Doubt: How a Handful of Scientists Obscured the Truth on Issues from Tobacco Smoke to Global Warming*. Bloomsbury Publishing USA.

Saad, L. (2014). A steady 57% in U.S. blame humans for global warming. Posted to the website of Gallup.com, March 18, 2014, available at http://www.gallup.com/poll/167972/steady-blame-humans-global-warming.aspx. Accessed June 8, 2015.

Shultz, G. P. (2015). A Reagan approach to climate change. *The Washington Post*, March 13, 2015, available at http://www.washington post.com/opinions/a-reagan-model-on-climate-change/2015/03/13/4f 4182e2-c6a8-11e4-b2a1-bed1aaea2816_story.html. Accessed June 8, 2015.

Yale Project on Climate Change Communication. (2015). Not All Republicans Think Alike about Global Warming. Available at http:// environment.yale.edu/climate-communication/article/not-all-republicans-think-alike-about-global-warming/. Accessed June 8, 2015.

Postscript: The Paris Agreement

As this book was reaching completion, national delegations from all over the world were meeting in Paris to negotiate a path toward addressing human-caused climate change. On December 12, 2015, they issued a landmark document: the Paris Agreement. One hundred and ninety-five countries, from the Maldives Islands to Saudi Arabia, from the United States to Indonesia, agreed on the importance of "[h]olding the increase in the global average temperature to well below 2 °C above pre-industrial levels and to pursue efforts to limit the temperature increase to 1.5 °C above pre-industrial levels" (Article 2, paragraph 1(a) of the Paris Agreement, p. 21; see United Nations, 2015, for the full text of the document). They also agreed on the general framework of how they were going to try to achieve this, and on how the richer countries, which are responsible for most of the carbon dioxide built up in the atmosphere, will help the poorer countries to withstand the worst impacts of climate change, and develop with less reliance on fossil fuels.

This extraordinary level of agreement—unanimous across 195 countries representing a wide range of economies and cultures—marks a departure from the acrimony and finger-pointing that has characterized previous international climate change negotiations. There are at least two plausible reasons for this. First, the science of climate change is now extremely difficult to refute, requiring contortions of epic proportions to do so. It is simply untenable now in the international community to undertake these contortions, and the Paris Agreement demonstrates this. Even major fossil fuel–producing countries, such as Saudi Arabia, recognize the seriousness of the situation.

Second, the approach followed in Paris, and the years preceding it, was very different compared with earlier international meetings. The last major international agreement on climate change, 1997's Kyoto Protocol, attempted to dictate the different levels of carbon emissions cuts that each country should achieve. These rigid, detailed targets and timelines stirred up resentment in the various individual countries and ultimately torpedoed the agreement. The U.S. delegation signed the Kyoto Protocol, for example, but it was never ratified by the Senate and therefore never became law.

For the Paris meeting, however, all countries were invited to submit plans for what they felt they could reasonably achieve. While the arguments at previous meetings resembled diners at an expensive restaurant trying to split the bill, the Paris meeting was more like a potluck dinner: the common goal is to feed everyone, so in that spirit, bring whatever you can. For Paris, instead of bringing food, national delegations submitted their own carbon emissions targets—known as *Intended Nationally Determined Contributions* (INDCs). Because the INDCs are nationally determined, rather than sent down from on high by a remote international organization, countries are more likely to follow through on them. And the Paris Agreement stipulates that all countries will meet again regularly to assess progress and try to ratchet up the carbon cuts. Instead of using international law, the Paris Agreement is trying to harness the power of peer pressure.

By any standard, the Paris Agreement was a remarkable achievement. However, there is still a huge amount of work to be done. As they currently stand, for example, the INDCs are unlikely to prevent the world from warming more than 2°C above preindustrial levels. Right now, the lofty rhetoric is not matched by action, or even adequate plans for action. The intention is that the peer-pressure, naming-and-shaming mechanisms of the regular meetings, and assessments that are to follow the Paris Agreement will bring the INDCs into line with the warming targets, but there is no guarantee that this will happen.

Furthermore, in the United States, at least, the actions needed to meet the INDC are not being safeguarded with new laws. Instead, they are being brought about through the actions of the executive branch of government, the presidency. The EPA's authority to regulate carbon dioxide as a pollutant is one example of how the executive branch can tackle carbon emissions without going through Congress, the legislative (law-making) branch (question 33). From a practical standpoint, it's understandable why the president would choose this path: it's highly unlikely that new laws on climate change would be approved by Congress. In fact, the Paris Agreement is an agreement, not a treaty, precisely because of the difficulty anticipated in getting a new treaty ratified by the Senate (the Kyoto Protocol, mentioned earlier, shows the challenges).

This means that climate science denial and misinformation still had a subtle but significant influence. In January 2016, the U.S. Senate failed to pass a measure stipulating that humans are contributing to climate change due to opposition from Republican senators who continue to reject the scientific consensus on human-caused global warming. So while climate science denial didn't have an explicit presence in the climate negotiations in Paris, its influence was felt in the fact that the U.S. Senate wouldn't approve an international treaty based on mainstream climate science.

Technically, the Paris Agreement is a part of an earlier, formal treaty, the United Nations Framework Convention on Climate Change, signed in 1992 on behalf of the United States by President George H. W. Bush and ratified unanimously by the Senate. That treaty aims to avoid "dangerous anthropogenic interference with the climate system," and the Paris Agreement now lays out how to do this—so there is no legal requirement for the Paris Agreement to be ratified by the Senate. However, precisely because the actions being taken to meet the United States' INDC commitments are not protected by law, it is at least possible that a different president, with different views about climate change, could reverse the actions. And there is no shortage of think tanks ready to tell a new president, and conservative politicians, that climate change is all a hoax. One recent study (Boussalis and Coan, 2016) found that the output of material from conservative think tanks aiming to undermine the scientific evidence for human-caused climate change was actually on the increase. As the study authors put it, " 'The era of climate science denial' is not over" (p. 98). Further, psychological research testing the influence of misinformation has found that arguments against climate change were effective in undermining the positive influence of scientific information (McCright et al., 2016). Climate science denial persists, and the misinformation associated with it is effective in lowering public levels of climate literacy and support for climate action.

Despite the tremendous advances of the Paris Agreement, then, there is scant opportunity for scientists, engineers, policy experts, climate science communicators, and ordinary concerned citizens to sit back and relax. Paris was a first step on a long journey, and the difficulties along the road will be considerable. Another important step in this journey is increasing climate literacy levels, as well as reducing the influence of misinformation. Achieving this goal requires an improved understanding of both the science of climate change and the techniques used to distort that science. This book hopes to contribute to achieving that crucial step.

FURTHER READING

Boussalis, C., and Coan, T. G. (2016). Text-mining the signals of climate change doubt. *Global Environmental Change, 36,* 89–100.

Kollipara, P. (January 21, 2015). Wrap-up: U.S. Senate agrees climate change is real—but not necessarily that humans are causing it. *Science,* available at http://www.sciencemag.org/news/2015/01/wrap-us-senate-agrees-climate-change-real-not-necessarily-humans-are-causing-it. Accessed January 28, 2016.

McCright, A. M., Charters, M., Dentzman, K., and Dietz, T. (2016). Examining the effectiveness of climate change frames in the face of a climate change denial counter-frame. *Topics in Cognitive Science, 8*(1), 76–97.

United Nations. (2015). *Adoption of the Paris Agreement.* 21st Conference of the Parties to the Framework Convention on Climate Change, Paris, France, available at http://unfccc.int/resource/docs/2015/cop21/eng/l09.pdf. Accessed January 27, 2016.

Index

Note: Page numbers followed by the letter *f* in italics indicate figures.

About the Authors

Daniel Bedford, PhD, is professor of geography at Weber State University, Ogden, Utah. He has been teaching about climate change to college students across the United States for over 20 years.

John Cook is the Climate Communication Fellow for the Global Change Institute at the University of Queensland. He created the website Skeptical Science.com, which refutes climate misinformation and won the 2011 Australian Museum Eureka Prize for the Advancement of Climate Change Knowledge.